PLYMOUTH
A NEW HISTORY
1603 to the present day

CRISPIN GILL

DAVID & CHARLES
Newton Abbot   London   North Pomfret (Vt)

Related works by the same author

PLYMOUTH: A NEW HISTORY: Ice Age to the Elizabethans
PLYMOUTH IN PICTURES
SUTTON HARBOUR

British Library Cataloguing in Publication Data

Gill, Crispin
    Plymouth, a new history.
    1603 to the present day
    1. Plymouth, Eng. – History
    I. Title
    942.3'58   DA690.P7

    ISBN 0–7153–7617–9

Typeset by Northern Phototypesetting Co., Bolton
and printed in Great Britain
by A. Wheaton & Company Limited, Exeter
for David & Charles (Publishers) Limited
Brunel House, Newton Abbot, Devon

Published in the United States of America
by David & Charles Inc.
North Pomfret, Vermont 05053 USA

CONTENTS

LIST OF ILLUSTRATIONS

MAPS AND FIGURES

JACKET PHOTOGRAPH

Aerial view from the south-west (Plymouth City Council)

CHAPTER ONE

THE PURITAN TOWN: 1603–42

PLYMOUTH was a Puritan town when James VI of Scotland became James I of England in 1603. Nor was it surprising, for Plymouth had been fighting Catholic Spain for thirty years and too many of her men had fallen into the fires and tortures of the Inquisition for there to be any love of Papistry. The seamen who came home from the sack of Cadiz in 1596 were laden with their loot from churches, rich altar books and prayer books, 'supersticious books' the records call them. On 15 December 1600 'there was burnte in the markett place 22 chests of the pope's Bulls and pdons'.

Drake and Hawkins were touched by the Puritan spirit, says A. L. Rowse, and Puritan sympathies he reports as widespread among the growing bourgeois of the English towns, especially the more prosperous merchants and tradespeople in commercial centres like Plymouth, and the other ports. In late Elizabethan days the only two records in St Andrew's, the parish church of Plymouth, of 'church briefs', a way of taking special collections for charity, were both to relieve the inhabitants of Geneva, that stronghold of Calvinism whose people were under pressure from the Dukes of Savoy. In that period too the town accounts show many payments for special preachers and lecturers, and at that time lecturers, who delivered the sermon after the incumbent had finished morning prayer, were the common mouthpieces of the Puritans.

Queen Elizabeth had given to Plymouth Corporation in 1572 the right to appoint the vicars to St Andrew's, and in 1603 they chose Henry Wallis from St Dominic on Tamarside. Perhaps they were unsure of him; he had to give a bond that he would resign the living if they so wished but they never did and when he died in 1632, still in office, a characteristic Puritan sermon was preached at his funeral. It is from the sermons of the day that were printed and survived that we can be so sure that we are dealing with Puritans.

Many survive from the pen of the Rev Samuel Heiron, for long vicar of Modbury. One which explained his 'Refysall of Sybscrpiton to the Books of Common prayér', was printed in 1607 in Holland, as is made clear in a handwritten note on the title page of a surviving copy, 'and sent over packed in the goods of an eminent Merchant of Plymouth, Mr T. Sherwil. No Bookseller daring to sell it, ye whole impression was given away . . . Some were dropt in the streets, and others left at the door of Scholars'. Yet Thomas Sherwill, this smuggler of dangerous books, was Mayor of Plymouth the following year and twice again afterwards; he was a Plymouth MP from 1614 until his death. His brother Nicholas was also three times mayor. 'Old Mr Sam. Heiron' had many sermons published in London and one, published in 1616, was dedicated to Sir Ferdinando Gorges, commander of His Majesty's forces at Plymouth, Sir William Strode of Newnham, Sir Warwick Hele of Wembury, Sir Christopher Harris of Radford and Mr George Chudleigh of Strachleigh (near Lee Mill, now a farm), who had been led 'to commiserate and to help the spiritual necessity of an vntaught Towne by procuring the establishment of a weekely Lecture in it'. This sermon was one in the series. Heiron was responsible for bringing John Barlow to Plymouth, where he was lecturer at St Andrew's from 1608 to 1619. Barlow had a national reputation and left Plymouth to join a renowned champion of nonconformists in Bradford. But he still returned to preach in the town and a 1632 book of his is dedicated to the Mayor and Magistrates of Plymouth.

Soon after Barlow left Plymouth the Rev Alexander Grosse became vicar of Plympton St Mary. In his fourteen years there a number of his Puritan sermons were published, several originally preached in Plymouth. He preached at Thomas Sherwill's funeral in 1631 and again that year at the funeral of Matthias Nichols, lecturer to the town. Grosse later moved to Bridford near Exeter, but in 1645 he came specially to Plymouth to preach at the funeral of John Cawse, who had just finished his second term as mayor.

THE MERCHANTS AND THEIR TRADE

We find the names of these Puritans constantly in the mayoral rolls and the lists of merchants in the town; it was a tight community. Thomas Fownes said that there were only twenty-four true merchant adventurers resident in Plymouth when he was mayor in 1620, but these were the ruling spirits. There were some like Parker and Rawlyn who had been active in the Caribbean privateering that brought so much profit to Plymouth in the last Elizabethan decades. Earlier Elizabethan names were fading out; Sir Richard Hawkins, after his ten years in Spanish prisons, largely retired to his new home near Slapton, and the Eliots, old Hawkins partners, were in their great house at St Germans, Port Eliot, built out of the old monastery. Thomas Drake, brother of Francis, and his heirs were country gentlemen at Buckland Abbey. There had been a Fownes with Hawkins and Drake at San Juan de Ulloa in 1568 but the 1620 mayor was a son of a Bristol man; there had always been close family links between the two ports. There was a Gayer mayor of Plymouth in 1592; three Gayer sons stayed in Plymouth and married respectively into the Fownes, Amadas and Sparke families (more Elizabethan Plymouth names) while two others moved to London and became important merchants there. John Gayer indeed became a director of the East India Company (born out of Drake's voyage of circumnavigation), a Lord Mayor of London, a knight, and a distinguished traveller in Persia. Some left, some moved in. Abraham Colmer came from Birmingham in 1599, for example, but established himself by marrying the daughter of Nicholas Sheere, a leading merchant.

The basic trade of most of these merchants, and certainly Plymouth's principal business, was in the Newfoundland fisheries. It was essentially a West Country trade dominated by Plymouth and Dartmouth, with Dartmouth holding the major share. Plymouth had fifty ships in the business in 1594, and sixty by 1631; they averaged 100 tons apiece and it has been suggested that they were each crewed by about forty men. To take 2,400 seamen out of Plymouth's estimated total population of this period of 7,000 seems a high figure but, even if overstretched, shows how vital the business was in Plymouth's economy. The ships sailed across the Atlantic in spring, set up wooden platforms on the beaches where the fish were split and dried, and returned with their catches in July and August.

Some cargoes came to Plymouth for home use or re-export to France, Spain, the Canary Islands and Italy. But many more ships went direct from Newfoundland to these countries, sold their fish, bought local goods and returned with the profits of a double turnover. Spanish ports had been denied English ships during the long Spanish war, but James had made peace in 1604, opening the ports of Spain and Portugal to English ships. They had been reaching deep into the Mediterranean since 1570 – 'voyages to the Straits', say the Plymouth records – and the Spanish war had not halted this business. The Sherwills were in the Mediterranean trade, and the Trevilles had a factor at Gibraltar.

The true exports from Plymouth's hinterland were tin, lead and woollen goods. Dartmoor tin production was falling in the early seventeenth century but was not negligible; most of it went out from Plymouth and some was shipped coastwise from Cornish ports for export overseas. Most of the western lead went through Plymouth, partly to Newfoundland in the fishery ships and the rest, with some of the tin, coastwise to London. Just as Plymouth was on the edge of the tin-producing areas, so with wool the main production areas were in east Devon and Somerset, better served by Exeter and even Dartmouth. But Dartmoor had large flocks of sheep, east Cornwall was a major spinning area and weaving was another cottage industry along the southern edges of Dartmoor. Tavistock, Buckfastleigh and Ashburton were all woollen towns and while even their output gravitated eastwards, Plymouth did get a share. The six mills which Sir Francis Drake had built beside his 1591 leat were originally planned to grind corn but by 1608 the two lower mills, roughly situated where Cornwall Street now crosses Armada Way, were fulling mills where cloth was cleaned and shrunk. The slopes above the mills were covered with racks for drying the cloth. The Tavistock and west Devon output was a rough cloth but the old 'kerseys' were gradually giving way to the new serges as the seventeenth century progressed.

The total volume of trade increased over the years, and Exeter and Barnstaple manufacturers sent some of their produce through Plymouth. The markets ranged from the Atlantic islands to Spain, France and the Low Countries. Through Plymouth too went slates to ports between Copenhagen and Cadiz.

The imports show a richer list: the three-hundred-year-old wine and salt imports from France, with paper, pitch, linen and canvas added; more wine, fruit and sugar from Spain and the Canaries, with iron ore as well from northern Spain; shipping stores from the Baltic (Eastland trade, the Plymouth records call this), rye from Lübeck and hops from Flushing.

Some was for local use, some was trans-shipped into coasting vessels for other English ports, just as the Exeter wool for export came round in coasters. Coal from Newcastle and south Wales, grain from the east coast, all the needs of the town came in by sea from the ports where they were available. The roads of England were still only fit for packhorses and Plymouth was not helped by a river on either side. Not until 1618–19 was a causeway driven across the mud-flats at Marsh Mills and a bridge built over the Plym – the 'Long Bridge' – to cut out the long haul round by Plym Bridge or the Ebb Ford (Efford) available at low tide from Crabtree to Saltram.

The economic life of Plymouth was based on the sea, as it had been for centuries. It is difficult to measure the amount of trade because not all the port books are available, customs returns are an imprecise guide, and in addition all the returns of the Cornish ports (apart from tin, unimportant) are shown in the Plymouth figures. There are also many goods, like the Newfoundland fish, exempt in certain cases. London of course dominated all English trade as it had for centuries and, in the west, Bristol and Exeter overshadowed Plymouth as merchant ports. In 1614–20 the London customs returns averaged over £100,000 and the best provincial figures were Hull £7,200, Exeter £4,500, Bristol £3,700, Newcastle £3,300 and Plymouth £2,900. Plymouth, about the twentieth town of the country in size of population, was the sixth port. In her best year of that period, 1617, she outstripped Newcastle.

NEW ENGLAND

But Plymouth still held the lead in American developments. The Newfoundland fishermen had very early on reached down from the Newfoundland banks to the American coast, the main ('Maine') land, searching for new fishing grounds. Ralegh had tried settlement in Virginia in 1585 and failed, but the idea persisted. In 1602 Bartholomew Gosnold built a fort on Martha's Vineyard, just south of Cape Cod, but one winter was enough for his men. In 1604 a group of French Huguenots settled in Nova Scotia, the first settlement to persist in North America. But the new start for Plymouth men followed George Weymouth's exploration of the New England coast in 1605. He brought home five Indians to Plymouth, three of whom he gave to Gorges, the Governor of Plymouth. Indian and African servants were already not uncommon in the town.

Gorges joined with Chief Justice Popham, a Somerset man like himself, Ralegh Gilbert, heir to the Ralegh patent for Virginia, and William Parker the old privateer captain, to form the Plymouth Company of Virginia. They received a charter from the King granting them all America between 41 and 45 degrees north; the London Company of Virginia also had a charter giving them all America between 34 and 38 degrees north. Roughly, Plymouth was given New England and the London Company was given Virginia. Plymouth sent out a ship at once but the Spanish, still claiming all America, captured it. Another ship went out the next year with two of Gorges's Indians as interpreters, Ralegh Gilbert as admiral and Captain George Popham as president. They endured a bitter winter and found nothing but 'extreme extremities', and in 1608 a relief ship brought them all back. Jamestown, which the London Company set up at the same time, survived to become the first unbroken English settlement in North America. Plymouth was to play a great part in keeping Jamestown going, though it was never very receptive to the pressures Captain John Smith, that great advocate of settlement, constantly put upon the town. Smith was a man of many adventures, chief among them his being captured by Indians and only saved from death through the pleading of the king's daughter, Pocohontas. She was to marry a Puritan settler, John Rolfe, who did much to set up the tobacco industry in Virginia. Rolphe brought her to England in 1616; they landed at Plymouth. Her father also sent home one of his men to spy out the strength of these white men; he landed at Plymouth with a large stick, meaning to carve a notch for every Englishman he saw!

One of the Jamestown support voyages led to the discovery of Bermuda. Sir George Somers sailed from the Sound in 1609 with nine ships and 600 passengers. Eight reached Jamestown but Somers was wrecked on Bermuda where he wintered. Soon after a permanent settlement was established.

But Plymouth ships were finding trade with the Indians more profitable than settlement. They were setting up trading posts for the summer months to buy fish and above all furs, but bringing these and their men home for the winter. The posts were used year after year, and some were acquiring English names. Gorges and Popham had Plymouth ships in this business, as did Robert Trelawny. His father had moved from St Germans into Plymouth in 1578, apprenticed for eight years 'to be enstructed in the trade of merchandize'. Through marriage the family were linked with the Hawkinses, the Sparkes and the Gayers. The younger Robert had a town house in Looe Street and was mayor three times. The Treville family also moved into the New England trade.

The Plymouth men sent Richard Hawkins out to survey settlement possibilities in 1615 but he found Indian wars ravaging the coast and went on to Virginia. Captain John Smith was sent out from Plymouth as well, but true to form he was hammered in a storm, captured by French privateers, and escaped from his La Rochelle prison the following year. He constantly upbraided Plymouth for lack of enterprise but knew the port's value; it was, he wrote, 'near as much trouble but much more danger to sail from London to Plymouth than from Plymouth to New England'. The Plymouth Company named him Admiral of New England but stuck to the trade. It made money with little sickness or fighting; in 1619 one Plymouth ship of 200 tons was on the coast for six weeks with 38 men and boys and sold the cargo of furs for £2,000. The next year John Smith said every seaman in the trade had £20 in his pocket for seven months' work. A stay-at-home craftsman would do well to earn £8 in that time, and he would have to keep himself as well.

With such profits it is not surprising to find a new charter being sought by Gorges and his friends in 1620, giving them all trading, fishing and settlement rights from 40 to 48 degrees north, from Atlantic to Pacific. While the negotiations were still in hand the first trespassers sailed into Plymouth.

They were separatists from the countryside between Doncaster and Gainsborough, Calvinists who, despairing of purifying the Church from within (the Puritan aim), became nonconformists. They had moved to Holland in 1607 to practise their religion in freedom but found their children growing up as Dutchmen. So they resolved to move to the New World where they could follow both their religion and their English way of life. They had a licence from the London Company of Virginia and had chartered two ships, the *Mayflower* and the *Speedwell*, for the crossing. The emigrants had assembled in Southampton where a number of English sympathisers joined them, put into Dartmouth for repairs, and again into Plymouth because the little *Speedwell* seemed unfit for the voyage. There they resolved that *Mayflower* would sail alone and on 6 September 1620, with 102 passengers aboard, she 'loosed from Plymouth, having been kindly entertained and courteously used by divers friends there dwelling'.

There is no evidence of any separatist body in Plymouth as early as 1620, but from what is known of the religious feelings of the town at that time it can be accepted that the clergy and the people would have understood them. Beyond their religious sympathies, they would have known that these Pilgrims were setting out across the Atlantic at the wrong time of year, when the Newfoundland and the Maine fishing fleets were homeward bound, and they would have known what hardships any settlers in New England would have to face. In fact this company of men, women and children anchored under Cape Cod on 11 November, found a place to settle across the bay, and did establish the first permanent English settlement in New England. As it happened their choice of settlement was a little harbour long used as a summer fishing and trading point;

Captain John Smith's map of 1615 of this coast called it 'Plymouth' and the new settlers kept this name in honour of their last English port of call.

But the Plymouth Company got its new charter and one of the first things the Pilgrims had to do was to regularise their position with the company. From now on settlement was encouraged and the Pilgrims found neighbours, not always welcome, arriving in small numbers round Massachusetts Bay to the north of them. Abraham Jennings, who had the biggest share of the import–export business in Plymouth in the year the *Mayflower* sailed, bought Monhegan Island off the Maine coast from Gorges soon after to support his summer fishing. David Thompson, who had been married in St Andrew's Church in 1613, settled in 1623 where Boston now stands, his new venture financed by Nicholas Sherwill and other Plymouth merchants. He built a strong house, made friends with the Pilgrims, and when he died in 1629 his widow married another Devon man, Samuel Maverick. From this Devon pair the famous Texas family of Mavericks has descended. In 1623 too the *Ann* embarked sixty settlers at Plymouth, mainly local people, who spent their first winter with the Pilgrims. Also in 1623 another Plymouth merchant, Leonard Pomeroy, sent his *Providence* up the Piscataque river to settle the first English in New Hampshire. Gorges and his partner Mason had divided their new charter lands between them, Mason calling his New Hampshire after his native county and Gorges calling his New Somerset.

PIRATES IN THE CHANNEL

When James I ended the Spanish war in 1604 he may have opened new trading areas to Plymouth merchants but at the same time he began to run down the navy and ceased issuing letters of marque to English privateers. For Plymouth seamen this had been good business and Plymouth merchants handled their prizes. Now, out of work, some privateers turned downright pirates and found Plymouth merchants still willing to deal with them. In the early years of the reign the Dutch were still at war with Spain and their privateers, notably the

Dunkirkers, were a constant scourge to our traffic. As the Dutch retired from the scene the galleys of Algiers, the 'Turks', long a Mediterranean danger, moved into the Channel in 1609 and with them the Sallee Rovers from the Atlantic coast of Morocco. Between 1609 and 1616 the 'Turks' took 466 English ships in the Channel. Some of the English pirates linked up with the Turks, notably John Ward who had long associations with Plymouth. He is said to have gone over to the Bey of Tunis and taught his men the techniques necessary for Atlantic work. On one occasion Ward sailed into Plymouth after a fight with Frenchmen and recruited replacements for his crew. In 1609 two men were paid 16d for watching at the Barbican to see that no food was taken aboard a pirate ship; clearly pirates used the harbour and had friends ashore. Even Sir Richard Hawkins, Vice-Admiral of Devon, was constantly accused of favouring the pirates. A true Jacobean mixture here, a Puritan town paying touring theatre companies and entertainers to go away; yet consorting with pirates; men of deep social conscience (as will be seen) working with heartless embezzlers.

Into this world came a breath from the past. Sir Walter Ralegh, languishing in the Tower since his framed trial for treason in 1603, was released to seek out his El Dorado in Guiana. He came into Plymouth with his little fleet in 1617, was entertained by the mayor, Robert Trelawny, and the town paid for a drummer to beat the men to their ships. In June 1618 he was back, his son dead and his expedition a failure. His friends advised him to fly but he went to stay with his friend Harris at Radford. His wife persuaded Ralegh that the King was intent on his death, and got him to agree to take passage in a ship for France. At dead of night they rowed across Hooe Lake and down the Cattewater to join the ship, but Ralegh would not go on. He went back to Radford, and so to London and death on the scaffold.

One man who watched his execution was John Eliot of Port Eliot. It was a turning point for him; from being a man about court and a protégé of Buckingham, that villainous favourite of the King, he came back to Plymouth to work. He became Vice-Admiral of Devon and set about the corruption and the pirates. A plan to attack Algiers, the main base of the Turks, had been talked about since 1617. In 1619 all ports were required to contribute to its cost. Plymouth's share of £1,000 was matched only by Bristol; even Exeter was only asked for £500. Plymouth said its losses to the pirates had been so great that it could not raise the money, but it tried hard to get the Cornish ports – its official outports – to pay their share.

In 1620 a fleet of twenty ships assembled in the Sound with Sir Robert Mansell as admiral. He was head of the Navy Board and according to Dr Williamson 'probably the most eminent master of graft in our history'. Sir Richard Hawkins was called out of retirement to join him; the fleet sailed to Algiers and achieved no more than a useless treaty with the Bey. The fleet came home next year, the men were never paid and Sir Richard died arguing their case in the Privy Council.

Sir John Eliot took on the local pirates. He visited the Torbay headquarters of John Nutt, the most notorious pirate on the Devon coast, captured his ships and imprisoned him. Nutt had friends in high places and Eliot not only saw him released but found himself imprisoned for his vigour, as Richard Hawkins had been before him. But Eliot, out again, kept at his work. He brought untried pirates in gaol in Plymouth to trial and hanged them; another twenty caught red-handed he hanged in a day. As MP for St Germans he was vocal in Parliament and hated both by James I and his son Charles, who came to the throne in 1625.

Eliot found a local enemy in James Bagge the younger. His father, another James, had moved from Poole to Plymouth some time before 1590 to further his privateering interests. He was mayor in 1595 and again in 1605, an agent of the Crown by 1597, and Collector of Customs for Plymouth and Fowey. He was also cantankerous and (one suspects) anti-Puritan: he called Sherwill 'a seditious fellow', threatened to break the neck of Thomas Fownes and called the 1613 mayor, John Scoble, an insolent knave. In 1614 the town replaced him as MP by Thomas Sherwill, and in 1615 the mayor and magistrates took further action and James Bagge was 'clean removed from the Bench'. Even then he got himself restored by suing in the King's Bench. But the old man moved into retirement, resigning his customs posts in favour of his son, buying a farm at Saltram and beginning to build the great house there before his death in 1624. Young James Bagge moved into prominence, an MP for Cornwall in the 1620s and the Plymouth tool of the King's favourite, Buckingham.

THE SPANISH WAR

In 1625 Charles I declared war on Spain and began assembling an army 10,000 strong at Plymouth. Bagge was victualling officer. There were billeting troubles at once; when the fleet came in it brought the plague and seamen were put ashore in improvised tents. Twenty Sallee Rovers were on the coast, no food ships coming in, the soldiers mutinous and plundering the countryside for food. Charles himself came down for ten days, knighted the young Bagge, reviewed the army on Roborough Down and received a purse of £150 from the town. There were many expenses, and the town was also building plague houses at Lipson and Mount Batten to house the worst cases.

Buckingham stayed on at Saltram till the fleet sailed in October; it was back into the Cattewater in two days in complete disorder. It sailed again a week later, failed miserably to take Cadiz or the Spanish treasure fleet, and all through December the ships were limping back into Plymouth with hardly enough men to stand watches. The army was ordered into billets in Plymouth, the soldiers half-naked, plague-ridden and starving. Conditions were so bad in the town that the commissioners of the army had to meet at Plympton. Nearly 500 seamen deserted for a mutinous meeting at Cawsand. Plymouth people were fleeing the town but, like the soldiers billeted in the villages around, they only spread the plague. It reached Buckland Monachorum and Sir Francis Drake, nephew of the great seaman, moved to his house at Meavy where the commissioners next met. By June 1627 they were writing to London that the plague was so far spread that all commerce had ceased, by July the mayor was writing that only two magistrates were left in the town. Local government was collapsing.

The fleet began to go in May but the soldiers remained till September; when they went they could not even carry their muskets. How many servicemen died is not known, but Plymouth lost between 1,600 and 2,000 people, a quarter of the population.

In Parliament Sir John Eliot launched a violent attack on royal mismanagement and sought to impeach Buckingham. The Plymouth scandal was the major ground. John Eliot led the attack; he was MP for Newport, Launceston, a pocket borough of Drake's. A childhood friend of Drake's was John Pym who had grown up at Halton, on the Cornish bank of the Tamar, and was now MP for Tavistock. (Drake's son married Pym's daughter in 1641). Drake became MP for Plympton and William Strode of Newnham, related by marriage to the family, sat for another Drake Seat, Bere Alston. The Plymouth members were Thomas Sherwill, that Puritan smuggler of sermons, and John Glanville, son of the great Elizabethan judge, of Kilworthy, near Tavistock.

When Charles tried to dissolve the 1625 Parliament it was John Glanville who moved the protest. When another Parliament was called in 1626 Eliot demanded the impeachment of Buckingham. It was common gossip in Devon that most of the money to feed the army at Plymouth had gone into Bagge's pocket. Bagge was not in the House when the member for Totnes, Sir Francis Seymour, called him 'the bottomless Bagge'. But both Buckingham and Bagge survived; it was Eliot who found himself imprisoned for eleven days and removed from his vice-admiralty. The office went to Bagge, already Vice-Admiral for Cornwall.

That autumn Plymouth had to build a house in the fields, away from the plague-ridden streets, for the mayor-choosing of Thomas Sherwill. Next spring they found another army assembling, this time to aid the Protestants of La Rochelle. Buckingham was in command, staying at Saltram while the same horror story was repeated: burglary, rape, murder, mutiny, plague. The fleet made two ineffective sallies to aid La Rochelle, the only result being that the Huguenots lost the town. The soldiers were left to winter in Plymouth, plague-ridden again, left in tents on the Hoe, shoeless and frostbitten in one of those bitter winters of the time. Merchants like Nicholas Blake were ruined; the mayor, Robert Trelawny, died in office.

After one mutiny was started outside the Guildhall a scaffold was erected on the Hoe to hang the ringleader, but the mob threw it into the sea.

When Parliament reassembled in 1628 it was Eliot and Pym who presented the Petition of Right which Charles was forced to accept. In the 1629 Parliament, when the House refused to answer the King's summons to the Lords, young William Strode was one of the two members who held the Speaker in his seat while Eliot finished his speech. It was the last Parliament for eleven years. Eliot was back in the Tower, to die there in 1632. Strode rotted in prison for eleven years, Pym applied himself to the New England settlements. James Bagge was even made Governor of Plymouth when Gorges resigned in 1629. But his run was nearly over. In 1634 he was denounced to the Star Chamber, a career of embezzlement over many years disclosed, and he was even said to have 'cozened the King himself' of £20,000 over billeting. No wonder the soldiers in Plymouth had fared so ill, the townsmen groaned so loud, and Saltram grown so fine. Now Bagge was ruined, and Saltram forfeit to the state until the debts were repaid. Yet when he died in London in 1638 he was still described as holding all his old offices.

His twenty-year-old son, George, asked for all these posts, but was only given the governorship of Plymouth on condition that he accepted a lieutenant named by the King. He turned out his uncle, another George Bagge, who had been deputy, but young George did not keep the post long. In January 1639 King Charles gave the post to one of his most experienced soldiers, Sir Jacob Astley, a fifty-year-old veteran of the Low Country wars. Young George was only left with Saltram and its debts.

POST WAR TRADE

Though Charles's overseas adventures brought much of Plymouth's normal life to a standstill, trade did not entirely cease. Some Newfoundland fishing went on, though Abraham Jennings, who supplied £642 worth of fish to the 1627 expedition, was still unpaid when he died twenty years later. There was also a brief revival of privateering; eighty ships of

Plymouth had letters of marque in the war years and many prizes were brought in. After the war, trade made an unsteady recovery, with tin and wool going out, but rather less than before the war, and wine imports rather more. But as with most provincial ports, the 1630s saw a failure to recover the pre-war levels of trade. Pirates were still a menace to commerce: the Turks caught the Plymouth fishing fleet in 1636 and took thirty prisoners.

All through the 1620s bodies of settlers sailed from Plymouth, with many from the town and the neighbourhood. In 1630 the *Mary and John* left Plymouth with about 150 people from the Dorset area who founded the town of Dorchester in Massachusetts. But that year saw the big move into New England when a fleet of ten ships from Southampton took out over 700 people, mainly from eastern England. They had their own charter of self-government, and from their town of Boston the modern state of Massachusetts was created. Gorges surrendered his New Somerset rights in 1635 and in time his land became the state of Maine. He is still honoured as its founder, and a tablet in St Budeaux Church – he lived in the parish, at Kinterbury on Tamarside – commemorates the link. It is still remembered that Robert Trelawny, son of Gorges's old partner, together with Moses Goodyear, son-in-law of Abraham Jennings, financed the founding of Portland, the capital of Maine. But in the 1630s New England became for Plymouth what it had originally been, a place for trade with the new settlers replacing the Indians. By 1637 the colonists had taken over all the fishing on their coast.

The Newfoundland fishing prospered, however, growing stronger than before the war. Plymouth played a leading part in gaining the 'Western Charter' of 1634 which gave the West Country ports control and considerable privileges in the fisheries, and by 1641 declared itself 'chiefly dependent on the fish trade'.

WEALTH AND BUILDING

In spite of all the problems besetting Plymouth in this first part of the seventeenth century it was not a poor town; at least it had rich and generous merchants. Early in the reign the old Tudor guildhall and the market cross beside it were removed and a new guildhall built. There were two storeys on the old guildhall site and the council chamber was on the first floor, supported by pillars over the old market cross area which was now a covered space where the market could be held, processions to church start and great events be announced as they had through Plymouth's history. The total cost was £794 8s 1d and detailed accounts down to the last nail survive.

In 1612 William Lawrence, a merchant of Foxhole (Vauxhall Street), left £100 in his will to Thomas and Nicholas Sherwill to build an orphanage, the money to be paid when his good ship *Jonathan* came home from the Straits. The Sherwills and other merchants gave money and endowments of property in and around the town and the Orphan's Aid was built in Catherine Street with the date 1615 over the doorway. Then in 1630 more money was raised to build the Hospital of Poor's Portion just below the Orphan's Aid. It was the first true workhouse; the need for it may be a comment on the distress left by Charles's wars with Spain and France. The corporation had control of it, and the doorway surmounted by the town arms is preserved in the gardens behind New Street. Thomas Fownes also built almshouses in Basket Street in 1628, yet when he died in 1637 he still left £9,000 in cash with which his son could set up as a country gentleman at Whitleigh. Young Trelawny was able to rebuild Ham in 1639, the building which just survives in corporation ownership. The Trevilles were able to buy Budshead at St Budeaux. The Sherwills acquired the Houndiscombe estate, stretching west of Mutley Plain from East North Road to Ford Park.

THE NEW CHURCH

But these Puritan merchants had not finished their troubles with King Charles when his foolish wars ended. In 1631 Plymouth appointed Thomas Forde, vicar of Brixton, to be the lecturer at St Andrew's. But with the King's support the high church party was gaining strength nationally, and Forde was a notable Puritan. The King ordered that he should not be admitted. Next year the vicar, old Henry Wallis, died after twenty-nine years in office. Plymouth nominated Alexander Grosse of Plympton, another great Puritan. The Bishop of Exeter refused to institute him, so Plymouth put up the already banned Forde. Not only was he banned again by King and Church but the King took back the advowson from the corporation and in 1634 his nominee was instituted, Dr Aaron Wilson, rector of St Stephen's, Walbrook, and a staunch Royalist. So Plymouth made Grosse lecturer. The King forced him to retire, and appointed Thomas Bedford. The new vicar was soon at loggerheads with his parish. He said the street market was overflowing on to church property, that the councillors had no right to pews in the church, or to appoint a churchwarden.

Within months Plymouth resolved to petition the King, on the grounds of the increased population of the town, that Plymouth be divided into two parishes and to permit 'some worthy and devoted Gentlemen, our neighbours' to build a new church. John Hele of Wembury offered a site, Sir John Gayer of London was among the prospective benefactors, Robert Trelawny was mayor and the not yet discredited Sir James Bagge chosen to present the petition. This was as diplomatic as the 'increased population' reason: Plymouth no doubt hoped for a church as Puritan as St Andrew's had been before Wilson. There were endless arguments over the matter until 1640 when Charles, under all-round pressure, was persuaded to give back to the corporation the advowson of St Andrew's, and permit the new church. The King said it was to be called Charles Church! The necessary Act of Parliament received royal assent in 1641 and building began at once, at the town's expense, on a site on the north-eastern edge of the then built-up area. (The dividing line between the two parishes zigzagged from the Parade to Old Town Street, and thence by way of Cobourg Street, East North Road and Tavistock Road to the town boundary, with Compton Giffard outside the boundary added to Charles parish).

So with interrupted trade, pirates, futile wars, starved mutinous armies, plague and religious strife, Plymouth had no cause to love King Charles. In the 1630s the town resisted the imposition of ship money less strongly than the rest of Devon; it could see the benefits of the resultant stronger navy with convoys for merchantmen and the qualified success of the 1637 expedition against Sallee. But Plymouth's neighbours, the dowager Lady Drake of Buckland Abbey and Richard Strode of Plympton, brother of the imprisoned William, were the Devon Hampdens in the ship-money disputes.

And when Charles eventually recalled Parliament in 1640 it was dominated by the Plymouth neighbours. John Pym led the House, John Glanville was Speaker. When this Short Parliament was replaced by the Long Parliament, Strode was back from prison. When the King came to arrest the five members chiefly opposed to him, two of them were Pym and Strode. Their chief defender was John Maynard, MP for Totnes and Recorder of Plymouth. The five escaped, but from that moment Civil War was certain. There was no doubt where the sympathies of Plymouth lay.

CHAPTER TWO

CIVIL WAR: 1642–6

W HEN the Civil War did come in 1642 there was a great searching of men's minds; many who had opposed the King in Parliament drew the line at fighting against him. In Cornwall Lord Robartes, whose father had bought the title out of the fortunes the family had made as merchants of Truro, and built the great mansion that still stands at Lanhydrock, near Bodmin, stayed with Parliament. So did Francis Rous of Halton, John Pym's half-brother, and Sir Alexander Carew of Antony House, just across the Tamar from Plymouth. Otherwise the Cornish MPs and gentlemen were almost solidly for the King, led by Edward Hyde, the MP for Saltash who became the great Earl of Clarendon. Among them was Sir Nicholas Slanning of Maristow, son-in-law of James Bagge and one of Plymouth's MPs.

Of the country members and gentlemen on the Devon side of Plymouth the notable declarations for the King were the Champernownes of Modbury, John Glanville of Tavistock, John Harris of Radford and Robert Trelawny of Ham. Trelawny, Mayor of Plymouth in 1640, was still trading in the town. He had declared for the King when still a Plymouth member and had been removed from office and twice imprisoned for his views, but once free he began moving his ships quietly down to Falmouth. Plymouth, like most ports – in Devon, Exeter, Dartmouth and Barnstaple – declared for Parliament when the war began; Devon was in Parliament hands and Cornwall held by the King's men.

When Charles raised his standard at Nottingham in August 1642 he had already sent for the Governor of Plymouth, Sir Jacob Astley, to be his major-general of foot. The Plymouth fort and Drake's Island were without a commander and the mayor, Thomas Ceely, took both over without any protest from the garrison. Had the King left Astley as his commander in the west, who knows what different lines the war might have followed. But Parliament sent a distinguished soldier, Colonel Ruthven, later Lord Grey de Ruthven, to command at Plymouth, and young Sir Francis Drake (he succeeded his father in 1641) raised a regiment called the Plymouth Horse. Sir Ralph Hopton commanded Cornwall for the King. In November he advanced on Exeter but, finding it too strong, fell back on Tavistock and moved against Plymouth, cutting off the town's water supply from Burrator. He drove in Ruthven's outposts and then with 2,500 men attacked from Plympton. But Ruthven held the narrow passage of Long Bridge for three hours and Hopton fell back. Alarmed for Plymouth, Parliament sent Lord Robartes to command the west and raised three regiments of foot soldiers and a thousand dragoons to defend the town. In December Ruthven successfully broke up a Royalist assembly at Modbury; then in January 1643 he advanced with the Plymouth force into Cornwall only to be badly mauled at Braddock Down, between Liskeard and Lostwithiel. The survivors fell back on Saltash but Hopton flung them back over the Tamar and Plymouth for the first time was closely besieged.

Under the Earl of Stamford, who with his Devon army had joined Ruthven in Cornwall, and the new mayor, Philip Francis, a hasty line of earthworks was built across the vital ridge north of the town, looking down on the mile-wide gap between the head of Stonehouse Creek at Pennycomequick and the head of Lipson Creek, where St Augustine's Church now stands. Five regiments sat round the town, but the Cornish would not cross the Tamar, without them the Royalists felt too weak to attack, and on 29 January 1643 unsuccessful attempts were made to arrange a local truce in a meeting at Ham House.

Parliament built up the Plymouth garrison by sea till it was estimated that there were 9,000 men in the town. The Royalists sat tight around, but their foraging upset the Devon countrymen who rose and attacked a concentration at Modbury again. As the defeated Royalists streamed into Plympton they found the main army on the move back to Tavistock; the Plymouth garrison had attacked to support the Devon men. Now a local truce was arranged that lasted from 28 February until 22 April.

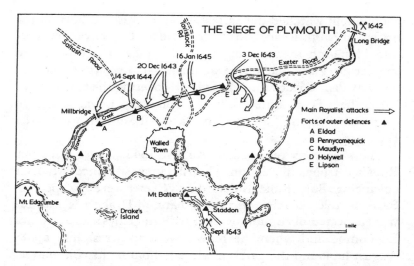

THE SIEGE OF PLYMOUTH. *The outer defences ran along the ridge overlooking the two creeks to the north and the Mutley Plain isthmus, with the forts commanding the roads.*

But Parliament disapproved of these local arrangements, sent commissioners and reinforcements into Plymouth to stiffen the Committee of Devon, in the town since the débâcle at Braddock Down, and the day after the truce ended there were Plymouth regiments fighting between Lifton and Launceston, and in the advance into Cornwall which was broken in the Battle of Stratton on 16 May. Leaving light forces to watch Plymouth, the Cornishmen advanced across Devon to besiege Bristol, but they had overrun their strength.

Plymouth, left in peace through the summer of 1643, built up its defences. The Elizabethan walls, such as they were, had been allowed to deteriorate; even the gates had been removed in 1620. Now the walls were repaired and the gates rebuilt, but the true defence of the town had to be further out. The key was the line of earthworks already built and it was now strengthened with five triangular forts. Ditches were dug and the earth flung inside to make ramparts, in turn topped with wooden stockades. Lipson Fort, roughly at the corner of Lipson Road and Queen's Road, covered the London road. Holywell Fort at the crossroads by Greenbank Fire Station dominated the second road, Maudlyn on the site of the Blind Institution controlled North Hill, Pennycomequick Fort at the present North Cross roundabout watched the Saltash road, and Eldad Fort, at the bottom of North Road, covered Millbridge. The only other ways into Plymouth then meant water crossings. There were two smaller forts in Stonehouse watching that waterfront, and two more at Prince Rock and Cattedown covering the Cattewater. An outlier, Fort Stamford above Turnchapel, was meant to control the Mount Batten peninsula and the entrance to Sutton Harbour.

The siege was resumed in August 1643. There were 900 Royalist troops based on Plymstock and Prince Maurice advancing; Barnstaple, Bideford and Exeter were all captured. Sir Alexander Carew was in command of Drake's Island. He was suspected of communicating with the Royalists at Mount Edgcumbe and when the mayor went to arrest him on 19 August he found the garrison already holding its commander prisoner on the beach. Carew was sent to London by sea and executed for high treason. New Parliamentary soldiers took command of Plymouth, Colonel James Wardlaw and Colonel William Gould. They launched raids on the besiegers at Hoe and Roborough, but Prince Maurice had taken Dartmouth and was advancing on Plymouth, the only place still held by Parliament in Devon or Cornall.

Fourteen of Maurice's regiments supported the 900 men already investing the town, billeted at Plymstock, Plympton, Buckland Monachorum, Tamerton and Cawsand. Royalist ships from Falmouth closed the sea approaches. For seventeen days Royalists battered the isolated Fort Stamford and after a heroic struggle the men there had to yield; they were allowed to march out with colours flying, bag and baggage. A Royalist battery was set up which could bombard the Hoe. An Oreston battery had already closed Sutton Harbour and with Stonehouse Creek closed by Mount Edgcumbe guns, Millbay had become for the first time in history the harbour of Plymouth.

It was a desperate situation. The bickering between townsmen and the imported military ceased, Colonel Gould took full command, and all the beleaguered took a solemn vow and covenant 'to the utmost of my power faithfully to maintain and defend the towns of Plymouth and Stonehouse . . .' Work

26

parties brought in timber from close at hand to strengthen the defences; a covering force at Thorn Hill chased a Royalist patrol back to Crownhill on 11 November but it was the last raid for a long time. The whole western army was tight round the town, with Prince Maurice setting up his headquarters at Widey Court, recently built by 'Yeoman Hele', of the newly rich legal family.

Then treason was found again. Ellis Carkeet, 'a malignant mariner', was arrested after trying to persuade the gunner at the Maudlyn to blow up his fort. Two of his accomplices, Henry Pitts, a wine merchant, and Moses Collins, a lawyer, fled to the enemy. They nearly brought the town down.

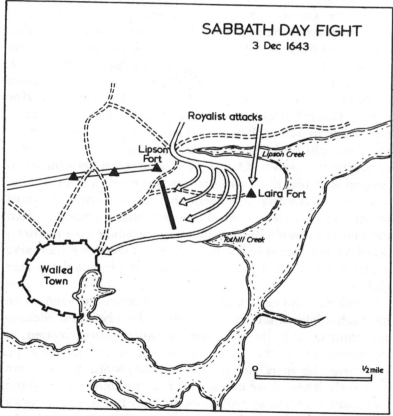

THE SABBATH DAY FIGHT. *A reconstruction of the tactics of the battle, with the black line representing the garrison's main stand against the Royalists' attempt to turn its defence line.*

Three hours before daylight on Sunday 3 December they guided 400 Royalist musketeers across Lipson Creek to take by surprise a little fort at Laira Point, where the Astor Institute now is. From Plymouth 150 horsemen and 300 musketeers streamed out to the rescue; they failed to dislodge the enemy and found Prince Maurice with his main force had advanced from Compton village around the head of Lipson Creek and, filing left, were moving up the northern slopes of Mount Gould. The rescue party charged the new threat without avail, and some Royalist cavalry broke through the disorganised defenders to reach the very walls of Plymouth. There they were all killed or captured and the main force of the garrison stood with their left flank resting on Lipson Fort. The Royalists held the Mount Gould peninsula; any retreat by the defenders would mean that the attack would be behind the fortified line.

For four hours the defence held. A small gun at what is now the top of Mount Gould Road worked havoc among the Royalist cavalry, and sixty musketeers moved along the southern slopes of Tothill to take the Cavaliers in the rear. Then, at the sound of a drum, Gould led the advance. Maurice, finding forces behind him, began to pull back. Retreat became a rout. The incoming tide was filling Lipson Creek and the Royalists barely extricated themselves. One body of a hundred horsemen was trapped and nearly all captured or drowned in the tide; the total losses of the attackers are unknown but the defenders had few casualties. Colonel Gould had one horse killed under him and another wounded; from that day the whole area has been called Mount Gould and a monument in Freedom Park marks the point from which he probably directed the Sabbath Day Fight.

Seventeen days later Maurice tried to break the defence line by night infiltration between the Maudlyn and Pennycomequick,. and three bloody assaults were needed to dislodge this force. But by Christmas Day he had had enough, and moved his men back to winter quarters at Plympton and Tavistock. They drove all the cattle in the countryside before them and hoped to starve Plymouth out. But 'there came an infinite multitude of pilchards into the harbour, within the Barbican, which the people took up with great ease in baskets

. . . such a circumstance never happened before'.

For the first six months of 1644 Plymouth built up its defences and sent foraging raids as far out as Roborough. Maurice moved his main force to attack Lyme Regis and a new commander, Sir Bevil Grenville, took over. A grandson of the Grenville of the *Revenge*, he was a cruel and vicious soldier of fortune, known as 'Skellum' Grenville after a treacherous desertion of the Parliamentary cause. He despoiled the country houses of the Parliamentary gentry, from Lanhydrock to Buckland Abbey, stole their revenues and hanged their villagers. By April he had his main forces in the meadows between Plympton and Marsh Mills, with another force at St Budeaux.

But Plymouth was in good fettle. Morale and discipline had been raised to new heights under Colonel Gould and after his death in spring 1644 his successor, Colonel Martin, kept up a vigorous offensive. On 11 May 1,500 men drove the Cavaliers out of Roborough and came back with 100 prisoners. Four days later an amphibious assault force landed at Cremyll, captured the peninsula from Millbrook to Maker, and set fire to Mount Edgcumbe House before pulling back.

Then in July the Earl of Essex with half the Parliamentary main army marched into Cornwall. The forces besieging Plymouth fell back before him, and Essex even called 2,500 men out of the Plymouth garrison into his army. But the King and Prince Maurice were on the heels of Essex; he was trapped and defeated between Fowey and Par, and the remnants of a shattered army took refuge in Plymouth.

Robartes, escaped from the Cornish chaos, resumed the Plymouth command, and eight ships of the Parliamentary navy under Vice-Admiral Batten were in the port. Fort Stamford had been retaken earlier and Admiral Batten had fortified the tip of the peninsula; it has been called Mount Batten ever since. Colonel Martin was buried in St Andrew's that October, like Gould before him; Plymouth took a heavy toll of its defenders.

The King reached Widey Court on Tuesday 9 September; his main army of 15,000 men and 28 'great guns' menaced the town. Each morning he rode down Tavistock Road with his staff and generals to be received on the southern slopes of

Hartley Hill with much ceremony and saluting. 'Vapourings', the veterans of Plymouth called it, looking across from their defence line; Vapouring Hill stuck as a name and there is still a Vapron Road there. Did Charles remember that nearly twenty years before he had led an army up that hill from Plymouth for manoeuvres on Roborough Down?

He launched his attack the following Saturday. Lipson had been tried, and the Maudlyn; now it was a frontal attack on Pennycomequick, with a side thrust across Millbridge. The battle raged from dawn till nightfall; sailors from the fleet played a heroic part in the defence of the line, and it was never defeated. Next morning Charles and Maurice rode away, and only the lodge gates east of the dual carriageway at the foot of Manadon Hill remain of 'Our Court at Widey'.

Robartes was left facing Grenville. In October the garrison captured Millbrook and Saltash only for Grenville to retake them. Grenville kept up the pressure all that winter, even though plague and cold were filling Plympton St Mary churchyard with his men. In January 1645 he flung 6,000 men against the whole line of Plymouth's defences, concentrating on the main forts. He did capture the Maudlyn but it was retaken and the Royalists were cast back down the hill to Mutley Plain; they lost 300 men there alone. In February Grenville captured the ruins of Fort Stamford only to be turned out again. In March he went off to the siege of Taunton leaving 2,000 men facing Plymouth. Robartes too was recalled, a Committee of Defence taking control in Plymouth. By December, as the Royalist cause collapsed, so the garrison moved out, capturing St Budeaux and even Buckland Abbey. Col Sir Francis Drake with the Plymouth Horse was with the army that Fairfax and Cromwell were leading westward.

There was one last piece of cloak and dagger; Fairfax did not want to advance into Cornwall with the Royalist concentration at Mount Edgcumbe on his flank. He sent his chaplain Hugh Peters (whose mother was a Treffry of Fowey) into Plymouth where Phillipa Coryton (the family is still at Pentillie) came in disguise to meet him. The two, fanatic Roundhead preacher and Royalist maiden, both disguised, made their way by boat and horse through the armies to Mount

Edgcumbe and back to Fairfax, with the assurance that the Mount Edgcumbe men would not move.

Parliament recaptured Dartmouth on 18 January, and that day the last Royalist marched away from the Plymouth siege. Fairfax advanced to Bodmin, on 12 March the Cornish army surrendered, and on 25 March Fairfax and Cromwell were welcomed into Plymouth; '300 pieces of ordnance were discharged to welcome them thither'.

CHAPTER THREE

COMMONWEALTH AND RESTORATION: 1646–88

THE resolution of Plymouth during its three years of siege may have been a vital factor in the final victory of Parliament, but it cost the town dear. St Andrew's parish registers show 3,000 deaths for the period, when a normal figure for the 46 months of war would have been 300. The town had suffered little physical damage but all its energies had gone into the struggle. For the last two years the Committee of Defence kept the town going by borrowing money, totalling from £2,000 to £5,000 a month, from the merchants, even the service leaders, against the next ship bringing in cash from Parliament. Even the funds of the town's charities were used. At the end of the war food was short and the soldiers' wages unpaid; it took two grants totalling £16,000 to clear the debts.

The countryside round had been stripped by the besieging forces. Plympton St Mary church registers show the death rate for the last three years of war up threefold; Leigham and Boringdon had been ransacked, Saltram damaged and all its gardens, orchards and woods cut down. George Bagge, already saddled with his father's debts, was a broken man, and disappears from view after 1654. Francis Drake retired from the command of the Plymouth Horse and set about putting Buckland Abbey and its ravaged estate in order; in 1650 he had to sell Werrington Park to pay his debts.

TRADE AND THE NAVY

Plymouth, with this ravaged countryside around it, could take little comfort from the sea. The Newfoundland fisheries had kept alive during the war, at a much reduced scale. In 1652 there were only five Plymouth ships on the banks, and this the trade on which the port ten years before had been 'chiefly dependant'. The New England fishing had been taken over by

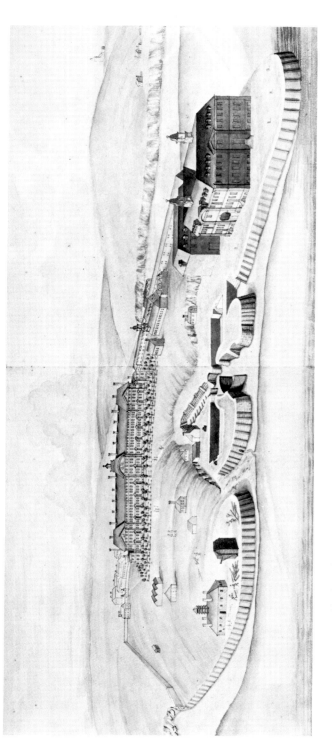

'A view of His Majesty's Dock-Yard at Plymouth taken from on board a vessel riding opposite the North Corner', from *A Survey of the Harbours and Dockyards of England*, 1698. In the centre is the square wet dock with the single dry dock behind it. To the left is a double-wheel crane and the smith's shop, to the right the 'Great Square Store House' with the hemp house behind and the rope walk running along the southern boundary. Behind the docks is the terrace of officers' houses. This drawing shows the dockyard in its original form; note the boats drawn up at North Corner, and the fact that the artist has sketched in houses outside the dockyard gates, although it is generally believed that the first houses were built in 1700, running from North Corner alongside the dockyard wall.

Above, 'A view of Plymouth Sound and yᵉ River Hamouze and Catwater taken from yᵉ rising ground above Mount Edgcomb . . . delineated 1697': a drawing by Edward Dummer, who was at the time supervising the building of the dockyard, which can be seen just right of Mount Edgcumbe House.
Below, 'The East Prospect of Plymouth', from *A Survey of the Fortifications in the Plymouth Division 1716*, by Col Christian Lilly. The drawing was made from Cattedown. Note the Victualling Yard below the Citadel.

the colonists before the war; thrown on their own resources during the war they had built their own ships and were carrying their own trade, reaching down to Virginia, Maryland and the West Indies, taking what had been the growth areas for Plymouth shipowners in the pre-war years. On top of that the remnants of the Royalist navy were at sea as privateers, with bases in Scilly and the Channel Islands until 1651. But Cromwell was building up the navy, which introduced a convoy system for merchantmen in 1649, crushed the Royalist privateers and within a few years cleared the Barbary pirates from the Channel.

More seriously for our shipping trade, the Dutch had taken over much of our foreign carrying-trade during the Civil War. The Navigation Act of 1651, forbidding foreigners to trade with our colonies, provoked the first Dutch war in 1652. Plymouth became a naval base again under Captain Henry Hatsell, who had commanded Drake's Island in the latter years of the Siege. He eventually lived at Saltram, close to the repair yards at Turnchapel and Teat's Hill. A hulk was also anchored in the Cattewater to house shipwrights, and stores were set up. The old castle became a hospital after de Ruyter mauled Sir George Ayscue's fleet in mid-Channel and chased him back into Plymouth. Later a house was taken over as a hospital and in 1654 a victualling establishment was established at Lambhay.

Once peace was signed with the Dutch, Cromwell launched a Spanish war which made Jamaica an English colony, kept Plymouth busy and frequently brought Robert Blake (who had commanded Lyme Regis as a soldier during the war) into the port as an admiral. In 1657, after crushing a Spanish fleet off Santa Cruz and dealing with the Sallee Rovers in their home port, he anchored in Cawsand Bay to die before he could come ashore. His heart was buried in St Andrew's Church beside that of Frobisher.

INDUSTRY

Industry also was helped by the navy. In 1665 their agent paid Thomas Teate the ropelayer £880 for 20 tons of cordage and Daniel Barker £962 for cable yarn – large sums for those days. A little earlier Teate had been buying land beside Sutton Pool which is still called Teat's Hill, and the town's largest ropewalk survived there until nearly the end of the nineteenth century. Barker was to be twice mayor.

Apart from the work engendered by the navy, there are signs of growing local industry. A yarn market had long been held weekly in St Andrew's churchyard where the spinners sold their yarn to the weavers. In 1653 the town built a proper Yarn Market in Old Town to serve them, though subsequent rents suggest that it did not do as much business as was hoped. The term 'clothier' begins to crop up in local records; these were the capitalists of the trade who bought the finished products and often financed the spinners and weavers who were small men working in their homes. Among those described as clothiers were new men of substance and members of old families, a Trelawny, and Harris of Manadon.

A new meat market, the Shambles, was also built down the middle of Old Town Street in 1657–8 with a Leather Hall above part of it. Here the tanners did business with the butchers and farmers; the manufacture of leather was the most important English industry after textiles and Plymouth had its share. The town seems to have had more than its share of brewers: indeed Captain Hatsell wished they could all be shipped to the West Indies, because their beer produced so much drunkenness.

RELIGION

The town was sufficiently recovered from the war to complete the building of Charles Church in 1657 (though the tower was only 20ft high) and to build a new grammar school within the Orphan's Aid in 1658. At the outbreak of the war the walls of Charles Church had reached roof height and it is thought that a canvas roof was improvised and the first services held there in 1643 by a Presbyterian chaplain to the garrison, Francis Porter. His communion table was in the nave and, to make it clear that this was a Puritan church with no altar, a door was built in the east wall. At the outbreak of war the town imprisoned the hated Dr Wilson of St Andrew's and sent him off to Portsmouth; on Wilson's death in 1643 the King named the lecturer, Bedford, as vicar. Plymouth then sent him packing by sea and appointed their own vicar, the saintly George Hughes. During the war all kinds of dissenters practised their religions freely but only the Baptists survived as a congregation. A Plymouth fuller, Abraham Cheare, whose father was tenant of one of the lower mills, became their pastor. In 1651 a meeting house was built in the Pig Market, the later Bedford Street, now roughly the frontage of Dingle's store on Royal Parade.

When two Quaker missionaries arrived in 1654 they marched into both St Andrew's and the Baptist meeting house to protest at the services being held. They caused an uproar, and two more Quakers who arrived the following year were arrested and sent for trial at Exeter. But a Society of Friends was established; they continued to protest in the older churches and neither fines nor imprisonment could check them. Arthur Cotton, a shopkeeper, and his wife Priscilla, and Nicholas Cole, a merchant, and his wife Mary, were early adherents, and the women made their protests and stood their imprisonment as much as the men. George Fox himself was in Plymouth in 1655 and there are prominent names among the Society's members: John Harris of Pennycross, John Light the clothier, and Elizabeth Trelawny, who became a regular correspondent with George Fox. For all their pacifism the Quakers brought a stormy atmosphere into Plymouth's religious life and in turn met much hostility from the other churches and the town leaders.

The Quaker unrest was paralleled by discontent in the countryside. The Royalist gentry, once they had settled the fines they had to pay for backing the losing side in the war, became restless. When the 'Sealed Knot' was formed in 1654 to co-ordinate the Cavalier efforts, they gave Sir John Grenville, son of the admirable Bevil and nephew of 'Skellum', the task of securing Plymouth as the first act in any rebellion. He actually found himself in gaol in Plymouth the following winter when the plans leaked out. They fizzled out in the abortive Penruddock uprising in the west in March 1655 when Plymouth hastily 'made up' the lines on North Hill, but the leaders were executed and seventy of the rank and file transported from Plymouth to Barbados. The rule of the major-generals was extended to the west and General Desborough took over the western counties. He had served Cromwell in the west before and visited Plymouth. St Andrew's Church was lining pews for him and his wife, Cromwell's sister, in 1652. In May 1659 Desborough was made Governor of Plymouth.

THE RESTORATION

Cromwell was forced into the near-despotism of the rule of the major-generals not only by the old Royalist–Episcopalians on the Right, but by the new forces of the Left, the Levellers, Fifth Monarchy men, Quakers, Anabaptists and Ranters. The old Parliamentary–Puritan men of the Civil War were the middle party now, and alarmed as much by the new Left as by the old Right. Fears for the future grew when Cromwell died in 1658 and his unpromising son Richard became Protector. Many old Parliament men like Robartes in Cornwall and Sir Francis Drake and John Maynard in Devon preferred the idea of a king to that of a left-wing republic. Of similar mind was William Morice who had bought Werrington Park from Drake and early in 1660 became Governor of Plymouth. (Seven years later he bought the Keyham, or Stoke Damerel, estate from the Wise family.) Morice arranged the vital meeting between his north Devon neighbour, General Monck, and the emissary of the King-in-exile, John Grenville. As a result Monck played the vital part in bringing King Charles II back to the throne in 1660. Monck became Duke of Albemarle, Grenville the Earl of Bath, Morice the King's Secretary of State and a knight. Maynard, the King's Serjeant-at-law, was also knighted and sat as MP for Plymouth almost constantly for the next thirty years. Morice was Plymouth's other MP, but in spite of his important part in the Restoration of Charles he retired into private life in 1668, saying that the King was debauching the nation.

Plymouth clearly had divided feelings about the Restoration, but the majority view preferred a king to the new Left. Charles was proclaimed in Plymouth 'with greate tryumph, the Cunditts Runing two dayes with wyne'. Apart from political concern, Plymouth had not prospered in the latter days of the Commonwealth. The wars had hit normal trade and though the needs of the fleet brought business the bills were not paid. By January 1660 the agent-victualler in the port reported six ships in the Sound with starving crews, and six more expected. His credit was exhausted and no one could go into the streets without being pestered for money. Wages for the navy were four years in arrears.

So Plymouth welcomed Charles II, but was aware of its past record in royal eyes. The £400 spent on a silver wine fountain for the King (it still has a proud place among the Crown Jewels in the Tower of London) was probably placatory, but its effect did not last long. In 1662 the Puritan mayor, William Allen, was removed from office along with six magistrates, thirteen councillors and the town clerk. The new mayor, William Jennens, was a 'church and king' zealot and applied the 1662 Act of Uniformity with vigour. Francis Porter of Charles Church conformed and kept his place but George Hughes of St Andrew's and his lecturer, Thomas Martyn, were ejected and imprisoned on Drake's Island, to be released after a few months and forbidden to come within twenty miles of the town. Abraham Cheare was in and out of Plymouth and Exeter gaols for three years before he too finished up on the island, where he died in 1668. Drake's Island became a notorious state prison; among its sufferers were Colonel Lilburn, one of the judges of Charles I, and later General Lambert, who had tried to set up a republic in place of the King's restoration. Both died on the island.

But the Puritans' spirit was not easily quenched. Driven from the parish churches, they formed their own, meeting in secret in private houses. The Rev Nicholas Sherwill of the old Plymouth family was one leader, Obadiah Hughes, son of the ejected vicar of St Andrew's, another. There had been ejections from both Plympton churches, from Tamerton, Brixton, Ugborough and many other villages; some of these pastors now came into Plymouth regularly to minister to the noncomformists. With the Declaration of Indulgence of 1672 five nonconformist ministers emerged to be granted licences, and a number of meeting houses were permitted. Sherwill led a congregation at the old town debtors' prison, now the gin distillery in Southside Street. Thomas Martyn, the ejected lecturer of St Andrew's, ministered in Green Street, near Charles Church. There was another congregation in Stonehouse, and the Baptists had survived, though their numbers were declining. The Quakers continued, though more quietly, mourning the death of some early leaders and the defection of others. They suffered most because they refused to hide, and met in the street if denied their meeting house.

The pattern of persecution seems to vary with the government of the town. Jennens was mayor until November 1663 and he regularly had Presbyterians, Baptists and Quakers in court before him. The persecution kept up until 1665, when even Sherwill had two months in gaol. After 1666 nonconformity 'seems to be winked at', to quote R. N. Worth, apart from a bad spell in 1669 when Jennens had some influence with the mayor. The Act of Indulgence brought real relief in 1672 and though it was soon repealed Plymouth paid no apparent attention and the nonconformists were left with far more liberty than the law permitted. When Jennens stood for Parliament in 1676 the first vote, that of the freemen, was so strong against him that he retired from the contest.

With the Toleration Act of 1689 came final freedom, and by 1704 the Southside Street congregation built a chapel in Batter Street. The later chapel buildings on this site are now part of the Virginia House Settlement. In 1689 the Baptists were still in the Pig Market. They had no pastor from the death of Cheare until 1689, when sixty-six members signed an invitation to a new minister. The Quakers, who had leased a house in Bilbury Street since 1675, bought the property in 1703 and were there with various rebuildings until 1918. The last building ended its days as a labour exchange and was demolished to make way for Breton Side bus station.

One group who had enjoyed this freedom before the Toleration Act were the Huguenots, French Protestants fleeing from Catholic persecution. Some forty or fifty reached Plymouth in 1681 and settled in both Plymouth and Stonehouse. The majority could accept the Anglican services of the day and at first both communities shared St George's Church, Stonehouse, a chapel of ease of St Andrew's. But the French communities grew and the Plymouth group were meeting in the old Marshalsea in Southside Street by 1706, and in 1710 built their own chapel in How Street. About 1690 the Edgcumbes found the Stonehouse community a chapel in Edgcumbe Street, and there was a third, Calvinistic, meeting house for them in Plymouth. The total community seems to have grown to about 700. Some were landowners, some very poor, but they found ways of earning a living. A French crew from Stonehouse took a Plymouth ship to Barbados in 1691; two started Plymouth's first paper mill, as early as 1710. But they were gradually assimilated into local life, and their anglicised names are still common in the city.

Charles Church was finally consecrated by the Bishop of Exeter in 1665, and Porter inducted. But that door in the east wall was walled up and the altar moved to the east end of the sanctuary. The walling-up is quite clear in the ruins that survived World War II, and in spite of this lapse the church Plymouth built for its Puritan conscience stayed a bastion of low churchmanship into living memory.

POST-RESTORATION TRADE

Plymouth's maritime trade, which had in common with that of the whole country picked up slowly during the Commonwealth, enjoyed thirty years of rapid expansion after the Restoration. It also changed direction. London, and to a lesser degree Exeter, merchants had moved into the Newfoundland fisheries with new methods, planting colonies of fishermen and sending out 'sac' boats with supplies and bringing back the fish. The Plymouth fishing fleet built up to twenty ships by 1677 and twelve were working on the sac principle, but the method took much capital which they had to borrow and the interest swallowed what profit they made. Plymouth had nearly abandoned Newfoundland by 1699 and though there was a revival in the eighteenth century it was short-lived. Plymouth vessels bought Newfoundland cod for south European markets until the end of the sailing ship era, but from the early eighteenth century this fishing was never a major Plymouth concern.

The new business was with the West Indies and the southern

mainland colonies. The Virginian tobacco trade was at first shared by Barnstaple, Bideford, Exeter and Plymouth. The West Indian islands, of which Barbados was the first to develop, started with tobacco but switched to sugar with coffee, cocoa, cotton and spices also in the smaller islands. They were fed by New England but the planters, in boom conditions, were getting luxuries, manufactures and cloth from England: the outward-bound cargoes were in small parcels so as not to swamp the small markets.

During the war years convoys escorted by warships sailed from Plymouth to the Americas and the Mediterranean, and up-Channel to the Downs. There were 56 ships in a 1666 convoy to Virginia and Barbados: a 1672 letter mentions 'the Straits fleet' waiting in the Cattewater for the weather. Customs returns for 1672 and 1676 show Plymouth in sixth place among English ports, with London roughly double all the outports put together and then Bristol, Hull, Dover, Exeter and Plymouth following in order; by 1679 and again in 1681 Plymouth was in fifth place. In the colonial trade alone she was outstripping Exeter and all the western ports by 1692, with 21 ships in the trade. Even Bristol only had 55. Exeter was sending serges by sea to Plymouth for export to the colonies, Spain, Portugal and Italy. Plymouth was the fourth English port for the Spanish and Portuguese ports in 1686, with 32 inbound ships and 42 out.

The West Indian links went beyond trading. In 1651 Francis Drake's brother-in-law, Charles Pym, went to look after the family estates in Nevis and Antigua; he was in Barbados in 1652 when the English fleet arrived, was one of the commissioners who surrendered the island to Parliament (it had been a Royalist stronghold), and in the reign of Charles II became a member of the Council for Foreign Plantations. George Bagge, brother of the Bottomless Bagge, turns up in 1667 looking for admission as a Poor Knight of Windsor (a military charity); he had been in Barbados. In his 1669 will Justinian Peard, Mayor of Plymouth in the last year of the Siege, mentions his interest in a plantation in Barbados. Peard was a North Devon man but he made enough money to rent what is now called the Merchant's House in St Andrew's

Street, then his own town house in Notte Street, and eventually to buy Cann House, Tamerton Foliot, as well. Peard was one of the magistrates removed from office after the Restoration; excluded with him was John Paige, because he had settled in Barbados. A Quaker meeting in 1677 was addressed by 'Katharine Norton, widow, late of Barbadoes'.

Count Magalotti, who arrived in Plymouth in 1669 in the court of that late Medici prince of Florence, Cosimo III, Grand Duke of Tuscany, wrote:

> The life of the city is navigation. The inhabitants export lead and tin in greater quantities than any other article, and with these they go to the Canaries and to the Western Islands. To Barbadoes, in the New World, and in every part of Europe, they act as carriers conveying merchandize from place to place at great profit to themselves. Hence it is that, in Plymouth, only women and boys are to be seen; the greater part of the men living at sea.'

He described how well supplied the town was, with all the necessaries and 'articles that administer to luxury and pleasure'. The town accounts tell the story: nearly £300 in 1666 to rebuild the Guildhall; nearly £100 in 1692 to build 'New Quay' – the Parade – and repair all the other quays; streets improved; exchanges for the comfort of merchants built on the Parade and the Barbican. John Lanyon left £2,000 in 1674 for the poor which with the Hele bequest of £500 some thirty years before founded Hele and Lanyon's School.

THE ROYAL CITADEL

Lanyon, a Cornish Royalist, had been appointed naval agent in Plymouth when Hatsell – a Commonwealth officer – was dismissed at the Restoration. In 1662 the Naval Board ordered the building of 'yards and buildings' at Plymouth when a fresh Dutch war was imminent, but in the event the war was concentrated in the North Sea and eastern Channel, and Sheerness Dockyard was built instead. In this 1664–8 conflict Plymouth had care of wounded seamen and prisoners of war, probably at Coxside, but Charles's mind was turning to coast

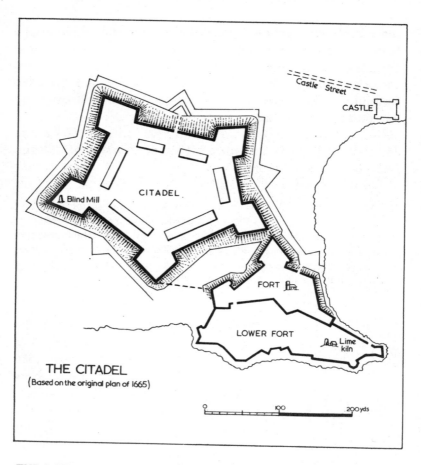

THE ROYAL CITADEL. *Sir Bernard de Gomme's original 1665 plan for the Citadel on Plymouth Hoe, a geometric star-shaped fortress alongside the Drake fortress of 1592–5. In fact the plans were changed to incorporate the Drake fort into the Citadel. Note the site of the medieval castle with its four towers, to the north.*

defences rather than ships at sea; he wanted a standing army. So in 1665 the commission was issued which led to the building of the Royal Citadel on Plymouth Hoe. Originally a self-contained conventional fort of the period was planned west of Drake's fort, with five bastions in the best Vauban style. Later the two eastern bastions were scrapped and the walls extended to take in Drake's fort, the old walls being built up to the new standard. A number of granite doorways from the old fort were used in the new building, and these with the irregular outline of

44

the eastern end alone remain of the Drake fort. Sir Bernard Gomme was the engineer and met some criticism over his unorthodoxy. Samuel Pepys in 1683, looking over the Citadel with a rival military engineer, wrote that 'De Gomme hath built very sillily'. But the new structure mounted 152 guns as against the old fort's 67. It is still one of the greatest fortresses of the period remaining in Britain and the gateway, attributed to Thomas Fitz, one of the nation's finest examples of baroque architecture.

The foundation stone inscribed 'Jo Earle of Bathe 1666' still faces the Hoe, and the walls were at an average height of 20ft in 1667. Twice that summer de Ruyter anchored in the Sound with a fleet of thirty Dutch ships, but each time kept well out from the Hoe. On the second visit the Earl of Bath sent out a flag of truce to say that the war was nearly over; the mayor and Sir Jonathan Trelawny went aboard the flagship amid much exchange of salutes. De Ruyter was back again in the Sound just after peace was declared. This was the year after the Dutch had towed the cream of our fleet out of the Medway; that they made no attempt to tamper with Plymouth shows their respect even for the half-built Citadel. Since its completion no enemy fleet has come into Plymouth Sound. The idea that it was built to cow a rebellious town was no doubt current in Plymouth and the Magalotti account of 1669 quotes it, but both the previous forts on Plymouth Hoe had all-round defence and they had not been built by suspicious monarchs.

The King himself was in Plymouth in 1671 with the Dukes of York and Monmouth to inspect progress. The King and his brother came again in 1676, this time with Samuel Pepys, the Secretary of the Navy, and on both visits inspections were made of the Cattewater and the Hamoaze, to see potential sites for the projected dockyard. But still no more was done.

THE LAST OF THE STUARTS

Though Charles might make flattering speeches in Plymouth, kiss merchant Allen's pretty young wife and touch for the king's evil, and though the corporation might make him costly presents, he did not have the town's love. His first act had been to pack the town council with his supporters. Within a couple of years there was a new town clerk, Edward Pollexfen of Kitley, near Yealmpton, who had been a stout Parliament man in the wars, a man who by the 1680s (when the terms Whig and Tory came into use) could be called a moderate Whig. He retired to Kitley in 1699 (his daughter Ann married William Bastard and the family is still there); his successor Robert Berry was another Whig. There were also devoted Tories like James Yonge. He learnt to be a surgeon in the navy, retired to his native Plymouth in 1670 to start in private practice and be surgeon to the little naval hospital, became a member of the council and eventually mayor. His diary gives a lively picture of the time, full of loyal sentiments with the Commonwealth years marked by a black mourning band which ends opposite the entry 'Cromwell ye great Rebell, went to ye devill in a tempest'. His family is still at Puslinch, looking across the Yealm to the Pollexfen descendants at Kitley.

For much of the rest of this century the parties seem to be about equally balanced in the council. When there was a dispute over a new vicar for St Andrew's in 1679 the two parties reached deadlock and the bishop put his man in, which 'caused great Animositeys'. There were things which upset both sides, like an early lawsuit. The Duchy of Cornwall owned the bed of Sutton Harbour, heart of the town's activity and wealth. It had always been leased to the town; early in the reign of Charles II it was leased to a Cornish cavalier and the ensuing lawsuit was not only lost by Plymouth but cost them some £2,500. It affected the ownership of all the quays, warehouses and private houses which the Plymouth merchants had been building out into the harbour for centuries, an activity which had speeded up with the new shipping boom. The Royal Citadel too spread over 41 acres of the Hoe which the town regarded as its own property. When the outworks reached into private property in 1679 payment was made, but the town land was just stolen. The royal visits were another drain on the town's purses.

The parish churches also had been forced to use services of a style forgotten for twenty years; it was an offence not to attend and early in the reign the Puritan conventicles were harrassed and oppressed. But the underground churches were never suppressed, though in a small town they cannot have been so very secret. Indeed in many mercantile towns the laws were increasingly ignored as Charles's reign wore on and public opinion increasingly turned against him. There is a gauge of Plymouth's attitude after the Rye House Plot of 1683; Monmouth, who was to have been put on the throne, fled to Holland, other leaders were executed or killed themselves, but two, Lord and Lady Landsdowne, took refuge in Plymouth.

King Charles, having successfully replaced the London Whigs by his own men, turned his attention to the provincial towns in 1683 and Plymouth was among the first. Only five aldermen voted against surrendering their charter; old Serjeant Maynard, still MP for the town and recorder, tried to stiffen resistance but Lord Chief Justice Jefferys, on assize in the west, advised them otherwise. When a new charter was obtained the following year (two members of the deputation died in London) it was met at Ridgeway, Plympton, with much celebration and ceremony. The King appointed in his charter all the officers, aldermen and councillors. But there had been two Whigs in the deputation; there were Whigs even among the men named by the King, and they were soon back in their old power-sharing position. Maynard was replaced as recorder by the Earl of Bath, but in practice Pollexfen served for him.

The accession of King James II was sharply followed by the Monmouth Rebellion. Plymouth was not directly affected but the method of its suppression did not go unnoticed. Within six months a group of Quakers from Plymouth and Stonehouse emigrated in the *Desire* to William Penn's new Quaker colony of Pennsylvania, where they planned to set up a woollen manufactory. James Fox, one of the leaders, was a member of the family prominent among West Country Friends ever since. They were soon to move into Philadelphia but their original settlement keeps the name of Plymouth Meeting to the present day.

James also looked at the Plymouth charter and the aid of the Earl of Bath was enlisted by the town. The earl swore that the town 'is now become as loyall as the garrison, which is no small reformation', and the 1684 charter survived. But the new King was rapidly alienating the Tories, and the Whigs had never wanted this Catholic King. When William of Orange landed at Brixham in 1688 his fleet came round to Plymouth. The Earl of Bath, in spite of his long allegiance to the Stuart cause, surrendered the Citadel, and arrested the loyalist Earl of Huntingdon, commander of the regiment in garrison. The troops declared for William of Orange. Plymouth was the first town in England to proclaim William and Mary, and the Black Book, the official civic record, has the entry, 'God wrought a wonderfull deliverance in these Kingdomes in rescuing us from Popery and Slavery . . .'

CHAPTER FOUR

PLYMOUTH DOCK: 1688–1750

THE accession of William and Mary meant the completion of the English Revolution that had begun with the Civil War. They were constitutional monarchs, invited to the throne by Parliament, and were to rule through Parliament. They also inherited from Cromwell and the later Stuarts a professional army and navy. No longer would England fight her wars at sea by hiring or commandeering private ships; now there was a state-owned fleet manned by regular officers and seamen, paid by Parliamentary vote.

Since Commonwealth days the naval wars had been with the Dutch, over trade, and mainly fought in the eastern Channel where the existing dockyards, from Deptford to Portsmouth. could serve the navy. The main need for a western port had been as a convoy base for the growing Atlantic and Mediterranean trades, and for repairing warships and refitting prizes.

Cromwell had established the hulk in the Cattewater; ten years later the Navy Board ordered the construction of yards and buildings at Plymouth, and the sale of the hulk. In December 1663 it was 'cried by the bellman according to custom, and put to the candle at £100, but no one would bid a penny'. No dock was built either, so the hulk was repaired, and in 1665 converted at least two Dutch prizes into English men-of-war. A map of that year shows the area between the entrance to Hooe Lake and Turnchapel marked 'the King's land fitting for a dock' and by 1667 the beaches there, and in front of the ropewalk on Teat's Hill, were being used to careen and repair naval ships.

But there was still no dock by the time William came to the throne. The Dutch wars were over, and while the Dutch had gone on fighting the French, we had taken back their maritime trade. William was the arch-enemy of the French and they now turned on us, aiming to restore the Stuarts. The naval harbour

which Richelieu had built at Cherbourg fifty years before and
Colbert had improved was fortified by Vauban in 1680–8. In
1688 too Louis XIV began building a great dockyard at Brest:
England more than ever had need of a western base to cover
these French arsenals.

After some debate in which Exmouth, Torbay, Dartmouth,
Bideford, the Cattewater (based on Turnchapel) and the
Hamoaze were all considered, the Admiralty decided on the
Cattewater. It wanted a stone dock (all earlier English docks
were of wood) but no one could be found at Plymouth to
undertake such a task. Ideas changed again and when in
December 1690 a contract was given to Robert Waters of
Portsmouth to build a stone dock, the site was fixed at Point
Froward, on the eastern side of the Hamoaze. The final
decision was urged by Edward Dummer, Surveyor to the Navy,
who planned and supervised the work and eventually increased
the size of the dock to be able to take first-rate ships and not just
cruisers, as originally planned.

A naval dockyard on the Hamoaze had originally been
suggested by Walter Ralegh. Charles I had considered Saltash
and his naval agent, Bagge, inspected a site with two Plymouth
elders. In 1671 Charles II with his brother James and Samuel
Pepys inspected all possible sites by boat – Sutton Harbour
(where naval ships had been repaired alongside Smart's Quay,
where the Fish Market now is), the Cattewater and the
Hamoaze. The latter site had its disadvantages, as a 1694
progress report makes clear:

> The passage into the River is very crowded, the Current false by
> many Eddyes, the tides on Springs rapid, the Soundings fowle, the
> Shores Dreadful, and the ready bringing in and carrying out of
> Shipps, too much commanded by the Course of the Westerne
> Winds.

But, goes on the same report, these disadvantages made it
equally difficult for the enemy to attack the yard, which it
finally called 'this supereminent treasure of the nation'. Buoys
were already being laid to mark the Cremyll narrows, and
pilots organised: a report four years later showed Plymouth in

Ships Returning with a Prize: a picture in the National Maritime Museum signed D. Serres, 1766. Serres was a French sailor captured in 1758 who settled in England and was later appointed Marine Painter to George III. The painting was made from Millbay before any docks were built; note how the ships are sailing through the Narrows under topsails, with a following wind.

Eighteenth-century architecture: engravings from Britton & Brayley's 1832 *Devonshire Illustrated*. *Above*, Fore Street, Devonport, looking down to the dockyard gates with a coach about to leave from outside the Royal Hotel. *Below*, the lecture theatre of the Athenaeum, with the chairman at the near table facing the speaker on the rostrum. Both these buildings were destroyed in 1941.

money terms as second only in value to Portsmouth among the English dockyards.

A good naval base required not only a sheltered dockyard but an anchorage whence ships could proceed to sea swiftly; Portsmouth had the advantage in the Solent over Plymouth Sound, disliked by every admiral from Blake onwards, until the Breakwater was built, as being too exposed. Still, Plymouth was the best choice in the west. Apart from a long record of supporting fleets with water, victualling and ship repairs, it now had the Citadel for its better defence, and was still the safest harbour. A breakwater had already been talked of in Torbay but there was no population to support a dockyard. Dartmouth was too dangerous an entrance in bad weather, and the Cornish ports seem not to have been thought of; Fowey was no healthier than Dartmouth and the Fal estuary too remote from London.

THE FIRST YARD

Sir Nicholas Morice, son of the Restoration Secretary of State, owned the chosen site, but he was only thirteen and his trustees would not sell. With difficulty they were persuaded to move from a one-year to a seven-year lease, but Nicholas when he came of age remained difficult, 'the greatest Jew in these parts'. It was said that he would not sell land for less than six times its normal price, so the leases continued. The land passed to the St Aubyn family through marriage in 1749 and though some later extensions were bought by the Admiralty the Crown did not finally become freeholders instead of leaseholders of all the dockyard until 1857.

Waters began work in 1691. Point Froward, the site of the original yard, can still be identified from a boat, the way most people see the modern dockyard. One cruises past Mutton Cove, the statue of King William IV and the covered building slip and then the waterfront turns sharply from north-east to north. That knuckle was Point Froward and just north of it a small cove was enlarged to make a wet dock and from the top of the dock a dry dock was cut out of the rocky ground. The rocky headland was levelled and the stone from the excavations and the levelling of the point used to build a flat area out into the stream north of the dock, with a sea-wall giving deep water berthing and two building slips. In 1693 Richard Annet contracted to erect the buildings. A row of thirteen officers' houses were set on a terrace looking over the dock, a large storehouse built on the flattened Point Froward, and a roofed ropehouse 1,056ft long ran back from the storehouse, at right angles to the waterfront. Various other storehouses and workshops were erected and when complete the navy had its most modern yard. A first-rater could be taken into the dry dock and two into the wet dock, while the great storehouse held all stores and equipment for forty ships of the line. (See drawing on p. 33.)

A wall enclosed the whole on the landward side by 1696. Then in 1727 a marshy area south of Point Froward was leased, bringing the total yard area to 54 acres. A mud dock which dried at low tide and a mast pond were made in the new area, and the recovered ground used for storing timber. A new dry dock was built in 1727 north of No 1 Dock, the new No 2 being a peculiar double dock, with one basin opening out of the other, but capable of taking two ships at once. No 1 Dock took its first ship, the *Weymouth*, in June 1695. The yard had launched its first ships the year before, the little 'advice boats' *Postboy* and *Messenger*. The first, *Postboy*, launched in April, was unlucky, captured by the French before 1694 was out. Both were probably built from the spare timber from the fourth-rate *Anglesea*, built (probably in the Cattewater) at the same time.

SUPPORTING SERVICES

The Ordnance Board rented the northern area of the yard in 1696 as a gunwharf, from which to supply ships with the guns, powder and shot. By 1708, when the navy presumably wanted more room, the gun wharf moved to Mount Wise, but in 1719 yet another site was leased and a gunwharf built to the designs of the celebrated John Vanbrugh, then in Crown service. The Gun Wharf and many of the buildings survive as the Morice Yard. Vanburgh's buildings are justly celebrated, but the earlier dockyard buildings made an impressive pile, as the

THE GUN WHARF TERRACE. *Officers' houses designed by John Vanbrugh and built in 1718 for the yard from which the Board of Ordnance armed the navy's ships. It is now part of the dockyard and called Morice Yard.*

original drawings show. Most have been replaced over the years in the natural course of development, and the Terrace, built for the officers, was destroyed in the World War II bombing, except for the northern end. One side-effect of the importation into the area of national architects and new techniques was the introduction of brick, hitherto almost unknown, into Plymouth building, and much more sophisticated architecture, particularly in the country houses built by the Plymouth wealthy after this time. Plympton House (1720) and Puslinch, built near Yealmpton in about 1726, illustrate the use of brick and the new elegance.

The Victualling Commissioners since they were appointed in 1654 had rented storehouses first at Lambhay and then at Coxside, in Sutton Pool. In 1705 they built a Victualling Office at Lambhay, in the shelter and protection of the Citadel, though the King's Bakehouse remained at Coxside until replaced by a new bakehouse at Lambhay in 1750. Not that any of their establishments had a good reputation. The first warship built in the dockyard, the fifth-rater *Looe*, joined the navy in 1696 and was sent to cruise to the westward. Her provisions turned bad; she made for an Irish port to revictual and on leaving struck a rock and was lost.

The 'Commissioners for Sick and Wounded Seamen, and the Exchange of Prisoners of War' also needed premises; by 1695 they had converted the old tidal mills at Millbay into a prison for 300 men. The sick who had been accommodated in Plymouth boarding houses (whose owners were also crimps, supplying seamen to merchantment and press gangs), or at one time in the old castle, were by 1690 in 'Plymouth Hospital', a building just south of the present Derry's Cross roundabout but then in open country. Even there they were complaining of ill-treatment and they continued to be billeted on the crimps or housed in converted storehouses, including some at Coxside, for another half-century and more.

In 1693 the first English chart of Plymouth Sound was published in *Great Britain's Coasting Pilot*, the work of Captain Greenvile Collins who had been appointed Hydrographer to the Navy by Charles II in 1682. Apart from the main harbour plan, there is a second of the Sound inset in the general Channel chart; the only other inset is of Portsmouth. In 1696 Henry Winstanley began building the first Eddystone Lighthouse, the first rock lighthouse in the world. Because of the French war a guardship constantly protected the men but, while she was away for a spell in 1697, Winstanley and his workmen were taken prisoner by a French privateer. They were all back within a month, Louis XIV sending them home with the comment that he was at war with England, not mankind. But in the great storm of 1703 Winstanley and his lighthouse were swept away. John Rudyerd built the second lighthouse in 1706–9 and this survived until destroyed by fire in 1755. Both these lighthouses were privately owned, the proprietors receiving the light dues collected by the customs officers.

THE OFFICERS AND MEN

In command of the yard was a Commissioner of the Admiralty, who in theory ranked with his brother commissioners in London. He had the central house in the Terrace, which looked down on the new dock, and the pecking order of his subordinate officers is shown by the ranging of their houses in the Terrace. On his right, in order, he had the Master Shipwright, the

Master Attendant (secretary), the Clerk of the Survey (civil engineer), the Shipwright Attendant, the Master Caulker and the Chirugeon (medical officer). On his left were the Clerk of the Cheque (accountant), Clerk of the Stores, Clerk of the Ropery, Master Ropemaker, Master Mastmaker and the Boatswain of the Yard.

The commissioners were serving naval officers posted to Plymouth. The first master shipwright, Elias Waff, was transferred from Portsmouth and it would be reasonable to expect a nucleus of dockyard officers and trained men to be appointed from other dockyards, were it not that the hulk had been at work in the Cattewater on and off for nearly forty years, and must have built up its own labour force. It is otherwise hard to explain why Plymouth Dock should have had 69 shipwrights and caulkers and 40 workmen and boys on its books in 1690 when not a stone had been laid in Hamoaze. It seems more likely that these were the men of the hulk, living with their families either in Turnchapel or Plymouth. Certainly a hulk was moved into the Hamoaze in 1689 and two other hulks, old French prizes, were brought down-Channel to serve as living quarters. But the transfer from the Cattewater was not completed until 1696.

A study of Stoke Damerel marriage registers for 1690–1715 shows that well over half the extra-parochial people getting married were from Plymouth and the neighbouring parts of Devon and Cornwall, a few from Chatham and Portsmouth, the other naval yards, and the rest from ports between Northumberland and Falmouth, with London most numerous. Many of these would be sailors in port, rather than settlers, but the evidence suggests that the new town which grew up around the dockyard drew mainly on Plymouth for its people, with the local immigration which had always fed Plymouth plus some skilled men from other dockyard and mercantile ports.

THE NEW TOWN

Men are not going to live aboard hulks if they can avoid it, and there are petitions in 1692 and again in 1697 asking for houses nearer the work. The January 1697 letter writes of the difficulties which our workmen undergo, by living too far from their business . . . of very great prejudice to his Majesty's service and a fatigue to them almost intolerable . . . this winter seems to have made all our avenues and passes thereto much more rotten and troublesome . . .

In 1695 Celia Fiennes went from Plymouth to Dock by boat, 'the nearest way'. It was a two-mile walk from Plymouth, either by way of the ferry at Stonehouse or across Millbridge, for a day's work which in winter was 6 am to 6 pm, in summer sunrise to sunset, with half an hour for breakfast and one and a half hours for lunch.

But not until 1700 would the Morice trustees part with any land for housing, and again it was on leasehold. The first house was at North Corner and then Cornwall Street stretched up, parallel with the north wall of the yard. By 1712 there were 318 men employed and by 1733 Plymouth Dock, as the new town was called, had 3,000 people. Because of the Cornwall Street development the Gun Wharf was separate from the yard. So the new town occupied a narrow strip running up from the waterfront between the two walls – a corridor which survives – and then gradually filled a gridiron pattern of streets of which Fore Street, leading from the yard gates, was the main axis and the furthest south. By the 1750s the workforce had risen to 1,000 and the town population to 4,000, and the town had spread north to Morice Square, east to the top of Fore Street and south by another couple of parallel streets. Daniel Defoe in 1724 wrote of the handsome houses of the yard officers and called the town streets spacious, as did another traveller, the Rev S. Shaw, in 1788. But, he writes,

as the inhabitants here are chiefly mechanics, &c, belonging to the docks, the houses are slightly built either of plaster or slate stone [he meant slate-hung] .. and will not bear a minute inspection, but have a good effect at a distance.

Plymouth Dock, in fact, was a working-class town. Within fifty years it grew from nothing to having nearly half as many people as its older neighbour.

The parish church, Stoke Damerel, was three-quarters of a

mile from the town, a lonely country church in the fields. Apart from the distance it could not cope with its suddenly swelling parish, though a north aisle was added about 1730 through the efforts of Robert Young, a clerk of the dockyard. In the 1740s both Whitfield and John Wesley preached at Dock in the open air a number of times. Though they attracted followers they were given rough receptions and there were no dissenting chapels until the second half of the century. There were no schools, no charities, and the market was in temporary wooden shambles outside the yard gates. According to Defoe there was a good cheap market at Saltash and people went there to shop 'by the town boat' rather than walk to Plymouth.

Plymouth Dock was outside the boundaries of Plymouth and was ruled by the county magistrates sitting in quarter session at Exeter. Magistrates living near the town would have conducted petty sessions for minor crime. The lord of the manor had his court. Other local government was in the hands of the parish vestry of Stoke Damerel, which seems first to have levied a poor rate in 1727.

Wages were small, ranging from 2s 1d a day for shipwrights and caulkers down to 1s 1d a day for labourers, but there was overtime, $7\frac{1}{2}d$ a 'tide' ($1\frac{1}{2}$ hours) or 2s 1d for a 'night' (5 hours). In 1693 a churchwarden put the master shipwright and several of his men into the spiritual court for working on fast days; a report to the Admiralty said that the men were so frightened that they would not work Sundays or holidays, a common dockyard practice apparently, and such a refusal had never been known before.

Men paid such wages could not afford to build their own houses and the developers of the new town seem at first to have been the yard officers, whose pay ranged from £100 a year for the master shipwright down to £36 for the boatswain. The clerk of the cheque in 1706 owned forty-two houses, and of these thirteen were beer shops. Seeing that the porter's lodge inside the yard gates also had a beer shop, part of the porter's 'perks', it is clear that there was one facility the new town did not lack.

What made the men even more poor was the system of paying; for fear of highwaymen, a frigate brought the money from London once a quarter for the wages to be made up. So every three months Dock had a spree, but in the intervening months the families ran up debts with shops and taverns whose keepers would be as alert to the frigate's arrival as their customers.

CORRUPTION

The one 'perk' that all yardees shared was the right to chips, in theory the waste ends of wood. In practice these chips grew so large that a size limit of 3ft was placed on them; it is said that most of the woodwork in the old houses of Devonport, stairs and all, is based on 2ft 11in timbers. Apart from these chips – and it was estimated at one time that enough wood went out of the yard in a month to build a sloop – there was straight pilfering of every kind of store. For the men it was a case of what they could smuggle out; for the officers it was a more complicated business of good stores being condemned or receipts signed with suppliers for goods that went other ways. It would not be surprising if the houses of early Dock were largely built out of yard stores. So much money could be made that large sums were paid to secure quite minor posts in the yard that offered opportunities for swindling. Another abuse was the overtime claimed; a 1710 clerk was paid for a quarter in which he apparently had only two hours off in every 240.

The Government was partly to blame for the frauds, through its tardy payment to the officers. Lanyon, for instance, Charles II's agent in Plymouth, complained at one time to Pepys that he was in great straits, for the government owed him nearly £8,000 which he had laid out on its behalf. Waters, the contractor who built the yard, did some £60,000 worth of work, was always kept waiting for payment and then received credit notes which he could only cash on the excise at heavy discounts.

Yet the agents seem not to have fared too badly. Bagge built Saltram House out of his years of office, though he lost it when found out. Captain Hatsell, Cromwell's agent in 1652, was quite soon able to afford to live at Saltram and was Mayor of Plympton in 1658. After the Restoration he was in custody in Exeter on rather vague charges, but in 1662 he was back and doing naval business, still living at Saltram and a trustee of the new Plympton Grammar School.

John Lanyon, a Royalist army engineer, had petitioned the King in 1661 for a job, pleading sadly reduced circumstances because of his loyalty. He was made naval agent at Plymouth and in 1664, with two other merchants of the town, offered Pepys £300 a year if he got them the contract to victual the garrison at Tangier. Pepys obliged, and got his money. In 1665 Lanyon was accused of dishonesty in his naval work and the clerk of the cheque in the port was refusing to sign Lanyon's bills. But the deputy governor of the Citadel assured the commissioners that this clerk was a worthless fellow, not fit for employment, who if he had an office at all kept it in a tavern. Lanyon, already a freeman of Plymouth, is described in local records as a merchant, was mayor in 1672–3, and when he died (oddly enough in Paris) the next year left large sums to charities in and around Plymouth. The almshouses he endowed (rebuilt in Victorian times) still face Charles roundabout. It was remarkable progress in fourteen years, but it may have been honest enough in the fashion of the times.

But certainly there was dishonesty in the new yard on a large scale. The storekeeper was dismissed in 1699. It was discovered in 1708 that the canvas contractor was supplying rotten ropes to the sailmaker for bolt ropes, the cause of several mishaps at sea. Then in 1711 the commissioner was replaced and the master shipwright, the clerk of the cheque and the storekeeper all dismissed. Twenty years later a number of yardees were on trial at Exeter for stealing. None of this was peculiar to Plymouth Dock. The chips and the scandals were common to all yards. And in its first sixty years Plymouth Dock did build or rebuild forty-eight ships, as well as coping with all the refit and fitting out of three strenuous naval wars.

CHAPTER FIVE

THE ADMIRALTY TAKES OVER:
1688–1750

IN his *Memoirs* James Yonge recorded '1690. In⁰ Paige. In this Gentlemans Mayoralty happened nothing memorable, but that the dock In Ham hoas was began . . .' Over the next twenty years he wrote 'nothing memorable' several times, and a century later Henry Woollcombe in his history of the town, still unpublished, suggests that Plymouth was asleep up to the beginning of the reign of George III. Indeed the town changed little outwardly; some avenues of elm trees were planted on the Hoe and about the town, a few houses rebuilt, the water supply was improved a little, a pond filled in. But the town was prosperous; trade kept up and people were busy. Underneath it was a vital period for Plymouth, the half-century in which the town was taken over by the Admiralty, that new branch of the civil service which Samuel Pepys had just created when Yonge made that 1690 entry.

TRADE

The commercial port of Plymouth was busy enough in this time. The town quay dues which had doubled between 1670 and 1700 more than doubled again by 1720. In number of ships and tonnage engaged in trade in 1715–17 Plymouth ranked fourth among English ports, and took third place in the trade with northern Spain, fifth place in the trade with southern Spain and the Atlantic islands, and sixth place in the Portuguese trade. In 1733 the port was trading with Virginia, the West Indies and the Mediterranean. There was at least one Plymouth ship in the slave trade.

But the gaps were great. In those 1715 figures London has 244 ships, Bristol 48, Exeter 30, Liverpool 23 and Plymouth 19. Defoe in his 1724 *Tour through Great Britain* called Bristol, the second largest town in England, 'the greatest, richest and best port in the country', and it was building new docks and wharves for her expanding trade. Even so Liverpool, which had been in the Atlantic trades since the mid-seventeenth century, had in 1715 opened the first wet dock in all Britain and by mid-century had outstripped even Bristol as a port. In the trade explosion of the eighteenth century Liverpool and Bristol, with industrial areas behind them to supply export cargoes and away from the war-torn Channel, took the lion's share. Plymouth marked time. Its little commercial harbour, Sutton Pool, was the subject of endless lawsuits over its ownership. Greenvile Collins's chart of 1693 shows its quay drying out at low tide, and in 1744 the fish house which stood where the two piers now are, and which gave some shelter to the harbour, was washed away in a storm.

Exports from the hinterland were limited; woollens overseas, some lead, tin and copper from Dartmoor to south Wales, paving stones and slates, some of which went to the American colonies. As the century wore on the coal imports from Newcastle fell, to be replaced by supplies from south Wales and increasingly from Whitehaven. The coasting imports consisted largely of corn, groceries, and other foodstuffs, together with household goods from London and other sources which supplied Plymouth and were re-shipped in smaller craft to West Country ports between Exeter and St Ives; road transport was negligible. In the same way a high proportion of the overseas goods on which duty was paid – tobacco, wine, sugar, fruit, ginger and Newfoundland train oil – was exported again coastwise. In the ten years 1722–31 Plymouth imported direct nearly 3 million pounds of tobacco, the bulk of which was re-exported, and it was still getting some tobacco by the 1750s. As the duties mounted on tobacco so the direct imports increasingly moved to Bristol and Liverpool where the richer merchants could find the capital required. The sugar crop too was drawn off to these ports. In 1750 Plymouth built its first sugar house for grinding cane (it was near the western end of the modern Mount Gould road, its ruins long thought to have been an old fort), when Bristol already had sixteen.

Yet foreign trade was growing in Plymouth in these years; in 1750 there were sixteen ships in the West Indies and another twelve sailing to the mainland American colonies, an improvement on the 1715 figures.

If the merchants of Plymouth sometimes contrasted the modest growth of their shipping trade with the meteoric rise at Bristol and even more at Liverpool, they still had a solid and important mercantile business, and alongside it a growing business which these other ports could not take away. War – and there were thirty-two years of war between 1688 and 1750 – might interrupt trade, and the press gangs were far more active than in the rival ports, but it brought compensations. There were captured enemy ships whose cargoes were auctioned before the vessels were converted to English use, and convoys of merchantmen which, whether inward or outward bound, wanted victuals, liquor and repairs. Ships could be weather-bound, or awaiting escorts, for weeks at a time, a useful extra market. Defoe in 1724 wrote, 'there are several considerable merchants and an abundance of wealthy shopkeepers whose trade depends on supplying the seafaring people that upon so many occasions put into the port'. It was, he said, 'the general port for receiving all the fleets of merchant ships from the southward, as from Spain, Italy, the West Indies, etc'.

Though the navy itself might be run down between the wars, as in the twenty-four years of peace after the Treaty of Utrecht, there was still the growing town of Dock that needed all manner of household goods, clothing and foodstuffs that Saltash market could not provide, and which had not developed its own mercantile community. In the peace years too the yard and its ancillary establishments were extended and built up; Plymouth merchants were shipping bricks from Southampton, bringing in timber, supplying the workmen to some extent and feeding them. The capital expenditure of the Crown in Plymouth in the century after 1660, from the building of the Citadel to the construction of the dockyard and its steady expansion, injected much cash into the Plymouth economy. The work of the yard and the Victualling Office at Lambhay, building and repairing ships, feeding crews, all brought contracts for Plymouth merchants and ship owners.

INDUSTRY

The Plymouth woollen manufactory reached its zenith in this time, largely through the enterprise of three generations of the Shepherd family, who came from Northampton about the beginning of the century. From their home at Coxside, looking down to the creek where they built a quay still called Shepherd's Wharf, they had storehouses and factories close by on the waterside, and more near the present Drake Circus roundabout, and in addition at Coxside they made glove leather from the sheepskins, converted the offal into glue, and produced thick 'foot oil' from various residues. They had half a dozen looms in private houses in the town, mills at Ashburton, Buckfastleigh, Totnes, Tavistock, and spinners in east Cornwall. Altogether the family had 4,000 people on their payroll and in Plymouth alone their weekly wage bill was between £500 and £600, plus the wages for the crews of their half-dozen coasters carrying the finished goods to London, for the East India Company. The balance was shipped direct from Plymouth to the Americas.

Commercial dynasties were established which have come down to modern times. Collier's the wine merchants were established in Southside Street in 1676 and the business is now part of the Dingle's company. William Moore the shipwright died in 1742 and the family business which continued until a century ago certainly had a shipbuilding slip alongside Friary Quay, in the north-east corner of Sutton Harbour, soon after the death of this first William.

SMUGGLING

The country financed its long wars with increasing taxes, and the principal source of revenue was the customs and excise duties. These seemed as iniquitous to the victims as income tax today, and there was little more shame in evading them than in our employing income tax advisers. From the dawn of trade there had been in Plymouth some evasion of duty on woollen goods, and uncoigned tin exported. But smuggling in the modern sense really began with William's French wars which denied English customers their brandy, wine, silks and fine lace. Very soon the Channel Islands, and notably Guernsey, became the entrepôt where these things could be bought, and Cawsand the main centre of the western smugglers of these goods. In Plymouth and growing Plymouth Dock they had the largest population and therefore the best market for their 'free trade'. It is hard to measure how fast this trade grew because the only records are of captured goods and smugglers and in the early eighteenth century the preventive service was little developed. But in 1732 the Plymouth tide-surveyor, who supervised the landguard, was murdered, and two men were executed for the crime. It was 'about the running of brandy' and their bodies were hung in chains at Crabtree, on the Laira estuary. This was usually done at the scene of the crime; one imagines that this was the landing point and perhaps the lonely Crabtree Inn, which disappeared when the dual carriage road was built in 1974 from Laira to Marsh Mills, was a smuggling base.

Apart from goods brought over from France, there was also the tea, tobacco and rum smuggled out of incoming ships into longshoremen's boats, and again Cawsand was admirably placed. As the duties mounted on these goods there was an even bigger business in deceiving the customs officers in the actual port landings, a practice made easier by the corruption of the age.

THE NEW FAMILIES

Customs service brought to Plymouth the founder of the town's dominant eighteenth-century family. John Rogers was the son of a Fifth Monarchy man who had been imprisoned for his libellous sermons against Cromwell, whom he had ardently supported until Cromwell made himself Protector, and grandson of the first Protestant martyr of Mary Tudor's reign. John Rogers, born in prison, married the daughter of a London alderman who probably used his influence to get Rogers 'a handsome place' in the Custom House at Plymouth, about 1670. It was in the last days when customs officers were not salaried but took their rewards in the fees they charged the owners of ships with which they dealt. It was possible to make fortunes. At any rate when Rogers was offered promotion which meant moving to Bristol, he 'quit that employ and continued as a merchant, to which he had been bred, and by his success therein arrived at a considerable fortune', to quote family records. 'He got his estate mostly by tobacco', they continue, although other reports attribute the fortune to pilchard curing. At any rate Rogers bought Wisdome near Cornwood in 1690, Ivybridge in 1692 and Blachford and other property in 1694. The family estates eventually stretched from the Harford slopes of Dartmoor down to Ermington.

No doubt his links with the Custom House helped him in the tobacco trade, but there was one disaster. His ship *Winchelsea*, laden with tobacco, struck the Eddystone Rock a few days after the storm of 1703 had destroyed the first lighthouse and she was lost with all hands. Rogers was already an important man in Plymouth, elected MP for the town in 1698 and then made a baronet by King William. In 1702 he was High Sheriff of Devon, this boy born in prison at Windsor, and in 1710 died of an apoplexy while smoking his pipe in a Plymouth coffee house. His family is still at Blachford, beside the stripling Yealm after its picturesque plunge out of Dartmoor.

This one-generation move from Plymouth business to country estate is remarkable only in its swiftness, but a new development at this time was of country families moving towards the merchant town. A native of Plympton, George Treby, was a successful lawyer, became MP for Plympton and its recorder, and then Recorder of London until he was removed by Charles II (who had earlier knighted him) for defending the City's rights. After 1688 he rose rapidly again, Recorder and Lord Lieutenant of London, Lord Chief Justice when he died in 1700. He had four wives as well, the last of whom was an heiress, and acquired much land in Plympton, including much of the old Priory land. He had just started Plympton House, splendid in red brick made locally and Portland stone, when he died in 1700. His son George, MP for Plympton by the time he was twenty-four, had finished the house by 1720 and the Trebys dominated Plympton for another century.

Plympton had changed little since medieval days. There were the hamlets of Underwood and Colebrook, St Mary's Church, just a few cottages beside Ridgeway at the Dark Street Lane junction, and the old town of Plympton St Maurice clustered under the Castle. Its rather obscure claim to borough status and a mayor had been clarified by a new charter in 1602 and a later 1692 charter gave the town a recorder and quarter sessions. It was reasonably prosperous, a little market town with some retired Plymouth merchants, and some of its citizens were merchants and ship-owners in Plymouth. Plympton Grammar School had been built in 1663–71 after various law suits over the bequests in which Plymouth gained some authority over the trust. Built in similar style with an arcaded front is the Guildhall of 1696, given to Plympton by Treby and the Strode family.

Close to the eastern side of Plymouth the Friary estate, which had been in the hands of the Sparke family since Elizabethan days, was breaking up. Through the seventeenth century the Sparkes had lived at the old Whitefriars rather like father-figures in retirement. Jonathan Rashleigh of Menabilly had inherited part of the estate through a Sparke marriage and on the death of the last Sparke in 1714 his son-in-law, another Cornish landowner, Sir John Molesworth Bart of Pencarrow, acquired the main part. From Rashleigh a Plympton farmer, Anthony Culme, leased 28 acres at Tothill in 1680 and ten years later his son bought it outright. By 1730 the Culme estate included Mannamead and Little Efford and when the last Culme died in 1804 they also owned Freedom Fields, most of Lipson, Compton and Laira. Their house at Tothill was one of the most pleasant in the area, standing just north-east of the present St Jude's Church and looking down the Tothill Creek to the Laira and the woods of Saltram. (See illustration on opposite page.)

Even more important for Plymouth was the Parker move into Saltram. The family came from north Devon and by a series of marriages to rich wives had leased Boringdon, just north of Plympton, by 1564 and finally inherited that manor and Woodford. George Parker bought Saltram as well in 1712 and could afford to lay out the grounds, and his son John created the

Above, Tothill House, home of the Culme-Seymour family, painted 1892. The site is approximately the bottom of Beatrice Avenue. *Below*, Barley House, home of the Elliot family until the 1860s. In the foreground is Stonehouse Lane, now King Street, and the site is just north of the present Frankfort Gate. The estates of these two houses long held back the urban spread of Plymouth.

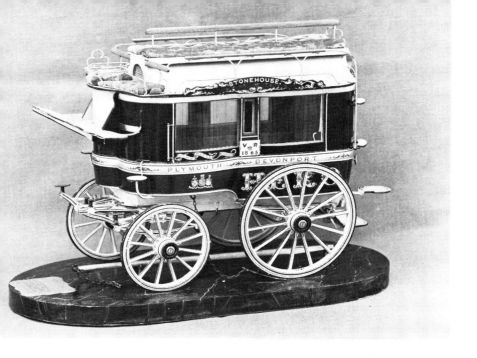

Above, a model from the Plymouth Room of Plymouth City Museum of the Plymouth–Devonport horse bus *Hero*, with an 1865 licence displayed. *Below*, the bridge at Camel's Head which linked Keyham and St Budeaux from 1827 until 1903, the switchback caused by its piles sinking in the mud. The 1902 photograph shows the terraces of 'by-law' houses beginning to cover the hillside beyond the 1890 LSW railway embankment.

great house largely as we know it today. John's son was created Lord Boringdon in 1784.

POLITICS

The landowners of the neighbouring countryside had real influence in Plymouth, even though the controlling element was the central group of merchants and traders, joined as the eighteenth century advanced by professional men, doctors and lawyers. Both Tories and Whigs kept their rich men's fingers in the Plymouth pie. The 1684 charter which Charles II forced upon the town gave them the Earl of Bath, Governor of Plymouth, as recorder. In the first list of freemen there were five peers, two baronets and a range of Tory landowners like Edgcumbe and Slanning (of Maristow). That charter also reduced the number of common councillors from twenty-four to twelve. The 1695 charter of William III restored the common councillors to twenty-four in number but brought in the Whigs, Sir Francis Drake as recorder, George Treby and three other baronets, and landowners like George Parker as freemen. Pollexfen, town clerk from 1665 to 1699, was basically a country landowner.

The importance of these appointments is shown by the method of local government, almost unique for a borough. The council as such rarely met, and administration was in the hands of the Court of Quarter Session. Here the recorder or his deputy, normally the town clerk, presided. The justices sitting with them were the mayor, the ex-mayor, and two senior aldermen. The grand jury of twelve was chosen by the aldermen from the remaining aldermen, the councillors and the freemen.

It was a self-perpetuating organisation. Freemen, who alone could trade in Plymouth, had either to have served an apprenticeship in the town, be eldest sons of dead freemen, or be elected by quarter sessions. From the freemen the aldermen elected the councillors, and the aldermen filled any vacancies on their bench from the councillors. In turn the mayor was elected annually by the councillors and twelve freemen, but the twelve freemen were chosen by two aldermen appointed by the retiring mayor, and two councillors elected by the freemen. Of the estimated 8,000 inhabitants of Plymouth in 1700 there were about 250 freemen.

Yet even in this closed shop the politics were as fierce as the comments in the contemporary records. Of William Cock, mayor 1702–3, Yonge says: 'A good church-man & a Tory, but of no parts, nor temper; he was R. Berryes Bro. Law, who had now screwed himselfe into ye Townclarks chair, and proved as Imperious, & Arbitrary as his Master Polexfen had befor him. He Governed this Mayor . . .'; of Thomas Darracot (1704–5): 'One whom we all thought honest, but he proved a Shuffler. Abetted the whiggs . . .' Yonge makes it clear that the Tories were churchmen, probably high churchmen; the Whigs were dissenters or had Presbyterian leanings. Captain Hambly's Book in the city archives is equally blunt: William Phillips, mayor 1746–7, 'when drunk was carried home in his cook's apron'.

The advantage swayed every year or two from one side to the other, and many men changed sides; over the years, as in national politics, there were breakaway parties in both Tories and Whigs, and rival factions. Several times in Plymouth there were evenly divided elections, as over the election of a new vicar for Charles Church in 1711 which had (as in the election of a vicar for St Andrew's in 1679) to go to the Bishop of Exeter for decision. It was almost the same story in 1732 over a new vicar for St Andrew's when the great Zachariah Mudge only secured the election after the Black Book had been consulted for precedents.

The election of Members of Parliament was further confused not only by party divisions but by the question of who had the right to vote. According to Yonge the two Members of Parliament for Plymouth were elected by the freeholders, but by the time of Queen Elizabeth the freeholders left the election to the corporation and the freemen, to avoid the cost of having to pay the members. In the general election after the Restoration the freemen and the freeholders enthusiastically claimed their old right and elected two members strong for the King's return. The corporation, old Parliament men, in turn elected more restrained supporters of the Restoration, but the

Committee of Privileges of the Commons gave the right to vote to 'the Mayor and Commonalty' and accepted the freeholders' men. So the freeholders were considered as electors.

Though this was the age in which party politics took shape, they were still not clear-cut or well-defined. Not only were both Whigs and Tories split nationally into opposing groups, but locally men were likely to weigh personal interests against these new ideas. It was a corrupt age too, and practices change; the old custom of presents from the corporation to a helpful member – a silver-gilt cup to John Sparke in 1679 for example – gave way to payments to the corporation. In 1710 the two men elected each gave a hundred guineas to the corporation. In 1721 there were twenty houses open to supply wine and strong liquor free to the voters, and two hogsheads of beer for 'the rabble'.

The first manager for the Whigs in south Devon was Sir Francis Drake, the third baronet, great-great-nephew of the Elizabethan hero, nephew of the Parliamentary colonel of horse. He was related to all the West Country Whigs, and by the end of his life had in his own control two seats at Bere Alston and one each at Tavistock, Dartmouth, Totnes, Plympton and Plymouth. His correspondence shows how the control was exercised: buying up property which carried freeholder's votes, using his influence to get a voter a place in the excise or the Custom House, filling a vacancy for an armourer in the Citadel. The Whigs and the navy were always close and a Drake of course would gravitate to the navy. A brother and a cousin were captains in the navy, and a niece married Sir Charles Trevanion, Commissioner at Plymouth Dock. Even so Plymouth was difficult to manage. In Lady Elliot-Drake's family history she says of this time that Drake never quite controlled Plymouth, and that the Whigs were always in a minority there.

Yet in spite of this view, and even though Charles II tried to pack the Plymouth Council with his friends when he came to the throne, the town was returning Whigs to Parliament within seven years. William of Orange's accession naturally gave the Whigs further strength, but ten years later his policies were upsetting the merchant class nationally and in 1698 John

Rogers and Charles Trelawny defeated the Whigs Parker and Calmady and set the Plymouth Tories rejoicing. The King made Rogers a baronet and so perhaps bought back his support; at any rate at the 1700 general election the Plymouth Tories secured the nominations for Charles Trelawny again and his brother.

Francis Drake retired from Parliament the next year and entered his management career in earnest. In 1705 Charles Trelawny kept his seat but Drake secured the other for Admiral Sir George Byng, a serving officer and staunch Whig. Byng promptly gave the command of a ship in his squadron to a Drake cousin! The admiral was to hold a series of senior posts in the navy for the rest of his life; when he was made Viscount Torrington two of his sons in succession took his seat (the third was the Admiral Byng executed for losing Minorca). The family held this Plymouth seat for thirty-four years.

Drake got rid of the Tory Trelawny in 1713 by securing the nomination for Sir John Rogers, the second baronet, as a Whig. 'A sensible man', said Sir Francis of him. Indeed when Drake died in 1717, Rogers became Recorder of Plymouth. The family held this office for eighty years, handing it down with the baronetcy as if it too were hereditary. But the second baronet was an unreliable supporter of the government and on a number of occasions voted the wrong way, so that in 1721, in addition to Byng, the government managers put up William Chetwynd, a junior Lord of the Admiralty. Rogers was going to stand and it looked as if Plymouth was to see its first contested election since 1698, but at the last minute he dropped out. The way the Rogers family could change their tune is shown by two pamphlets which survive at Blachford. Neither is dated but one proclaims 'The Admiralty for Plymouth for ever' and urges a vote for Rogers or 'you'll disoblige the Admiralty your only friend'. The other opens 'Rise up sinking Plymouth' and in verse attacks the navy as no friend to the town, principally for having built a brewhouse at Millbrook instead of beside the Victualling Office at Lambhay.

George Treby of Plympton succeeded Drake as the government and Whig manager in Devon, controlling not only Plymouth and one of the Plympton seats but five other Devon boroughs. He was a candidate for the mayoralty of Plymouth in 1727 but Sir John Rogers had shortly before persuaded the previous mayor to add seventeen freemen, improperly, to the list. His son John (who never bothered with trade after he had made the grand tour) also stood for the mayoralty, and both polled an equal number of votes. At one point the two candidates drew their swords on each other and a fight was only averted by the alarm of a fire in Gasking Street. The town had no mayor from 17 September until the following 12 March, when the council chose Rogers by order of the King's Bench.

It is not easy to follow the Rogers's politics; the second son William was 'bred a merchant' and became Collector of Customs in Plymouth, while the third son Frederic joined the navy a few years later. Yet when Robert Byng resigned his seat in 1739 and the government candidate was Charles Vanbrugh, one of Byng's captains and brother of the Gun Wharf architect, John Rogers stood against him and Plymouth had its first election since 1698. Rogers raked in every freeholder he could find, 'faggot votes', and won; probably the 'Rise up sinking Plymouth' pamphlet is of this date. But Vanbrugh went to petition, and the House of Commons decided that the 'Commonalty' of the 1661 decision meant the freemen only, not the freeholders, and Rogers was unseated in favour of Vanbrugh. Not for another forty years were the freeholders of Plymouth to try to claim their rights, and the Admiralty and the government went on nominating the men they decided Plymouth should send to Parliament. When Captain Charles Saunders RN was returned in 1750 a contemporary wrote that 'though neither a man of figure or character [he] was readily accepted by the vile scoundrel Alderman in places, and their lacquays the Common Council – one half of both benches having made themselves *slaves and dependants* on the board of Admiralty by getting into places'. It was unjust about Saunders; he commanded the fleet at Quebec when Wolfe captured the city and was later Pitt's First Lord of the Admiralty for a short spell. Yet one of the Plymouth seats was held by one naval officer or another from 1705 to 1754, and the other had been at the government's disposal since 1713. For twenty-six years it was held by Arthur Stert of Membland, who steadily served one government after another, had a secret service pension and helped manage the West Country elections. In Plymouth he was said 'to have a precarious interest of his own with the Corporation', and he paid the rent for the Shepherd factories and stores for all the time he was in the House.

The dockyard, the customs service and the Citadel always had enough jobs, contracts, fat commissions and other inducements to keep a majority of the 200-odd freemen happy. Politically Plymouth was a rotten borough, in the pocket of the Admiralty and the government. In business it was finding it easier to make money out of the dockyard than by the old-style trade.

CHAPTER SIX

THE GREAT AWAKENING: 1750–1815

PLYMOUTH was dead by 1750, and only began to wake up with the accession of George III, wrote Woollcoombe in 1810. The three major factors in the revival seem to have been the extensive Crown building programme in Plymouth which grew out of the long French wars, the coming of the turnpike road link with London, and the discovery by the county gentry with Plymouth interests that they could make money out of the developing town.

With brief intervals Britain was at war with France and various of her allies from 1738 until 1815. Increasingly the theatre of war was not the Narrow Seas but the Atlantic, the Mediterranean and the West Indies, with Plymouth the most strategically placed naval base. So Plymouth prospered. When the Seven Years War broke out in 1756 Captain George Rodney was senior officer at Plymouth and all that spring he was driving the dockyard and the ships' companies. Invasion was feared and defence lines around Dock, from the high ground by the present Devonport Hospital to Stonehouse Creek, were started at once. Behind the lines half a dozen squares of small barracks were built, and in 1757 'the best wages in the county' were being advertised as far away as Sherborne for fifty masons and bricklayers to build barracks at Dock. By 1759 over £25,000 had been spent on local defences.

Land had been bought at Stonehouse at the outbreak of war for a naval hospital, but more land was later bought from Lord Edgcumbe and building began in 1758, on the shores of Stonehouse Creek. The first patients were transferred from the old hospital at the bottom of George Street in 1760 and when the hospital was completed in 1762 it was the first in England built in small blocks, so that groups of patients were isolated from one another. With landing steps down to the water's edge, sick and wounded seamen could be landed directly from boats: the steps were in use until about 1919 and still survive, along with the graceful grouping of the wards and the officers' quarters.

During the same time the dockyard itself was being expanded across the 'New Ground' to the south. The original ropehouse which had formed the southern boundary of the yard was demolished to open up the New Ground, and another ropehouse built on a north–south line. In the New Ground a mast pond, new store, mast and boat houses were established, and two building slips on the site of the present slips. A new road was made down to Mutton Cove, the little basin still at the southern boundary of the dockyard. On the other side of the yard a third dry dock, the North Dock, was added in 1762, and more building slips. Improvements to the yard went on for another ten years, and in that time over £153,000 was spent.

Much of this work went on in the uneasy peace period of 1763–76, when the navy was much run down by political neglect. The War of American Independence (1776–82) stirred things up very sharply. A Franco-Spanish fleet off the port with an invasion army threw Plymouth into a panic in 1779. New gun batteries were hurriedly built all around the Sound, and a blockhouse at Higher Stoke. New barracks for the Royal Marines were built in Stonehouse, in 1782–3. When the force had been raised in 1755 the Plymouth Division was billeted round Sutton Harbour, with an orderly room in Southside Street, since occupied by the Parade Printing Works, and with the New Quay as rallying point and parade ground. That quay has been called the Parade ever since. As the force grew so companies were billeted out, in Dock and as far afield as Modbury, Plympton and Tavistock (on the main routes into Plymouth). In 1781 the new barracks were started, again on land bought from Lord Edgcumbe, a long block for the men running along the western water's edge of Millbay with the officers' quarters at right angles at the two ends. The block survives, with the officers' mess still in the south wing and senior officers' dwellings next door. It was first occupied in 1783. The familiar block on Durnford Street and the wings which completed the barracks square were not added until 1857. Railings separated the original parade ground from Barrack Street, which disappeared with the Victorian extension, but not before it had acquired nine public houses and a brewery.

In 1789 work on the fourth dry dock, the New North Dock, was started. It was planned as the biggest in the country, and George III came down to see it under construction. A classical summer house on 'Bunker Hill' still marks the spot from which he admired the view. The King, it is said, asked why the new dock was being built even larger than designed and was told that the French were building a new ship, the *Commerce de Marseille*, which was even longer than the design length of the dock. So it was being made big enough to take her; she was indeed captured at Toulon soon after the outbreak of war in 1793, and was the first ship to enter the new dock.

Preparations for war had long been in hand. Under the authority of the Duke of Richmond, Master-General of the Ordnance, a second wall was built around the town, behind the main line with its barracks and the civilian houses. He also moved the seat of the Governor of Plymouth from the Citadel to a new house at Mount Wise, built as Government House but since 1934 known as Admiralty House and the seat of the Commander-in-Chief. The first governor to occupy this house was General Lord George Lennox, Richmond's brother. It was a rewarding post, 'the first military appointment in Great Britain', so not only was there a smack of nepotism about the appointment but Richmond was accused of building a comfortable house for his brother 'economically with the public money'. Richmond upset a lot of local people, particularly because his new wall cut them from the little foreshore left, and to placate them he built Richmond Walk, which still runs along the waterfront from Mutton Cove under Mount Wise. Not until 1820 was another residence, now called Hamoaze House, built for the port admiral at Mount Wise. In 1810 a start was made in turning the landward defences of Dock into a moat and masonry wall, but this was abandoned at the end of the war in 1815.

With the outbreak of war in 1793 Plymouth was full of troops, some accommodated during the summer in camps at Roborough and Maker. In 1794 Shepherd's woollen manufactory 'behind Frankfort Place' – roughly where Dingle's now stands – was made into a barracks, and another built beside the Millbay prisoner of war establishment. After extensive campaigns in the West Indies, Plymouth was flooded with sick and wounded soldiers in 1795. Many died, a temporary, inadequate hospital at Friary could not cope, and the Naval Hospital would not take soldiers. A direct result was the building in 1797 of the Military Hospital, on the northern shores of Stonehouse Creek facing the Naval Hospital, following a similar pattern of small blocks, four in this case, linked by a massive colonnade. The building is now used by Plymouth Education Authority.

As the war progressed, so did the number of French prisoners mount. Apart from Millbay and converted establishments at Coxside, there were prison hulks in the Hamoaze. Conditions worsened until in 1805 Thomas Tyrwhitt, close friend and servant of the Prince of Wales and an enthusiastic 'improver' of Dartmoor who had already built himself a house at Tor Royal and founded the new settlement of Princetown, proposed building a prison there. It reputedly cost £200,000, and in 1809 it received its first 5,000 prisoners from Plymouth.

The last, most elaborate and expensive scheme of all began in 1812 when the Breakwater was started. It had been suggested by Admiral Lord St Vincent as early as 1779, when captain of the *Foudroyant*. He, Hawke, Hood and all the great admirals of the time found Cawsand Bay dangerous as an anchorage and preferred Torbay. When St Vincent became Commander-in-Chief Channel Fleet in 1806 he forced the Admiralty to consider various remedies, of which the present Breakwater was eventually chosen. When St Vincent resigned in 1807 things were forgotten again but work eventually began in 1812. It was not completed until 1848 and had cost £1,500,000.

After a century's inflation sums of money mean little in modern terms, but the Crown did invest a great deal of cash in Plymouth between the middle of the seventeenth century and 1815. Local labour and local stone were employed, and each finished project meant local employment or wages spent locally. At the head of the Office of Works were distinguished architects – Sir William Chambers, for instance, who built Somerset House – and they not only provided Plymouth with an impressive and often overlooked collection of great Georgian buildings, but again set new standards for local builders and developers.

For centuries overland communication and transport in England had been so bad that wherevei possible coastal shipping was used. The King's Post, in which relays of horsemen rode post-haste with messages of government, was opened to public letters on payment in 1635. John Codd started a packhorse system between Plymouth and London in 1722. But the old system whereby each parish had to maintain its roads was never going to satisfy a developing nation, and in 1663 the first Turnpike Act was passed. In this a private trust could improve a length of road and recover its costs by charging a toll. At the toll houses there were gates, or pikes (long poles) which were turned aside to permit passage after the toll had been paid. So the new roads became known as turnpikes. As the increasing number of French wars after this date made coastal shipping a prey to enemy ships, so the pressure for new roads mounted. Much of the Great North Road, and the roads from London to Bristol, Harwich and Portsmouth were completely turnpiked by 1750, with many other main roads nearly complete.

By 1753 there was much lobbying for the Great West Road, to Plymouth and Falmouth. There was much traffic in wartime, it was argued, and in peace new roads would attract 'such persons of fashion and fortune as make various tours in England for pleasure, health and curiosity'. Many would settle in Devon and Cornwall if they could get to London comfortably. There was opposition, some from farmers, but by May the Acts had been passed which would permit turnpikes all the way to Exeter. It had been agreed that the improvements would be left to the major towns on the route, each town trust concerning itself with its approach roads. The Exeter Act, for instance, allowed them to improve the road west as far as Chudleigh Bridge. In 1755 the Ashburton Trust was permitted to turnpike the road from Chudleigh to (South) Brent Bridge and in 1757 came an Act for improving the high road from

Brent Bridge to Gasking Gate, Plymouth – the Plymouth East Trust. The Great West Road followed the line of the old post road to London, more or less the present A38 to Exeter and A30 on to London.

The new road was constructed in 1758. Before that time the usual route from Plymouth to London was through Tavistock and Okehampton. The old south road was only ten to twelve feet wide, 'more like a river bed than a road', wrote Woollcoombe, and if a horseman met a packhorse he had to go back to a gate to let the packhorse pass. Invalids could join a coach at Exeter! The new road, wrote Marshall in 1796, was well-formed but too narrow, and the lofty hedges were an intolerable nuisance to travellers. In spite of this John Bignell, the landlord of the Prince George Inn on the corner of Stillman Street and Vauxhall Street, had a diligence running to Exeter weekly in the first year the road was open. The journey took twelve hours. Two years later a 'machine' was plying between the White Hart, Old Town Street, and Exeter, and by 1785 there were mail coaches on the road.

Once the main road to Exeter was turnpiked, others were improved. The Modbury turnpike through Yealmpton and Brixton to the main road at Plympton was authorised in 1759. In 1760 the Cremyll–Liskeard road, through Crafthole, Polbathic and Trerule Foot, continued the Great West Road into Cornwall and subsequent Acts that year took the road on through St Austell, Lostwithiel, Truro and Falmouth to Penzance. This Cremyll route had been the post road into Cornwall at least since 1600, but it was challenged by a new 1761 road from Trerule Foot to Saltash which continued, on the Devon side, to Weston Mill. In 1761 too there was an Act to improve the roads out of Tavistock which authorised roads to Callington, Launceston and Lydford, and above all through Horrabridge and Rock (Yelverton) to Plymouth. A branch road from Manadon Gate took a spur to Plymouth Dock, and this became the new town's main road to London.

With communications so improved from Plymouth and Dock to the outside world, it was time to look internally. A map in Devon County Record Office, from the Bedford Papers, refers to a Turnpike Bill for improving the roads out of

Plymouth in 1756, but this seems to have been replaced by the Plymouth East Act of a year later. Apart from improving the Plympton road, it also showed improvements planned to the road across Cattedown to the Oreston passage, to Stonehouse Lane (through King Street and Stonehouse High Street to the Cremyll Ferry), and to the old Dock road by way of Cobourg Street, Pennycomequick and Wilton Street, as well as the road from Pennycomequick through Milehouse to Saltash. At best this was patching, but a major change came in 1768–73 with the building of Stonehouse Bridge, which linked Dock and Stonehouse. Like the new roads it was subject to toll. Pedestrians paid ½d return, and so for the rest of its days it was the ha'penny gate. By 1775 the first diligences were running from Plymouth to Dock by way of Stonehouse Lane and the Bridge, but the road cannot have received the proposed 1756 improvements. In 1784 a Bill seeking a turnpike from the western edge of built-up Plymouth to Stonehouse Bridge was presented to Parliament. A Dock petition extended the road up the hill to reach the Dock town gate, but a petition from the Mayor and Corporation of Plymouth asked for the road to be extended right through the middle of Plymouth to meet the Exeter road at Gasking Gate, from the Bridge through Stonehouse to the Cremyll Ferry, and from the Dock Gate right through Dock to Mutton Cove (which by now also had a ferry to Cremyll). It was impertinent, for the turnpike trust would be responsible for maintaining these roads, and the House of Commons rejected the petition – the appellants were themselves responsible at least for the road through Plymouth.

In 1791 Torpoint Ferry started operating, with passenger boats operating from North Corner, between the dockyard and the Ordnance Wharf, and horse boats running from Pottery Quay, the present Devonport landing stage. The horse boats had a platform between two hulls and a ramp enabled horses, carts and carriages to be taken aboard. The 1760 Cremyll–Liskeard Act had permitted a spur from Crafthole to Torpoint and this road with the ferry made a much shorter route into Cornwall than the old Cremyll crossing. In 1800 this became the post route, with the mail brought across the ferry and loaded into the waiting Truro coach.

Improvements were also going on to the east of Plymouth. In 1784 Lord Boringdon had built an embanked carriage drive from the Longbridge at Marsh Mills to his fine house at Saltram. This kept the tides out of Plympton marshes, which had stretched right up to St Mary's Church. On the other side of the estuary he promoted the Plymouth Embankment Company which enclosed the Laira marshes, and these two embankments made it possible for the Plymouth Eastern Trust in 1802–9 to avoid the old steep route over Lipson Hill with a new embankment road from Plymouth to Crabtree, and thence from Longbridge straight to the foot of Ridgeway, cutting out the previous route winding along the northern edge of the marshes. Plymouth celebrated the 1810 Jubilee of George III by making a new road from Breton Side to Embankment Road and so the present line of the main road was established. A Jubilee Inn on the present Exeter Street still commemorates the development.

Thus by the end of the Napoleonic wars Plymouth had good communications in all directions. The London mail coaches were making the journey in two days even before the last improvements, and by 1797 a man called Rosedew, who provided the post horses on the road, was building Beechwood House near Cornwood out of the fortune he had made. It was subsequently bought by Lord Seaton, one of Wellington's generals at Waterloo, and his descendants are still there.

THE COUNTRY GENTLEMEN

The last male Morice – the family which had owned all the manor of Stoke Damerel since 1667 – died in 1749. He left the manor to his elder sister's son, the twenty-three-year-old Sir John St Aubyn, fourth baronet, in 1749. Like his father this St Aubyn sat for various Cornish constituencies all his life but, though a Tory, was never as far to the right as his Jacobite father. On his death in 1772 his fourteen-year-old son succeeded him, a colourful character in trouble over his extravagances even before he left school, the father eventually of fifteen bastards by two different women, a lover of the arts and sciences and a patron of John Opie, the Cornish painter. After the St Aubyns inherited Stoke, Dock began to blossom; there was clearly more freedom in granting leases. A market was built in 1762 and talks started with Plymouth to improve the town's water supply (though this was not done till the building of the Devonport Leat in 1795–6). Dock Theatre opened in Cumberland Street in 1762 (the site is now Cumberland Garden, overlooked by Theatre Ope and the Shakespeare Hotel), and decent hotels like the Fountain and the King's Arms developed in Fore Street just outside the dockyard gates. The town began to spread south to George Street, Pembroke Street and Prospect Row, where villas with views across to Mount Edgcumbe were built. The fourth baronet did offer £200 a year to Plymouth in 1766 for a water supply, and he did build Stonehouse Bridge with Lord Edgcumbe in 1767, but the destruction by fire in the last century of the estate office and its papers makes it difficult to trace the extent of the family influence in the development of Dock. But the rateable value of the town increased from £4,000 in 1750 to over £20,000 in 1800, and apart from the expansion of the town proper the two village suburbs of Stoke and Higher Stoke began. Though they kept the leasehold system of the Morices, the St Aubyns vastly increased their revenues from the development of their manor, and it is hard to doubt that they actively encouraged it.

Their neighbours in Stonehouse, the Edgcumbes, in the eighteenth century collected three titles. Richard Edgcumbe, a close friend of Walpole's and a minister in his governments, was the Whig political manager for Cornwall and was made a baron in 1742 to prevent his being examined by the House of Commons over his political machinations in Cornwall. He was succeeded in 1758 by his eldest son Dick, who sat in Parliament to keep the influence warm but had no interest in politics. As a young man he lost his daily twenty guineas at White's Club, made a reputation as a wit, remained a bachelor and had four children by Ann Franks, a beauty of the day. One of the Plympton seats was Edgcumbe-owned, and Dick, himself an artist, became the first patron and encourager of Joshua Reynolds, son of the Plympton Grammar School headmaster. His younger brother George went off into the navy and was a midshipman in HMS *Romney* with Byron and Rodney. All three became admirals and lifelong friends. George had reached captain's rank with a distinguished naval record when he succeeded his brother in 1761.

Like the St Aubyns, the Edgecumbes also made the most of the building boom. Father had sold the government the land for the Naval Hospital, son George was a partner with St Aubyn in building Stonehouse Bridge (which by the end of the century was making them £2,000 a year profit). In 1773, the year the bridge was completed, he leased out the land on which Durnford Street and Emma Place were built, with imposing houses for the new élite of Dock. Durnford Street was named after the fifteenth-century heiress who had brought Stonehouse and Maker to the family, Emma Place after Lady Edgcumbe (who was the Archbishop of York's heiress). He had already removed the barrier gates at the top of High Street, by the new hospital, and at the top of Chapel Street, the start of the new Durnford Street. The High Street arch became a decorative feature in Mount Edgcumbe Park, on the carriage drive above Redding Point.

In 1780 Lord Edgcumbe, now a full admiral, sold the land for the Royal Marines Barracks to the government and the year after, in compensation for the damage the new defences of Plymouth Sound had done to his woods, was made Viscount Mount Edgcumbe and Valletort. In 1789 he became the first Earl of Mount Edgcumbe and the following year, with Reginald Pole Carew of Antony, launched the Torpoint Ferry. When the first earl died in 1795 Stonehouse had grown from a village to a town of nearly 4,000 people, almost a quarter the size of Plymouth itself. The second earl, a dilettante amateur actor and musician and Tory MP, saw Stonehouse still growing and one of his daughters is remembered in the name of Caroline Place.

The Sir William Carew who built Antony House in 1710–21 was another Jacobite who in 1715 was in preventive detention in the Citadel at Plymouth. He and his successors lived very quietly after this, but the estate passed in 1771 to eighteen-year-old Reginald Pole, of the political and wealthy east Devon family and also closely related to the politically powerful Rashleighs of Fowey, the Morices and half the great families of

Above, one of J. M. Rendell's two ferries on the Torpoint crossing. There was a vehicle deck on either side of the engine room of all the ferries until 1925. The first-rate screw battleship astern is believed to be HMS *Conqueror*, launched at Devonport in 1855 and wrecked in 1861. *Below*, aerial view of Stonehouse with Devil's Point and the Royal William Victualling Yard in the foreground, Stonehouse Creek with the new Mayflower marina to the left and Millbay Docks right. In the docks a Roscoff ferry is partly hidden by the grain silo.

Above, the last hustings in Plymouth, at the 1868 general election. Candidates addressed the crowd from the temporary platform in front of the Theatre Royal, and voting was in public. It was a notorious campaign; Stuart Lane, the Conservative candidate, failed on his second attempt to break the Liberal domination, and was showered with mud and rotten eggs. *Left*, a late-nineteenth-century drawing showing how the Elizabethan houses were degenerating into slum tenements.

Cornwall. He added Carew to his surname, became an MP for Fowey and a privy councillor, much improved Antony House and park in best eighteenth-century style, and regained family land lost after the Civil War.

On his estate was the land opposite the growing dockyard, and at Tar Point, as it was first known, grew a little community of marine tradesmen: blacksmiths, carpenters, shipwrights and boatmen. They came mainly from Plymouth. Two rope walks were built. The Carews had kept Tar Point field – it is believed that the name came from the practice of tarring boats on the beach – clear with an eye to housing development, and helped obtain the 1760 Cremyll–Liskeard Turnpike Act with its spur to Torpoint. There had been an unofficial ferry to Devonport since 1730, and by 1748 the Passage House had been built. But not until 1774, after young Reginald Pole Carew took over, was Torpoint field formally laid out for development as a housing estate with a regular grid pattern of streets like Dock. As at Dock even the type of house built was controlled – a very early form of planning. By 1784 there was 'scarcely any gound left untaken', and in 1785 two more fields were laid out and provision made for a church and a market. As it turned out there was no Anglican church in Torpoint until 1819 but a visit by John Wesley in 1787 led to a Methodist chapel by 1792.

But the major development was the start of a Torpoint Ferry proper. Pole Carew had to bring in Lord Mount Edgcumbe, who had the right of passage over the river between Cremyll and Saltash. St Aubyn would have been a more likely partner but though he was a cousin of Pole Carew's and this branch of the Poles had their home in Stoke Damerel, St Aubyn was not happy with the rival town of Torpoint. Once the ferry was in business he tried to injure Torpoint by manipulating the times and charges. But St Aubyn did become a partner in the ferry within a few years, by 1794 the Liskeard mail was being carried on the ferry and by 1796 there were two rival coaches running from Torpoint to Truro and Falmouth. There were about 1,500 people living in Torpoint by 1811.

Even more important to Plymouth was the second Lord Boringdon at Saltram who succeeded his father in 1788 when he was only sixteen. He embanked Chelston Meadows to make a carriage drive to the ferry he created where the Laira Bridge is now, built two slips at Turnchapel in 1793, where many ships were buil: for the navy, and laid mooring chains in the Cattewater in 1809 which added much to the commercial facilities of the port. He was active in the House of Lords from an early age but played a full part in rebuilding the trade of Plymouth at the end of the French wars, becoming first president of the Plymouth Chamber of Commerce in 1813 and a leading light in establishing the Exchange in Woolster Street the same year. He was created Earl of Morley in 1815, and Plymouth named a street in his honour.

NAVAL INFLUENCE

The landed families also developed an interest in Plymouth through their naval members. Admiral Lord Edgcumbe was Commander-in-Chief Plymouth in 1766–70 and again in 1773. For fifty-five years the Commissioners of Plymouth Dock had strong local connections. Frederic Rogers was another younger son sent into the navy. A captain at twenty-four, Frederic became the Commissioner of the Dock in 1753, built himself Hoe House in Hoe Lane in 1758, was Mayor of Saltash in 1768, and succeeded his brother at Blachford and in the baronetcy in 1773. Two years later he retired on pension. He was followed as commissioner by Captain Paul Ourry, son of a naturalised Huguenot from Blois. Ourry was Captain Edgcumbe's lieutenant in a series of ships, became a captain in 1757 and fought a number of notable single-ship actions. No doubt through the Edgcumbe connection he met the Treby family of Plympton and in 1749 married the daughter Charity. When his brother-in-law died, Paul Ourry's wife inherited Plympton House and Paul became MP for Plympton in 1763, was given command of a guardship at Plymouth and in 1775 became Commissioner at Dock. There is a neat description of Captain Ourry entertaining Admiral Rodney in 1781 in the Commissioner's House in the yard, before Rodney sailed off to the Battle of the Saints: the two old men sitting on either side of the fire, both crippled with gout. Captain Ourry died in office just over a year later, but for him and Rogers it must have been a comfortable life, with authority in Dock and large country houses not far away.

Seven years later, in 1789, came another commissioner with strong local links. Captain Robert Fanshawe's mother was a sister of Captain Sir Frederic Rogers, his father an admiral and his home at Stone Hall, the big house overlooking Stonehouse Pool. 'One of the finest seamen in the Navy', he became an Admiralty MP for Plymouth in 1784 and only resigned in 1790 on being appointed Commissioner of the Dockyard. He remained in that office until 1815, and was twice Mayor of Plymouth.

Thankes, just north of Torpoint, became the home of another naval officer, Thomas Graves, who in 1713 settled there with his new wife Mary Warne, whose father had just bought the property and who ran the naval brewery at Southdown. Graves died a rear-admiral and his son, another Thomas, had a chequered naval career which finished gloriously with him the admiral commanding the van under Lord Howe at the Battle of the First of June in 1793. He was wounded and served no more, retiring to Thankes with a peerage and a pension of £1,000 a year. He had inherited the house in 1755, had two spells as Commander-in-Chief Plymouth after that time, and died at Thankes in 1802. The family were there all through the nineteenth century but sold the house in this century. It was rebuilt at Portwrinkle as the Whitsand Bay Hotel.

Admiral Sir Charles Morice Pole, younger brother of Carew Pole at Antony, was born at Stoke Damerel in 1757 and was MP for Plymouth 1806–18. The great Edward Pellew gained his baronetcy for his gallantry at the wreck of the East Indiaman *Dutton* under the Citadel in 1796 (he had himself hauled out through the surf to the wreck and restored order with drawn sword). Pellew had been on his way to dine with Dr Hawker, the vicar of Charles, when he heard of the wreck. Lady Pellew bought Hampton House in Ebrington Street in 1804, and lived there until 1811. Her husband was made Viscount Exmouth in 1814 and was Commander-in-Chief at Plymouth 1829–32. Admiral Howe and his wife lived for a time in How Street. Collingwood, Nelson's second-in-command at Trafalgar, stayed with his family at the Fountain at Dock and a letter of his gives a charming account of the family entertaining Nelson beside the fire.

Tobias Furneaux of Swilly was Wallis's second lieutenant in his 1766–8 voyage round the world and commanded the *Adventure*, Cook's second ship in his 1772 voyage. He was the first man to sail round the world in both directions. He died young, at Swilly, and was buried at Stoke Damerel.

James Hawker, of the Plymouth family of wine merchants, entered the navy in 1744 and reached post rank. Three of his daughters married naval officers, one of them the one-armed Michael Seymour. Beaumont House was the Seymour home from 1798 until 1814, during which time Michael won much fame and a baronetcy in single-ship actions. His brother-in-law, Edward Hawker, became an admiral. His son John Seymour married Elizabeth Culme, whose family were neighbours at Tothill. When Elizabeth died in 1841, Sir John took the name of Culme-Seymour, to keep the Culme name alive, and both names survive as Mannamead street names on old Culme land.

SOCIAL AND INTELLECTUAL LIFE

This mixture of county, naval and Plymouth families led to a considerable social life. In an advertisement of 1785 'The Nobility and Gentry are respectfully acquainted that the Long-Room, near Plymouth, will be opened for their reception with a CONCERT and ASSEMBLY on Thursday the 12th of May next . . .' The Long Room with its tepid bath and 'a machine to bathe in the open Sea' had begun its fashionable life in 1766, on the Stonehouse shores of Millbay. It ended its social life in 1804 when a wooden-hutted barracks was built round it, but the Long Room itself survives, an elegant red-brick ballroom used by the Royal Marines as a gymnasium. Nelson in 1801 found he had 'given much offence' by not attending an assembly there. The Prince of Wales (later Prince Regent and then King George IV), the Duke of York and Prince William (later Duke of Clarence and eventually King William IV) gave a ball there in 1788. Prince William, captain of the frigate *Pegasus*, had been ordered to Plymouth to get him out of the clutches of a woman;

his brothers visited him in defiance of their father, and Prince William further upset the family peace by falling in love with a local girl, Sally Winne. He was staying with her father, George Winne, a merchant who encouraged the affair because he hoped to become agent-victualler to the fleet. He had to be content with becoming Mayor of Plymouth in 1791–2. The Prince was packed off to sea again, out of harm's way. Prince William probably saw more of Plymouth than any other member of the royal family before or since. At one time he lodged in Ordnance Street, between Morice Square and the gate of the Gun Wharf. He was a guest at dinner parties at many of the great town houses, and his name survives in street names and pub signs. As a young man he probably honoured too the assemblies at the Fountain in Fore Street, Devonport, the Old London Inn, Vauxhall Street – and, with his tastes in lechery, other less salubrious haunts.

In 1789, the year that William became Duke of Clarence, the King himself visited Plymouth with the Queen and his three eldest daughters, but for them it was a round of Saltram and Mount Edgcumbe, a sham battle at sea and a trip up the Tamar. Saltram, where the royal party stayed, was the great centre of fashion and from a diary in the Saltram archives a picture survives of the social round of the day, and the snobbery. In 1790 Lord Valletort (heir to the Earl of Mount Edgcumbe) and his wife were staying at Saltram for the Plympton Ball. 'The aldermen's wives do not like that the freemen's wives should go to the ball,' wrote fifteen-year-old Theresa Parker, and in 1796, 'Government House and the Dock Ball, which amused us extremely. Such figures! such waists! such heads! as I never saw before . . . two of the best we discovered to be Stonehouse milliners and we saw them hard at work in their shop the next morning.' Lord and Lady George Lennox at Government House were of course great social figures; after all he was a great-grandson of Charles II, even if on the wrong side of the blanket. In 1798 Theresa Parker was at a 4pm dinner in a tent on Staddon Heights. 'Mrs Bastard brought Lady Onslow and General Grenville; we met the Lennoxes and Lord Fortescue.'

The year before Mrs Siddons, appearing at the Plymouth

Theatre, was dined at Saltram and Theresa found her 'very pompous'. Plymouth's first theatre in Hoegate Street had been replaced in 1758 by a building at the top of the newly developing George Street, which called itself the Theatre Royal after being honoured by George III and his family in 1789. All the great actors of the day played there and at the Dock Theatre.

It is a clue both to the social life and growing wealth of Plymouth that the corporation could in 1810 hold a competition for the design of a new theatre, hotel and assembly rooms, on a site at the bottom of George Street. The winner was an architect practising in Pall Mall, John Foulston. The massive block with its two Ionic-pillared porticoes was built in 1811–13 and cost £60,000. The hotel had over fifty bedrooms, the theatre could seat 1,192 people and the assembly room measured 80ft by 40ft. Foulston settled in Plymouth, building himself the long-vanished Athenian Cottage on the west side of Townsend Hill. With his new public and private buildings, and his planning of new streets, he created a neo-classical elegance in the Three Towns, as Plymouth, Stonehouse and Dock were beginning to be known.

So with balls, assemblies, theatres and dinners, Plymouth had its smart social life. There was also an artistic and intellectual life, often overlapping the social. Young Reynolds dining at Mount Edgcumbe was a fellow guest with Captain Keppel, the future admiral, who was bound for the Mediterranean. Keppel offered Reynolds a free passage and so enabled the painter to make his vital early visit to Italy. Reynolds, later established in London, became a close friend of Dr Johnson and brought him on holiday to Plymouth in 1762. They stayed with Dr John Mudge, fourth son of the vicar of St Andrew's. John, a little older than Reynolds, practised in Plymouth as a doctor all his life but was sufficiently distinguished in his profession and his other interests to be made a Fellow of the Royal Society in 1771. John's elder brother Zachariah was a brilliant watchmaker who retired to Plymouth in 1771, became the King's watchmaker in 1776 and was eventually awarded £2,500 for his work on chronometers. Their father, the vicar, a great Hebrew scholar and preacher, so impressed Johnson that he wrote Mudge's obituary for the *London Chronicle*. Reynolds called him the wisest man he ever knew. Another friend of this learned circle was John Smeaton, the engineer and another FRS, who was in Plymouth from 1756 to 1759 building the third lighthouse to stand on the Eddystone Rock.

Smeaton lodged in Notte Street with William Cookworthy, the great Quaker-chemist who discovered china clay in Cornwall and made the first true English porcelain. Captain Cook, who sailed from Plymouth on his three great voyages of discovery, was a frequent guest of Cookworthy's, and he brought the young scientist Joseph Banks with him in 1758. Banks, for so many years in after life the President of the Royal Society, was sailing with Cook on his first great Pacific voyage. Another dinner guest and friend of Cookworthy's was Captain John Jervis, later the Admiral Lord St Vincent who built the fleet that Nelson was to lead. 'Whoever was in Mr Cookworthy's company', said Jervis, 'was always wiser and better for having been in it.' Jervis had met Cookworthy at Lord Edgcumbe's dinner table; how the social, intellectual and naval sides of eighteenth-century Plymouth life intertwined! Many of these men live still in the portraits of Reynolds, who had his first studio over the milliners' shop of his sisters in Dock and produced thirty portraits there and many landscapes. He was much in Plymouth 1744–9, but then moved to London and became the first President of the Royal Academy. He was followed to London by another famous Plymouth painter, James Northcote, who arrived with a letter of introduction from John Mudge.

The meetings of these men were not confined to private houses. John Mudge was a leading light of the Otter Club which met for literary discussions at the Pope's Head, at the top of Looe Street, in the building now fittingly enough the Plymouth Arts Centre. The odd name comes from the club's origin in a group of men who bathed under the Hoe together. Dr Mudge was also president of another club which met at the Bunch of Grapes, in Kinterbury Street. In 1810 the Plymouth Proprietary Library was formed, and Foulston designed its original library, built in Cornwall Street in 1812. The organisation if not the building survives. So does the Plymouth Institution, founded by Henry Woollcoombe in 1812, which again had Foulston for the architect of its classical Athenaeum, built next to the Theatre Royal in 1818–19. The Library of Plymouth Law Society was founded in 1815. Plymouth Medical Society, again still flourishing, was founded in 1794 in the new Globe Hotel at the top of George Street. It too had its library. From its members came the foundation of Plymouth Public Dispensary in 1798, the first real source of medical aid for the poor. A legacy from Dr Charles Yonge of the Puslinch family paid in 1804 for the dispensary building in Catherine Street. In 1815 the Dock and Stonehouse Public Dispensary was built in Chapel Street.

Apart from the literary groups which began meeting in the leading inns, there were freemasons. The early records are unreliable but there seems to have been a lodge in Dock as early as 1734 and two more in Plymouth by 1748. St John and Fortitude were warranted in 1759, Friendship in 1761, Harmony and Brunswick in 1778, and Charity the next year. One lodge with clear records to the present day is Sincerity (No 189) which was formed at the Three Crowns on the Parade in 1769 and, after using the Mitre and the Rose and Crown in Plymouth, moved to a succession of Dock inns before returning to Plymouth in 1829. There seems to have been a strong mercantile or naval background to the early lodges, for some were formed in other ports and later moved to Plymouth. The warrant of Fidelity (No 230), for instance, founded in Rotherhithe in 1799, was used at Kingsand in 1810 and has been in Plymouth or Devonport since 1817. Prince William was initiated into Lodge No 86 at the Prince George Inn in 1786, two months before the freedom of the town was presented to him 'at Mr Winne's'.

THE CHURCHES

The Church of England went along quietly enough in the eighteenth century, blessed by two powerful leaders. Mudge at St Andrew's was a strong high church man with no love for nonconformists or Methodists, in spite of a dissenting youth.

He only preached once a month. After his death in 1769 his curate John Gandy succeeded him and remained vicar until 1824 – two vicars covering ninety-two years. Gandy was 'a beautiful example of a Christian pastor' and a wit; John Wesley, visiting St Andrew's in 1775, was impressed by the 300 communicants. At Charles Church John Bedford, great-grandson of the first lecturer at Charles, was succeeded in 1784 by his curate Robert Hawker, who was vicar until his death in 1827. Hawker, originally a surgeon with the Royal Marines, was an evangelist who entertained John Wesley at his table and sympathised so much with the Methodists that he was reported to the bishop. A high Calvinist and a nationally popular preacher, he founded Plymouth's first Sunday School in 1787 and built the Household of Faith in Vennel Street, near Charles, in 1798 to house his school. He ministered unflinchingly to the sick soldiers brought home in 1809 in the retreat from Corunna; a thousand died of fever in a converted barn at the Friary and 3,000 Plymothians died in the same contagion. St Andrew's had an organ by 1735 but Charles had only an unsupported choir until 1821: organs until then were lumped with ornaments, a little Popish. But the present stone spire was added in 1766.

To serve Dock's growing population, Stoke Damerel Church was enlarged in 1750 though the Admiralty, asked for help, would only give masts for pillars and such-like supplies from the dockyard. But it was a long way from the town proper and two new churches were built in the town by public subscription, St Aubyn in 1771–2 and St John in 1797–9.

When Whitfield first came to the Three Towns in 1744 he found the nonconformists 'low and afflicted'. They were split by endless schisms which were to continue on and off for the rest of the century. The Congregationalists in their Batter Street chapel were shaken by Unitarianism but they finally settled down with Christopher Mends, a Trinitarian, and the Unitarians moved to Treville Street. To fight the West Country's tendency to Arianism (the heresy which denies the full divinity of Christ), the London Congregational Fund Board moved their Western College from Ottery St Mary in 1766 to Radnor Place, Plymouth. It was rebuilt in 1861 on Townsend

Hill and its buildings still form the northern side of Western College Road. The Baptists had a revival about mid-century and replaced their Pig Market chapel with one in How Lane in the 1780s, when Dock had its first Baptist chapel in Pembroke Street, with a daughter chapel in Morice Square.

A Tavistock convert of Whitfield's, Andrew Kinsman, moved to Plymouth in 1745 and married Ann Tiley, who gave the land on Bretonside where the 'Old Tabernacle' was built. A later split led to the 'New Tabernacle' being built in Norley Street in 1797; these two chapels became the ancestors of the present Sherwell Congregational Church. The two Wesleys at first left the Three Towns to Whitfield but began visiting in 1746 and were here many times before John's last call in 1789. They too found constant division which they worked hard to heal, but the first Methodist churches were Lower Street in Plymouth in 1779 and Ker Street in Dock in 1786, followed by Morice Square in 1811. Methodism was stronger in Dock than Plymouth, but in both communities all the nonconformists were not only constantly at loggerheads among themselves, but oppressed by the naval and military authorities who regarded them as centres of disaffection. A Unitarian chapel built in George Street, Dock, so offended the dockyard authorities that it was closed in 1806; the building is still there as the Old Chapel public house. These were rowdy towns, and the mob, service and civilian, was happy to heave stones and start riots where they felt authority was on their side. The nonconformist history of eighteenth-century Plymouth is not happy.

There were Roman Catholic priests in 1792, a building registered for worship in Dock in 1801, and a chapel built opposite the gates of the Naval Hospital in Stonehouse by 1807.

The growth of the navy brought Jewish pedlars to Plymouth, and a small community had settled by 1740. Little Isaac, a Jewish pedlar, was murdered near Plymstock in 1760, and the Jews were very much the butt of seamen, who accused them of cheating. But the Plymouth Synagogue, the oldest Ashkenazi foundation in Britain outside London, bought three gardens near the Citadel as a burial ground, and in 1762 built the synagogue which still stands behind the Guildhall. Many of the Jews had settled as shopkeepers or jewellers by the end of the century, and Abraham Joseph, the most important slopman in the Three Towns, held a royal appointment to Prince William.

TRADE AND COMMERCE

The business life of the Three Towns was greatly helped by the foundation of banks. John Baring of Exeter, who with his brother Francis was building up the great European banking firm of Baring Brothers in London, was a brother-in-law of the first Lord Boringdon. He launched the first bank in Plymouth in 1772, known as Baring, Lee, Sellons & Tingcombe and later as the Plymouth Bank. The year after came Harris, Harris, Tanner & Herbert, which became the Naval Bank. Dock's first bank was founded in 1788 by Elford, Elford & Hartwell. They were, apart from the Baring link which did not last long, very local affairs based on the capital of the partners rather than the great national institutions we now know. The partners chopped and changed over the years, and there were several more private banks in both towns by the turn of the century. By making credit available, and issuing bank notes, they facilitated business life very considerably.

The business life of Plymouth had changed very sharply under the pressure of the French wars, and nowhere is this better shown than in a book published in 1816 by William Burt, secretary of the new Chamber of Commerce. Over the centuries Plymouth had grown on foreign trade. In 1814 Burt was writing that while Plymouth in the past year had imported coastwise 1,550 tons of sugar from other home ports, only 33 tons came direct from the West Indies, and this state of affairs applied to nearly every other commodity. Virtually all the coal came in non-Plymouth ships. The Cawsand and Kingsand pilchard fishery employed 50 men, the Plymouth trawlers 112 and the hookers about 50; the Newfoundland fishing was dead.

The port had, in fact, 'become the greatest emporium for prize ships and goods, of which, during the war, many millions sterling have been sold here'. Another 1814 letter-writer, remembering the Parade piled high with overseas imports, 'the property of merchants, particularly the great Mr Morshead', and the revival of the port's Newfoundland fishing in 1763, said that fishery and all commercial enterprise in the port was stopped by the outbreak of the American war in 1766. 'Wealth flowing in from the lucrative channel of prizes, and prize goods without hazard . . . consequently all trade is stagnated.'

The prize business had reached large proportions much earlier. Advertisements in the *Sherborne Mercury* for 1757, during the Seven Years War, show ships and their cargoes being 'sold by the candle' almost daily, sometimes two a day, at Pinham's Coffee House on the Parade by Francis Fanning, the broker. 'A thousand barrels of fine French flour and a large quantity of biscuits, lately taken by His Majesty's Ship *York*' in mid-June; seven ships auctioned between 9 and 16 June the same year including the 550-ton *Invincible*. In the eight and a half years ending 29 September 1801, 948 captured ships were brought into Plymouth. By 1813 there were 110 registered prize stores around Sutton Harbour, many specially built during the wars and still surviving, often dated. There was no point in normal trade, investing in ships, when the war brought enemy cargoes into port without risk to the merchant. The money involved was more than the Plymouth men could finance. Increasingly they became agents for the wealthier men of London, Bristol and Liverpool.

But if all normal trade was suspended for these 'speculative adventures', what was happening to the Plymouth ships? Vancouver in his 1808 *General View of the Agriculture of Devon* said that Plymouth had 245 ships totalling 15,574 tons and employing 1,105 men. In 1815 there were seven shipbuilders around Sutton Pool, six in the Cattewater and six adjacent to the Hamoaze, employing about 300 men and building twenty to thirty vessels a year. They were supported by fourteen ropewalks and a dozen sailmakers. Even Bristol had a smaller fleet, though of much larger vessels. Some of the ships were coasting but the bulk seem to have been privateering, private warships out for prizes. The Admiralty lists of privateers only give the port of registration for the American War of Independence but eight Plymouth ships appear. The first licence in 1777 went to the 70-ton *Swift* with a crew of sixteen but by the end of the war bigger and stronger ships were engaged, with the *Plymouth* and the *Devonshire Hero* both having

SPANISH PRIZES

will be Sold at THE BROKERS NEW SALOON, late the

MAYORALTY HOUSE, PLYMOUTH
on Friday the 2nd August, 1805
at 11 o'clock in the forenoon

The good Spanish Ship
Pura Y'Limpia Conception

Burthen about 200 tons, square stern, with a neat figurehead, copper bottom, and from her appearance no doubt can be entertained of her being a fast sailer. She has two decks, well calculated for the fish and fruit trades. Detained by H.M. Ship-of-War, Repulse, commanded by The Hon. A. K. Legge - now lying in Cattewater, and there to be delivered.

Also the good Spanish Brig
Santa Mariana

Burthen about 80 tons, a strong handy vessel for the coasting trade of culm or coal. Shifts without ballast and may be sent to sea with a small outfit, being well found in her principal stores. Detained by H.M. Ship-of-War, Diamond, Captain Elphinstone, now lying in Sutton Pool.

Immediately afterwards will be sold - all the warlike stores and other valuable items landed from the enemy Frigates Medea, Santa Gertrudes and El Infanta Don Carlos - consisting of Anchors, Cables, Rigging, Sails, Masts, Yards, and other parts. Junk, Double and Single Blocks, Iron Ballast, Muskets, Pistols, Cutlasses. 101 Guns (being 6, 18 and 24 pounders). Round and Grape Shot, Gunpowder in barrels and other ordnance. Also Legars, Half Legars, Casks and sundry other articles. The above vessels and goods are condemned as droits to His Majesty.

For viewing the same and catalogues, or for further particulars, application to be made to Edward Lockyer, Esq. or Messrs. Symes.

Thomas Lockyer,
Sworn Broker.   Plymouth, July 17th, 1805

PRIZE AUCTION POSTER. *Captured ships and cargoes up for sale during the Napoleonic Wars. The Mayoralty House was in Woolster Street and the door survives in a garage. The Lockyer family, who made their fortune in this kind of business, are much concerned in the sale.*

crews of 100. There are few local references, as if it were not a matter to be proud of, but 'many fortunes were made'.

Even the bigger craft in the smuggling fleet based at Cawsand had privateering licences from the times of the American war. The open boats, ostensibly seine net fishing for pilchards, were available with their six-man crews to meet ships at sea but could also cross the Channel. They could carry six tons of brandy at a time, but the three-masted luggers and the bigger cutters could carry much more, 600 to 800 eight-gallon spirit casks as well as tea and tobacco. In 1804 the Plymouth Collector of Customs estimated that 17,000 casks of spirits were smuggled into Cawsand every year. There were fifty craft in the trade by 1815. The Channel Islands were their main sources until 1767 and though Guernsey was still used until 1805 the main trade moved to Roscoff, which the French made a 'free port' in 1769 and which Napoleon later encouraged as a source of information as well as trade. There were some notorious battles in Cawsand Bay between smugglers and revenue men; in 1788 Henry Carter, the 'King of Prussia', barely escaped though he lost his cutter, and in 1798 the men of the *Lottery* of Polperro opened fire on the revenue men and killed one.

Manufacturing in Plymouth had gone the way of commerce. The Shepherd family were out of the woollen business and just a small white serge business remained. The manufacture of fine porcelain by Cookworthy, which had employed up to sixty people, only lasted from 1768 to 1774 and was then moved to Bristol. By 1815 there were two earthenware potteries at Coxside, employing just over fifty people. The canvas makers and the tanners produced more than the town needed, but otherwise the little industry just supplied the local inhabitants and the shipping business. Sutton Harbour had been improved in the 1790s by the building of the two piers at the entrance, and after long disputes over harbour rights the local businessmen had formed the Sutton Harbour Company which in 1812 leased the Pool from the Prince of Wales for £6,000.

INDUSTRIAL REVOLUTION

The real employer and source of wealth for all the Three Towns was the dockyard. Vancouver in 1808 reports 2,741 men employed in the yard, with a total wage bill of £191,153 a year. The actual 'take-home' pay of even the labourers was 16s a week. No wonder it was hard to find labourers in the country districts around, for though they were busy feeding the ships and the Three Towns their wage was only 7s a week. Even dockyard pensioners – 380 in 1808 – had nearly 5s a week, and to become an 'established' man in the yard, which meant a pension, was regarded as security indeed.

With the towns growing fast the major shore employers outside the yard were the housebuilders. Six or seven master builders in Plymouth alone employed some 350 craftsmen, and had built 500 houses in the ten years up to 1815. Robert Bayly, who married the daughter of Captain Brabant of the Island House on the Barbican and inherited his business as a merchant and shipowner, started a timber company at Coxside in 1780 which survives as Bayly-Bartlett. The town was expanding slowly, eastwards with Brunswick Terrace and other houses along the new Exeter road and towards Coxside, northwards ('Charles Town') to Regent Street and north-westwards ('New Town') along Saltash Street towards Coburg Street. The old Pig Market became Bedford Street, George Street was a residential area reaching down to the Royal Hotel and Theatre, and Lockyer Street, like much of the Hoe slopes and those north of the town, was dotted with middle-class villas. The old village of Stonehouse had its new Durnford Street gentility to the south. Dock was virtually filled within the lines and, with the start of the Torpoint Ferry, development began at Morice Town, behind the ferry landing area. The first house was built there in 1796 and to bring in the needs of Dock three 'canals' were cut, lined with wharves by 1812 and soon backed by coal yards, breweries and a pottery. The ferry landing beach is still called Pottery Quay, and the southern 'canal', filled in, is under the hoarding-enclosed space between the two ferry roads.

Dock had outgrown Plymouth by 1801, and increased its lead by 1811. The figures are:

	Plymouth	Stonehouse	Dock	Total
1801	16,378	3,807	23,787	43,972
1811	21,156	5,174	30,083	56,616

Plympton had 2,166 people and Plymstock 1,633. But whereas the country districts had about six people to each house, old Plymouth had 9.2 and Stonehouse 9.5. In newer Dock the figure was 7.2; the towns were growing faster in population than houses could be built for them. By 1815 there was talk of uniting the Three Towns and the new thoroughfare planned by

Foulston which linked them all in 1815, across the old Sourpool marshes, was called Union Street. The Three Towns, which had grown under the one impetus and formed one urban area, were now in effect the fifth largest provincial town in England; their previous ranking through the centuries had always been about twentieth. The only larger towns were Manchester, Liverpool, Birmingham and Bristol, in that order. Even Leeds was smaller. Plymouth with its neighbours was one of the new towns of the Industrial Revolution, with all the problems that entailed.

It was not always peaceful. In 1797 crews of the ships at Dock mutinied along with the men at Spithead and the Nore; the men of the *Powerful* set some officers adrift and came ashore with others to lock them up in the 'Black Hole' in Fore Street. Admiral Lord Keith put down the mutiny quickly and bravely; fourteen ringleaders were hanged and many more flogged. Soon afterwards three marines were shot on the Hoe for seditious plotting. There were riots in the yard and the streets of Dock in 1780 and again in 1801 over systems of work and food shortages.

The *Grand Gazeteer* of 1759 nicely describes eighteenth-century Plymouth:

> . . . in its most flourishing wicked time of what some call a good red-hot war with France, when indeed 'tis too much over-stocked with inhabitants newcome from Ireland, Cornwall and other parts, and gathered Flocks of Females, charitably inclined to solace money'd sailors in distress; and that they may do it honestly . . . marry them ex tempore, possibly half-a-dozen in as many months. The true Plymothians are in the main allowed to be as polite, genteel, religious and worthy a people as those enjoyed by any other place. [But in war] the vast resort of the necessitous, the rapacious, the lewd, by land, and of the half-mad Jack Addles from the sea, the scenes are altered much.

Against this there was the elegant, sophisticated society of the gentry and the professional classes. They all flocked to see Napoleon when he was brought into Plymouth Sound after Waterloo, aboard the *Bellerophon*. It was the end of a near-century of war, and the dawn of a new era for the Three Towns.

Above, the hub of nineteenth-century Plymouth. The Lockyer Hotel (right) and Derry's Clock still survive, but the Royal Hotel went in the Blitz and the 1843 building down the hill, the Bank of England branch, was demolished after the war. Such provincial branches were uncommon; the presence of one in Plymouth is a testimony to the town's commercial importance. *Below*, the Promenade Pier under the Hoe, another Blitz victim; note the horse tram in the foreground. At the time of this photograph, August 1905, the Aeolian Opera Singers were appearing, but in all but the best of weathers it was a trial to get to the pier. The warship is the cruiser *Terrible*.

Between the wars: *above*, east coast herring drifters crowd the Fish Market quays with commercial sailing vessels moored in the Pool. *Below*, Drake Circus looking into Old Town Street, the site of the present pedestrian shopping complex of C & A.

CHAPTER SEVEN

POLITICAL REFORM: 1750–1835

THE growth of the Three Towns, and the development of their intellectual life, naturally enough led to resentment at the medieval control of affairs. In the new towns of Stonehouse and Dock the old manorial direction prevailed; both were privately owned, and properties only leased, so in both towns authority was exercised by the manor court. With no freeholders, there were no parliamentary voters. Local government came from the county magistrates in Quarter Sessions – at Exeter. Dock did in 1780 get a body of commissioners to care for the poor and see the streets were policed, but a new Act was needed in 1814 to obtain further powers. Electors were those who paid over £8 a year in poor rates. Commissioners had to qualify with £50 a year in property or £100 in personal income and were elected for life. There were also a number of ex-officio commissioners like the lord of the manor and his steward, the Yard Commissioner, the Port Admiral, the rector, and neighbouring landowners. With the population steadily growing and the town's pride expanding, a town hall designed by Foulston was built in 1821–2 at the top of Ker Street, and in 1823 a petition for a new name was addressed to King George IV: a town bigger than Plymouth resented being called Plymouth Dock. The King accepted the suggestion of the name 'Devonport' for the town. The townsmen celebrated exuberantly, and raised more money to build, again to Foulston's design, a column beside the Guildhall to celebrate the new name. After the Municipal Corporations Act of 1835, Devonport was the first town to apply for a charter and the first town to be so incorporated, on 29 November 1836. Even so the application was not made without great local debate, for many feared it would bring amalgamation with Plymouth.

THE STRUGGLE FOR PLYMOUTH

Local government in Plymouth at the end of the eighteenth century had not changed from the old system of a mayor and corporation, with true administration in the hands of the borough quarter sessions. Members of Parliament were government nominees who were never opposed; in fact the freemen had only had to vote in an election once between 1698 and 1780. In return every government post was seen as a perk to be distributed by the council. Viscount Barrington who was a Plymouth MP for twenty-four years (1754–78) without ever fighting an election and was a kind of permanent minister whoever was in power, observed in 1774 when Secretary for War that Plymouth Corporation was making a recommendation for every employment that fell vacant, and told them that 'they could not have them all'.

It is interesting to see new kinds of people as Mayors of Plymouth. In addition to the merchants who had tended to dominate the council, there were now more lawyers and surgeons, and also two pursers in men-of-war who had become merchants, officers of the Victualling Yard, the dockyard (even one commissioner) and the customs service.

In 1766 Quarter Sessions appointed a committee to watch, pave and sweep the town but it did not work over-well and in 1772 an Act of Parliament was obtained which gave rated householders the right to elect thirty-eight commissioners for life, and to fill vacancies that occurred. It was the start of reform, and that year the borough Quarter Sessions transferred its administrative powers to the mayor, aldermen and councillors.

The commissioners began zealously, paying watchmen – eight and a corporal in summer, eleven and a corporal in winter – to patrol the streets at night with halberd and bell, calling the hours and the weather. They lit the main streets with 250 oil lamps, and began to widen streets to cope with wheeled vehicles. The old town gates were also demolished where they delayed traffic. These commissioners were freemen, and it is clear that they sometimes sat with the council in decision-making. The freemen began to flex their muscles, and by 1789 were claiming the right to elect aldermen, who held the real power. They were just defeated, and the following year the freeholders of the town, remembering rights their fathers had claimed, began again to seek parliamentary votes. So a three-cornered struggle started which became increasingly complicated as individuals varied their arguments and changed sides. The majority of the freemen wanted power over aldermen, but they did not want to lose what power they had to the freeholders.

There was further reform in 1799 when a Lands Committee was formed, and a paid officer took over the handling of corporation finances, instead of a councillor elected annually as receiver, a practice that went back to the earliest days. The freemen were meeting regularly to further their claims, and from the name of the inn where they met they called themselves the Leg of Mutton Club. In 1802 they claimed the right to elect the mayor, fought it successfully through the law courts, and in 1803 elected the brewer John Clarke Langmead. (He gave Plymouth its first lifeboat, to celebrate the victory.) Then the freemen instigated an examination of by-laws and established their right to elect the aldermen, councillors and officers of the corporation as well. A resolution to give financial control to a committee of the mayor, the past mayor and nineteen people elected annually by the freeman was passed, and this Committee of 21 became the real power. These decisions were reached in the new guildhall just completed by the Lands Committee (a building 'neither elegant nor efficient' which survived at the end of Whimple Street until 1941), and a diarist wrote jubilantly that 'the first use of the new Guildhall was to overturn the old Corporation. The aldermen are now cyphers.' But the victorious freemen were not going to dissipate their new strength, and set up a small committee to examine very carefully any new admissions of freeholders to their ranks.

Next year a Market Committee was appointed. For centuries the stalls had clustered around St Andrew's and in adjacent streets. Now property was bought on the then northern edge of the town and new markets built. It cost £10,000, but the tolls by 1809 were £900, and it lasted Plymouth with one rebuilding until its destruction in 1941. The top of New George Street now covers the site. In 1809 it was decided to build a new theatre, hotel and assembly rooms and £50 was offered as a prize for the best design. So cheaply did Plymouth bring Foulston into the town!

Henry Woollcombe, a lawyer of an old family, emerges at this time as the leader of the reform group – 'the founder of almost every institution in Plymouth at that time', wrote Edwin Welch, a city archivist of recent years whose patient researches unearthed all these affairs. Woollcombe was backed by the Lockyers – Edmund Lockyer, mayor in 1803–4, is described in a manuscript history among the Rogers papers as 'of low origin, but got rich by being a government contractor'. He handled the disposal of prize ships and cargoes. Various Lockyer sons became captains in the Royal Navy and active in Plymouth affairs, and Lockyer Street was so named to honour Lockyer's fight for Plymouth's rights to the Hoe. Another reformer was the fiery ex-naval surgeon, George Bellamy, who in the battles going on with the military authorities about the ownership of the Hoe really stormed the barricades.

But personalities began to clash. The town was overspending on its building projects, and cutting back. The old arguments between freemen and aldermen revived. The Committee of 21 bought a specially designed medal and chain which it presented to the mayor in January 1816, to mark the successful reform of 1803, and the Lord Mayor of Plymouth still wears it. But it did not resolve the new arguments, which dragged on over the years. The struggles for parliamentary votes running at the same time complicated issues, as did the refusal of Sir William Elford, Recorder of Plymouth since 1797, to give up his office even though he had moved away to Totnes in 1825. Arguments mounted, the Shoulder of Mutton Club split and died, and not all Woollcombe's astute attempts at compromise brought any peace.

But with the passing of the Reform Act of 1832 – which concerned parliamentary elections – came peace. Many new freemen were created. With a final compromise of January 1833 the right of electing the aldermen finally passed to the freemen. Elford resigned, and Woollcombe was elected recorder. All by-laws were repealed, a new administration and new committees created. 'We have not visited any corporation in the west of England so well managed in all respects', said a report of 1835. But the report was made under the new Municipal Reform Act, under which the short-lived administration finally disappeared in favour of the new universal plan. John Moore the shipbuilder, elected in 1834, was the last mayor under the old charter and the last mayor to wait (only an hour now) after his nomination for any objection from the Prior of Plympton, a tradition surviving from the days before the priory was closed down in 1539.

PARLIAMENTARY REFORM

The freeholders moved into the parliamentary field as soon as the unpopularity of the government nominees gave them a chance. On the death in 1778 of Barrington, who had looked after the freemen's claims for twenty-four years, Lord North gave the seat to his relation, Viscount Lewisham. The other MP since 1771, old Admiral Hardy, was the Commander-in-Chief Channel Fleet who had let the French fleet into Cawsand Bay in 1779 and done nothing to move it out. When he died the next year the Admiralty nominee was Sir Frederick Lemon Rogers, son of the former Dock Commissioner and, of course, Recorder of Plymouth. He had won £60 in a three-day cock fight in 1773, had twenty-seven horses and twenty-four couples of hounds in his stables at Blachford, and was eventually to die of gout. In the by-election John Culme stood as a champion of the freeholders, petitioned against Rogers's election, and when he was still rejected stood again in the general election at the end of 1780. Lord Lewisham, afraid of fighting an election, did not stand again. Admiral Darby, a tool of Lord Sandwich's, had the Admiralty nomination, Rogers the government ticket. The freeholders also put up the locally popular Admiral Rodney, but neither be nor Culme could shake the establishment.

There were two new government men at the 1784 general election, Captain Fanshawe (whose mother was a Rogers) and John Bastard of Kitley. John Macbride, a naval captain who had risen by his own ability and was much admired for 'winging the French in their own ports', successfully stood against the

Admiralty nominee, and John Bastard finished third. Captain MacBride, who sometime lived at Leigham House, was instrumental in getting the government grants for the piers which still enclose Sutton Harbour. He remained a thorn in the government's side, opposing 'the infamous and expensive projects' of fortifying Plymouth and Portsmouth, and held the seat till 1790 when Rogers stood again and defeated him. MacBride's petition was of no avail; he went back to sea, rose to be a full admiral, and his name is still remembered by the public house overlooking the Sutton Harbour piers.

In 1796 the freeholders came back with William Elford the banker as their champion, fighting Rogers and the Admiralty's Captain Gardner. Rather that fight, Gardner found another seat, and Elford joined Rogers in Parliament. Rogers was a government man and Elford was 'by no means disapproved of by it'. When Rogers died the next year he was replaced by another government man and Elford was given the recordership. Two years later there was a baronetcy for him; he may have been a freeholders' man to start with but he was being bought over. In the 1802 election, when the freemen were winning municipal power, the government only nominated one man who dropped out when it was seen that the freeholders' men, Elford and Philip Langmead (father of the 1803 mayor, a popular and respected local man) were going to win. They were returned unopposed but four years later Langmead resigned his seat a disillusioned man. The Prince of Wales promptly put his friend Tyrwhitt into his place.

Elford is a strange character to elucidate. Of the old west Devon family he had followed his father at Bickham (now Lord Roborough's home), was a friend of the younger Pitt, a renowned whist player at Bath, a Fellow of the Royal Society and an exhibitor at the Royal Academy from 1774 to 1837. In his early days he was a great friend of Henry Woollcombe, but after the Plymouth Bank, which Elford now owned, crashed in 1823 with £70,000 deficiency it was clear that he had been running an insolvent concern for years and Woollcombe broke with him completely. But it is clear that in the 1806 general election the government, which thought it had bought Elford, still found him too independent. He was a candidate again, with Thomas Bewes, a leader of the freeholders, who spent a lot of money on this election. They were opposed by Tyrwhitt for the Prince of Wales and Admiral Sir C. M. Pole (brother of Carew Pole of Antony) for the Admiralty. The official men won, petitions did not dislodge them, and from that time until 1831 there were no freeholder candidates. They had shot their bolt. After this the Prince's men and the Admiralty men were regularly returned without opposition. Indeed in 1812 and again in 1818 Elford was supporting the Prince's man.

But just as the Establishment brought Elford to heel, so Admiral Pole was disciplined in 1818. Pole was a good local member, as befits a native. In 1812 he had helped to pass the motion in the House of Commons which granted £80,000 to start work on the Breakwater. In 1817 he was pressing the government to expedite the work on the Breakwater, to compensate for the shortage of work in the dockyard. At all times he spoke 'with the freedom of a man independent of party', and upset his Admiralty colleagues by his attacks on inefficiency. Perhaps that is why in 1818 he found himself opposed by the Comptroller of the Navy, Admiral Sir Thomas Byam Martin (son-in-law of Captain Robert Fanshawe, the former MP). Pole found himself a very poor third.

But though the freeholders had found it fruitless to put up candidates for Parliament, they and the rest of the Whig reformers found plenty to do. There were as many property owners in Plymouth with the right to vote for the Devon county members as there were voters for the Plymouth members. In the county as in most rural seats the landowners had most influence but their influence was scattered and it was not easy to get voters to Exeter. The greatest influence was exerted by the Duke of Bedford and Earl Fortescue, and both had sons who were strong reformers. Lord John Russell, who eventually became the leading reformer nationally, was first returned for Tavistock. Viscount Ebrington, Earl Fortescue's son, captured one of the Devon seats for Reform in 1818 and the Plymouth freeholders gave a dinner in his honour. Ebrington lost in 1820 but the Bedfords gave him the Tavistock seat and Lord John moved to Huntingdonshire. When Ebrington captured a Devon seat again in 1830 the Plymouth reformers met his carriage at the eastern end of the town and man-hauled it through the streets to the Royal Hotel and a victory dinner.

That was at the general election which followed the accession of William IV, the Duke of Clarence so beloved in the Three Towns and thought to be in favour of Reform. Indeed Devonport, which had asked for a Member of Parliament in 1827 when the rotten Cornish borough of Penryn had its member taken away, directly petitioned the Duke of Clarence for enfranchisement on a formal visit he paid in 1828. In the 1830 election, when the reformers swept the county seats but boroughs like Plymouth went on sending back the official nominees, the reformers of Plymouth and Devonport united in a mass meeting addressed by Thomas Bewes, Dr Cookworthy (son of the Quaker-chemist) and Dr Woollcombe from which a petition urging Reform was sent to the Plymouth MPs. The first Reform Bill was presented to Parliament in March 1831; when it was defeated there were public protest meetings outside the Royal Hotel in Plymouth and Devonport Town Hall.

The Prime Minister, Earl Grey, went to the country. Devon returned Lord John Russell and Viscount Ebrington – who both have streets named after them in Plymouth – and in the town Admirals Byam Martin and Cockburn were opposed by the Hon George Eliot, a strong reformer protesting 'against nomination'. Eliot was the popular hero but the crowd had no votes. The sitting members won. At the close of polling not even an escort of 120 soldiers could protect Cockburn who had his head cut by a brick, and the mayor had to read the Riot Act twice. Grey's new ministy carried the Bill through the Commons in July but the Lords threw it out in October. The bench of bishops was much blamed; Dr Phillpotts, the new and very Tory Bishop of Exeter, told the Duke of Wellington that the spirit in Plymouth was tremendously bad. He had been asked not to go there to consecrate a new church because he 'would be in the greatest danger'.

The Bill went back to the Lords in spring 1832, and when on 12 May Plymouth heard of more temporising there was despondency everywhere. Flags were half-masted. Four days later a meeting of 26,000 people from all Three Towns met in the Bull Ring under the Hoe to support the Bill. On 4 June it was finally passed. Ten thousand people marched through the streets in procession, under triumphal arches, and another celebratory meeting was held in the Bull Ring.

During the passage of the Bill, which virtually gave the vote to occupants of houses worth £10 rent a year, whether freehold or leasehold, the future of Devonport had been debated in the Lords. The Bill made Stonehouse and Devonport into one constituency, with two members. One noble lord said they should be linked with Plymouth because otherwise Devonport would simply become 'another Government borough'. This raised Plymouth fears that St Aubyn patronage would then prevail. The Earl of Morley spoke for separate constituencies, supported by Earl Grey 'as a former resident of Devonport'. Their view prevailed, and at the general election of 1832 Devonport and Stonehouse returned their first members, Sir George Grey (nephew of Earl Grey) and Admiral Codrington, the hero of Navarino. Devonport did become a government brough. It was almost as if the Admiralty, losing its Plymouth seat, took over Devonport, and its men, Liberal or Conservative, dominated till the later Reform Acts. The local reformers did put up a candidate against them in 1832, George Leach, but with no success and after the election his friend Woollcombe was sued for libel, fined and sentenced to a month in prison.

In Plymouth the leaders of the reformers, Thomas Bewes and John Collier, were both elected. Admiral Byam Martin was nominated but found the contest so hopeless that he withdrew; so they were finally unopposed. A new era was born. Locally and nationally the old names of Tory and Whig disappear. Plymouth had a Conservative Association by 1837 and a Liberal Association soon after. The Liberals, heirs of the reformers, had their heyday. The Conservative candidate, C. J. Mare, was top of the poll in 1852 but was unseated for bribery. For two years from 1859 another Conservative, Viscount Valletort, was a member. Apart from that the Liberals held Plymouth right up to the second Reform Act, in 1867.

So ended the greatest period of political excitement the Three Towns have ever known. What had started in Plymouth as a slightly squalid struggle in which the freemen sought to take power from the aldermen, but did not want the freeholders to share that power, became a broader-based struggle for democratic rights, as it was in Stonehouse and Devonport. The final success after all only meant 1,461 Plymouth voters in a town of 30,000, and 1,768 Devonport and Stonehouse voters in a population of 44,000. Not till the 1867 Reform Act, which gave the vote to all rate-paying occupiers and those occupying lodgings of £10 value, was the franchise really widened. Only then, and with the replacement of open voting at the hustings by the introduction of the ballot box in 1872, did 'influence' really lose its weight. But to this day the lord mayor's medallion, and the tablets in the Bull Ring under the Hoe, mark a very determined fight for a greater freedom which, in Plymouth's municipal affairs at least, was won ahead of the national fight.

CHAPTER EIGHT

THE AGE OF STEAM: 1815–1914

THE brewers, eternally prosperous, brought the first steam engines to Plymouth: Langmeads' for their Hoegate Brewery in 1797 and Richard King of Notte Street in 1810. As motive power, steam was first seen when the paddler *Thames*, built on the Clyde, called in the summer of 1815 bound for London on the first open sea voyage of any British steamer. But no one in the years following the Napoleonic Wars would have predicted that these new engines would transform the whole country, and the Three Towns with it. In 1815 there were three towns separated by and enfolded among estuaries where fields sloped down to the tide; by 1914 it was one tight urban area running back across the hills with docks and factories lining all those estuaries.

Yet it started with depression. With the end of the war the navy laid up 200 ships in a month, six out of every seven seamen were discharged, the dockyard was run down, and Plymouth found its great trade in enemy prizes utterly vanished. The workhouses were full, there were 7,000 paupers in Plymouth 'receiving doles at the church doors', and by 1818 a road was being built from the Citadel gateway round under the Hoe to Millbay to make work. An 1823 national directory said that little business was in progress in Plymouth, there was scarcely any employment for the poor, and nearly an eighteenth of the population were receiving relief from the town. In the financial crisis of 1825, when up and down the country seventy-nine banks shut their doors, both Shiells & Johns of Devonport and the Elfords' Plymouth Bank failed; a desperate time.

GOVERNMENT WORKS

Yet even before the end of the war the government had begun a programme of major work which hardly halted for a century. The Breakwater was the first. Work began in 1812 with the purchase of a 25-acre quarry at Pomphlett. The engineers were John Rennie and Joseph Whidbey, who had been sailing master of *Discovery* on Vancouver's 1792 exploration of the Pacific. They laid rails in the quarry to move the stone, just as Smeaton had done in Millbay in 1756–9 when he was building the Eddystone Lighthouse, but they also had barges fitted with rails on to which the trucks ran – the world's first train ferry – and as the Breakwater rose above the sea they laid rails on the top to take these trucks. When Rennie died in 1821 Whidbey continued to supervise, living in Bovisand House above the reservoir and the little harbour built there to water ships in the Sound. The lighthouse at the western end was first lit, and the Breakwater finished, in 1844, with nearly 3½ million tons of stone used in its construction.

In 1820 Sutton Harbour received its most distinguished edifice with the building of the new Custom House, designed by David Laing, pupil of Sir John Soane and architect also of the new Custom House in London. John Rennie was also designing the new Royal William Victualling Yard at Stonehouse which was built between 1824 and 1835 by his son, later Sir John Rennie, at a total cost of £700,000. It covers 14 acres and is one of the greatest engineer-designed buildings in the country – certainly the most splendid complex in Plymouth. The Duke of Clarence laid the coping stone of the sea wall and his giant statue as King William IV still stands over the entrance gate.

By the time this was complete Devonport had already built its first steamship, the 813-ton *Rhadamanthus*, in 1831–2, but she had to sail to Woolwich to have engines fitted. The old South Yard, geared for sail, could not furnish the workshops or the kind of dock needed for these new beasts, and so a new steam factory was planned. But just as Cornwall Street had grown up along the north wall of the old yard, meaning that the later Gun Wharf had to be built separated from the yard it served by the North Corner projection, so the Torpoint Ferry slipway flanked the northern side of the Gun Wharf and the Steam Factory was also cut off. Work began in 1844, when already a quarter of the Royal Navy's ships had steam power. The first steam pile-driver in the world, designed by James Nasmyth, was used to build a coffer dam nearly a third of a mile long in the river. The area behind was pumped dry, and in this two basins were created, with three docks opening from South Basin. The Factory, a magnificent quadrangle of granite and limestone containing all the vital workshops, covering 10 acres, was built behind the North Basin. As the work cut into the hillside behind the old waterfront the masses of excavated material filled the space between the basins, and also Keyham Creek, which originally reached nearly to Milehouse. Work on the northern part of the new yard was delayed while a site was found for the powder magazine built there in 1784. Plymouth would not have explosives stored at Mount Batten, Stonehouse opposed a Millbay site, and eventually it went to Bull Point, next to the existing Kinterbury powder works. Not till 1854 was the new dockyard completed. It was even treated as a separate yard, with different hours of work and pay until 1876. A tunnel was built in 1854–6 to move horses and carts from one yard to the other; not until 1876 was it turned into a railway tunnel.

But before the Steam Yard was completed the government was worrying about the safety of this western base. So in 1853 the inner defences of Devonport, halted in 1816, were completed, and the old squares behind the lines replaced by Raglan Barracks in 1854–8, named after the commander in the Crimean War, which in those years brought great activity to Devonport. Then the imperialist ambitions of Napoleon III across the Channel alarmed Palmerston's government, and in 1860 both Portsmouth and Plymouth were ringed with forts. Bovisand, Breakwater and Picklecombe commanded the entrance to the Sound, Tregantle and Scraesdon aimed to prevent an enemy paralysing the dockyard from the Rame heights, and a ring of forts from Tamar to Plym and on to Bovisand covered the landward approaches. All told twenty-nine forts and interlocking batteries were built. The line of the Tavistock road was altered to allow the fort commanding it to take the hilltop and it was named after a pair of houses called Crown Hill removed from the summit. The nearby hamlet of Knackersnowle gradually took over that name, and in 1891–2 barracks were built there for the troops manning the defences.

The South Devon Militia had new barracks built on the edge of Plymouth, at Mutley, in 1840. With the Napoleon scare the

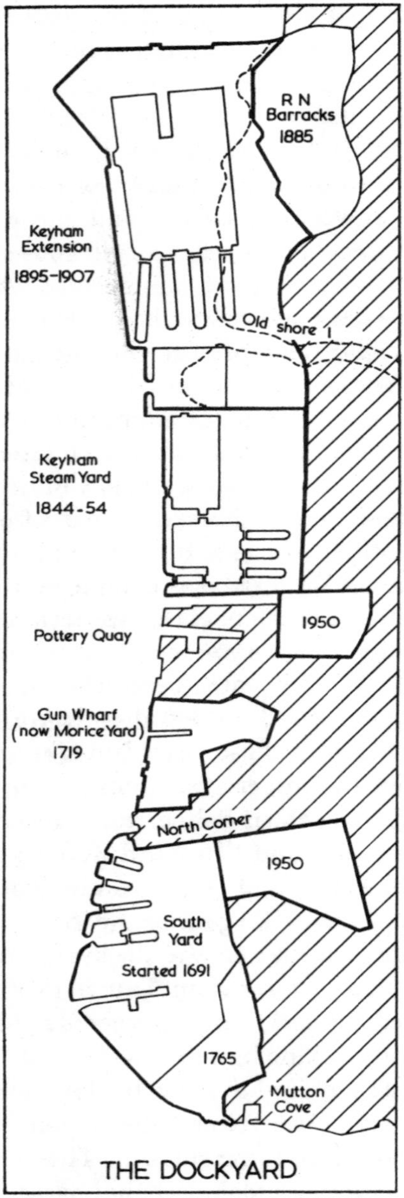
R N
Barracks
1885
Keyham
Extension
1895-1907
Old shore
Keyham
Steam Yard
1844-54
1950
Pottery Quay
Gun Wharf
(now Morice Yard)
1719
North Corner
1950
South
Yard
Started 1691
1765
Mutton
Cove
THE DOCKYARD

THE GROWTH OF DEVONPORT DOCKYARD. *The original shore line of the Keyham Extension yard shows how the dockyard was extended out over the mudflats, as were the South and Keyham yards.*

Volunteers, disbanded in 1814, were reformed and the Plymouth battalion was the second most senior in the country. Their headquarters were destroyed when Plymouth built a new guildhall and so a drill hall was built for them in 1870 on the southern side of the old Millbay prisoner-of-war barracks. The Durnford Street block of the Royal Marines Barracks was added in 1867, doubling the size of the establishment.

In the late 1850s the docks in South Yard were reshaped and enlarged to cope with the new steam vessels. But the navy's needs were changing fast, its ships changing from floating gun platforms into complex vessels with new weapons and armour. These needs were signalled by the building in 1879–81 of the Royal Naval Engineering College on the edge of the Keyham Yard, its architect the E. M. Barry who had just completed his father's rebuilding of the Houses of Parliament. The fleet was outgrowing the existing yards, and in 1896 the Keyham Extension was started, contiguous this time with its predecessor and adding another 130 acres to the existing 140 acres of dockyard. It was opened in 1907 when the Prince and Princess of Wales steamed in aboard the commander-in-chief's yacht *Vivid*. A tidal dock of $10\frac{1}{2}$ acres led to three graving docks: there was another closed basin of 35 acres and a sea wall 5,000 feet long. Two-thirds of the new yard had been below sea level. Over 4 million cubic yards of mud had been removed; infill was obtained by dredging the Skerries Bank in Start Bay and so much was removed that the beach at Hallsands changed its pattern and the village was washed away in a 1917 gale.

Apart from ships, the seamen were changing. Continuous service for ratings had been introduced in 1853 but men were still housed between commissions in old hulks. Some of these remained in the Hamoaze as training ships until well into this century but in 1884–9, with a second phase in 1898–1903, the Royal Naval Barracks were built beside the Keyham Extension. The men were borne on the books of HMS *Vivid* until 1934 when the 'ship's name' was changed to *Drake*. The nickname of 'Jago's Mansions' came in 1926 when the command supply officer, Mr. Jago, originated a system of central cooking and dining halls in place of the navy's traditional cooking by messes.

MANUFACTURING INDUSTRY

The pioneer who led Plymouth into the new chemical-based industries was Thomas Gill, younger son of a Tavistock banking family of the old-fashioned kind, owning mines, quarries and lime kilns. Thomas, striking out for himself, had realised that lime-burning was not far removed from the new French method of making soda ash and other alkalis needed in industry. Lime, heat and brine were the basic requirements and at Millbay he had a lime kiln beside the sea. So in 1818, at the age of thirty, he started an alkali and soap factory at Millbay. Very soon the Stanfords had a glass factory next door, also based on soda ash, and in 1823 the United Gas Company was also established there. Its street lights in 1832 were a boon; though Plymouth had long had oil lamps they were so feeble that the first meetings of the Plymouth Medical Society were fixed for evenings with a full moon. By 1845 United Gas had to give way to new companies, the Plymouth & Stonehouse on part of a pottery at Coxside and a Devonport company at Keyham. But Millbay was established as a factory area; an iron foundry actually preceded Gill's soap works by a few years and, passing through various hands and various waterside sites, did not end until the closure of Willoughby's in 1969.

Gill prospered; he was the first Reform mayor in 1832, Liberal MP for the town 1841–7, and in 1856 incorporated the Millbay Soap, Alkali & Soda Company with himself as managing director. The yellow bars of soap bearing the Plymouth coat of arms were familiar until well into this century.

Another bright young man of the time, William Bryant, retired from the excise service when only thirty-three and with another Quaker, Edward James, started making starch and refining sugar – again with new chemical processes – in Mill Lane in 1838. This of course had been an industrial area since Drake's first corn mills and the later woollen mills. These two were also factors for lucifer matches and Bryant began experiments with a third Quaker, Francis May, making their own matches. They succeeded in burning down the factory, but Bryant and May went off to London to try again, founding the still famous Swan Vestas company.

Wartime Plymouth: *above*, dancing before Drake's Statue on the Hoe, a morale-booster begun by Lady Astor in the worst of the 1941 bombing. *Below*, families moving out of the city for overnight shelter during the 1941 Blitz – a photograph taken at the top of Alexandra Road, Plymouth.

Wartime destruction: *above*, St Andrew's Church, the Guildhall and the municipal buildings stand roofless with an American anti-aircraft gun in Old Town Street, in a sea of rubble. *Below*, looking from the Guildhall tower across George Street; only the *Western Morning News* building still stands.

Bryant's brother James had also opened in Mill Lane in 1838, refining sugar with John Burnell. Then in 1844 the Bryant brothers and Burnell began a soap factory in Sutton Road, Coxside. They sold the Mill Lane refinery in 1856 to the British & Irish Sugar Refining Company which was to prosper for thirty years, at one time paying about half the customs receipts of the port. Not until 1886 was it finally closed by a change in duties which made it unprofitable.

Edward James, that first Bryant partner, was also diversifying. He began a starch factory in Sutton Road (with Burnell a later partner) and this too became a national concern. James established a close personal friendship with another Quaker soap-maker, Isaac Reckitt of Hull, whose firm took over the Plymouth factory in 1905. Imported rice was the major raw material and Robin brand starch, blue, washing powders and black lead had wide sales.

The neighbouring Bryant–Burnell soap works had become the West of England Soap Works in 1857 but this was taken over in 1863 by the Victoria Soap Company, started in 1858 at Millbay, and all production was concentrated there. This was to run until 1896 when the competition of the neighbouring Millbay Company and lack of drive saw the Victoria Company bankrupt and taken over by the New Patent Candle Company. This too had been started by William Bryant, and its Sutton Road factory grew to 20,000sq ft. The candle company, keeping up to date, began importing Royal Daylight petroleum in 1881. It was also to take over Millbay Soap in 1908, but in turn was swallowed up by the giant Lever Brothers in 1913.

So to Mill Lane and Morice Town were added the new industrial areas of Millbay and Coxside. At Millbay Thomas Gill was also quarrying limestone. He took his workings right up to the edge of the corporation land on the Hoe, and he and his successors literally sold all the western end of the Hoe. In latter days the little West Hoe harbour was built to ship the stone away, with a light railway running through a tunnel and through the former reading rooms and baths which are now the Royal Western Yacht Club premises. By 1880 the terraces of houses had been built on the quarry floor, and little West Hoe Park was later established under the quarry cliff face.

The demand for stone by the numerous building enterprises was enormous, and quarries also stretched along the waterfront from Coxside to Prince Rock. The rumble of the Cattedown stone carts through the streets was a familiar Plymouth sound for decades. As level stretches were created beside the Cattewater and the quarry faces moved back, so these areas became extensions of the Coxside factory district. Harvey's tar distillery was started on the eastern shore of Deadman's Bay, and then in 1846 Charles Norrington began to make the newly invented superphosphate fertilisers next door. In 1870 James Gibbs opened a similar plant just east again, and two years later Burnard, Lack & Algar opened acid works. The acid was used in treating bones to make fertiliser, and soon they were making fertiliser as well.

On the other side of Sutton Harbour George Frean, a miller from Ashburton with interests ranging from granite quarries to patent cement, bought the King's Bakery at Lambhay when the navy moved its baking to the new Victualling Yard. With two flour millers, Daw and Serpell, he began making biscuits. In a year or two, in 1857, Frean set up in London making biscuits with the two nephews of a Devon man who had built up the major tea business of Peek Brothers. So was born one of the great biscuit firms, Peek Frean, but the name of Serpell, who by 1864 was alone in the Lambhay business, was equally well-known. In 1899 Serpell's son moved the whole business to Reading and both firms have now been absorbed in the two large biscuit combines.

Printing grew steadily. By 1851 the names of both Latimer and Brendon appeared in directories – names still of national repute for book work – and by 1891 there were 500 men in the trade.

The brewers who had plied their trade too vigorously to please the service authorities in earlier centuries continued to prosper. An odd source of capital came from two brothers Scott, whose father had been a Jacobite fugitive from Scotland after 1745 and reached south Devon by way of France. The two brothers, naval officers, used their joint £4,782 prize money to buy the Hoegate Brewery in 1826 from the Langmeads, who had earlier been joined by the Elliots of Barley House. The grandson of the elder brother was Robert Falcon Scott who died after reaching the South Pole in 1912; he had been born at Outlands, Milehouse, the family home until 1924. The small breweries multiplied in the Three Towns but the three main Devonport concerns merged into the Tamar Brewery at Morice Town, to be eventually taken over by H. & G. Simmonds of Reading. A group of Plymouth brewers were similarly merged into Plymouth Breweries in 1889, concentrating in the former Regent Brewery, Stonehouse. Both groups have now been taken over by the Courage empire. One result was to free Wilson's purpose-built Bedford Brewery in Alexandra Road, which in turn became the Beechwood food factory of Brown Wills & Nicholson, a firm founded by William Burnell in 1797.

ROAD TRAVEL

In the years after 1815 coach travel reached its zenith. Plymouth East Trust much improved its road in 1819, straightening the length to Plympton and cutting off bad corners beyond. Some of the lost corners can still be seen, such as the Ivybridge loop to the old bridge in front of the London Inn, and the loop under the Bittaford viaduct. Longbridge was rebuilt in 1835 to a width of 24ft. The Earl of Morley, finding his Laira Ferry inefficient, called in the young J. M. Rendel, a Telford-trained engineer who had settled in Plymouth, and his Iron Bridge was opened in 1827, the second longest iron bridge in Britain at that time. The Modbury Trust made a new turnpike by-passing Plymstock, and 'respectable' coaches, *Celerity* and *Defiance*, were using this Totnes route to Exeter and London. By 1830 there were eleven major coaches a day leaving the Three Towns for London, Bath, Bristol, Portsmouth and Falmouth. Going east they started at Devonport, calling at Plymouth fifteen minutes later. *Quicksilver*, first away at 6 am and using the Ashburton road, reached London in 24½ hours, about the fastest coach in Britain. *Subscription*, the other flyer, left at noon, used the Totnes route and made London in 26½ hours.

Steam came to the Torpoint crossing in 1826 with a craft specially built at Stonehouse, but the *Jemima's* 12hp engines

127

could not keep her nose to the beach for unloading and in 1834 a steam-driven chain ferry, a new invention of Rendel's, was successfully brought into service. By 1836 the west-bound coaches were using this ferry, instead of passengers crossing on foot to join Torpoint-based coaches, and there was also a Rendel steam ferry at Saltash.

COASTING STEAMERS

In 1822 the Plymouth & Portsmouth Steam Packet Company was formed and in 1825 it put two steamers, *Sir Francis Drake* and *Brunswick*, into service. The 113-ton *Drake* had been launched by Hill of Cattedown two years before as a schooner and was converted in the same yard to steam in 1825. Both steamers went into regular service to Portsmouth, Falmouth and the Channel Isles on bi-weekly runs. Ten years later they were meeting competition from the London Dublin & Belfast Company and the Liverpool St George Company: the coasting steamers were to be important for goods and passengers for the rest of the century. *Sir Francis Drake* continued her Channel Island service until 1873.

THE RAILWAYS ARRIVE

There were big crowds for the launching of the *Sir Francis Drake* and the *Jemima*, but nothing like the excitement caused by steam trains. Thomas Tyrwhitt was the driving spirit behind the 1823 horse-drawn Plymouth & Dartmoor Railway: it was going to transform Dartmoor but never did. Granite came down for major London works and the surfacing of the Breakwater but only the Johnson brothers, who worked the line and had the Breakwater contract, made any money from it.

But after the success of the Liverpool & Manchester steam trains in 1830 every provincial town wanted a railway link with London. In 1833 Bristol merchants formed their Great Western Railway Company and to link with that came the Bristol & Exeter Company; in 1834 at a meeting in Plymouth Guildhall £20,000 was subscribed to build what was first called the Plymouth, Devonport & Exeter Company. Southampton merchants had similarly formed the London & South Western Company. The lines from London to Bristol and London to Southampton both opened in 1840; the Bristol & Exeter was in operation by 1844, and in that year the Plymouth company – now called the South Devon Railway Company – got its Act of Parliament.

Even Paul Ourry Treby pulled up the hunt to watch the first 'steamer' go down Hemerdon Bank in 1848. There was a temporary station at Laira before the completion to Millbay in 1849, but as the lines crept west so did the coaching services wither. By 1844 the *Defiance* was transferring its passengers and mail to the LSW at Andover and the *Nonpareil*, *Telegraph* and *Great Western* to the Bristol line at Beam Bridge, west of Wellington, then the terminal point. There was even fiercer competition when the line reached Exeter, with Plymouth coaches racing there in $3\frac{1}{2}$ to 4 hours. Old Bligh, who had driven a fancy team of four greys to Ashburton at an average $10\frac{1}{2}$mph each day, finished up driving a horse bus from the temporary Laira station into Plymouth.

Ten years later, with the opening of Brunel's Royal Albert Bridge at Saltash, the Cornwall Railway completed the Plymouth–Penzance link and a month later, on 15 June 1859, the South Devon & Tavistock Railway was in business. The GW had invested in both these companies and by 1876, as the LSW crept westward, the GW had absorbed them all. That year the LSW, with running powers from Lydford over the Tavistock line, reached Plymouth, sharing a temporary new station at North Road with the GW and building a spur which cut off Millbay and went on to the new Devonport LSW station. The competition, and GW management, woke up the old line which the SDR had not worked very hard. It was stirred into further animation when the LSW got its own line down to Tavistock and along Tamarside to reach Devonport in 1890; this killed the river boat traffic and the new drive at last started cutting into the coastal shipping traffic. The following year the LSW had extended its line to its new Plymouth terminus at Friary; using the old Plymouth & Dartmoor as a front it had built the ugly railway bridge beside the Iron Bridge in 1887 and by 1892 had a station at Plymstock. The GW was frightened that the LSW would reach out to Torquay; there was much in-fighting and eventually the GW won the line from Plymstock to Yealmpton in 1898 while the LSW had opened a line from Plymstock to Turnchapel the previous year.

THE NEW DOCKS

Brunel persuaded the merchants of Bristol who built the GW that the western terminal was really across the Atlantic, and they had Brunel's revolutionary steamship *Great Western* sailing for America by 1838, even before their railway line was built. Within a few months Southampton was laying the foundation stone of the largest tidal dock system in the country. Between them, and even better placed for the Atlantic crossing, was Plymouth, a port which both rival towns set out to dominate or eliminate. Liverpool too was in this steamship race, and the St George Company, already putting coasting steamers into Plymouth, played a part in sending the *Sirius* to get into New York just before the *Great Western*. On her second eastbound voyage *Sirius* came into the Cattewater to land passengers and mail. Already an industrial pioneer and a political leader in the town, Thomas Gill saw the signs and the following year announced that he was building a pier at the entrance to Millbay capable of taking the largest steamers – in fact Brunel's *Great Britain* used it in 1845 on her trial voyage. Gill also became chairman of the South Devon Railway Company. The railway's first dock plan at Plymouth was an improved Sutton Harbour which Brunel himself designed, but when the Admiralty vetoed those plans the railway switched to Millbay, replanning its terminus there instead of at Eldad, and in 1846 largely financed a Great Western Dock Company for which Brunel designed the complex we now know. The following year the LSW promoted a railway to reach Plymouth, and invested money in Sutton Harbour. Gill was out of the struggle; he had sold his pier to the new GW Dock Company and been ousted from the railway board because he had supported the failed 'atmospheric' system of motive power.

By 1850 Millbay Docks had their railway link, their own Custom House and the Pier Hotel, were recognised as a government mail packet station and saw the first mails embarked. In 1874 the GW became outright owner of Millbay Docks and steadily improved the facilities, notably adding the deep-water West Wharf in 1880.

But Sutton Harbour hopes rose as the LSW crept westwards; the Improvement Company set about buying the harbour from the Duchy of Cornwall and did at last get parliamentary approval for dock gates. But as soon as the LSW reached Devonport in 1877 it ran a branch line down to Stonehouse Pool, where another improvement company was formed and commercial development accelerated. It did get a line all round Sutton Harbour in 1879 (the GW improved its spur to Coxside at the same time) but the LSW simultaneously built a line along the Cattedown waterfront. So Sutton got two new rival docks at the same time as its rail link; though it added new quays to the north and east and built a new fish market, by 1896 the railway interests were elsewhere.

Cattewater was the new success story. Commissioners were set up to regulate matters. The Admiralty built Batten Breakwater in 1882, the channel was dredged, Burnard & Algar built Cattedown Wharves in 1888, Victoria Wharves were started and Turnchapel Wharf built on the south side at the end of the new LSW line in 1897. That year Plymouth Corporation promoted a Bill to deepen the Cattewater up to the Iron Bridge and create a new dock complex. The Admiralty, which had never liked the commercial development of 'its' port, produced requirements which effectively killed the Bill. There were also fears of 'municipalisation' and when the corporation built Prince Rock Wharves in 1906 the merchants prevented their full use. Schemes to improve the Cattewater continued to appear for another twenty years but its haphazard quay development, single rail link and inadequate road system remain to this day. Yet by the early 1880s it was handling more trade than Sutton Harbour, although not as much as Millbay.

There was one last railway battle for the maritime trade. In 1904 the LSW built Ocean Quay under Mount Wise, at the end of its Stonehouse Pool line, to steal the liner traffic from the GW in Millbay. The GW then started a cross-Channel service from Plymouth to Brest to hit the LSW Southampton–Le Havre service. Not until 1910, when the GW stopped its service and the LSW gave up its liner competition, did the fighting stop. If neither side had won all Plymouth's maritime trade they had effectively divided it; there were four local port authorities, an over-riding Admiralty, and rival merchant groups. Bristol and Southampton had both soared ahead of the commercial port of Plymouth.

THE CARGOES

With the advent of the steamship, and particularly after the real development of its efficiency in the 1870s, world trade increased by leaps and bounds and ships grew steadily bigger. With that growth the commercial port of Plymouth steadily increased the value and tonnage of cargoes handled, though not its percentage of the total trade. All its new wharves were kept busy right up to 1914 but the navy held the deep-water berths and the others were never developed enough to handle the largest ships.

In the post-1815 depression Sutton Harbour tolls fell until 1822 but then began to climb to a peak of £2,000 by 1830. Then came a fresh recession, but by the end of the decade business was booming again. By 1844 there was direct trade with the West Indies, the Baltic and the Mediterranean, timber coming in from North America, and a strong coasting business. The registered fleet totalled over 21,000 tons, and nearly 400 ships were entering the port each year. By 1850 Plymouth was the busiest port in the English Channel. The fleet had grown and the number of vessels entering was up tenfold. By 1857 there were sugar from Havana and Brazil, hides and tallow from Buenos Aires, wine from Cadiz and Oporto, brandy from the Charente and up to £80,000-worth a year of palm oil, cochineal, ivory, pepper and gum from West Africa. As late as 1860 Plymouth ranked sixth among English ports. The ten-year annual average number of vessels entering was 1,060 in foreign trade and 4,650 coasting, although the port's fleet was beginning to decline.

The Plymouth wharves show a steady increase in business for the rest of the century but by 1876 Plymouth was down to twelfth place, and by 1914 it was not in the top twenty. There was a record year in 1896 with imports and exports valued over £2 million but for most years until 1914 the annual figure was about the £1¾ million mark. The bulk of this was in imports – grain, manures, sugar, timber and, much fluctuating, petroleum products at Stonehouse and Cattedown. The only real export was china clay from Lee Moor.

FISHING

A similar story comes from Plymouth fishing. Trawling was introduced soon after 1815 and Sutton Harbour had thirty trawlers by 1820. The arrival of the railway in 1849, ten years before Penzance station could serve Newlyn and twenty years before Brixham had its rail link with the London market, put Plymouth into the West Country lead. There were sixty trawlers by 1850. The trade doubled between 1878 and 1888 with vessels even landing in Millbay and moving their catch to the Sutton market by handcarts. The new fish market was in business by 1896. That year Plymouth had its first steam trawler, the *Reginald*. Chant & Paddon built up a fleet of six in the next ten years. But the development of steam trawlers and the opening up of distant fishing grounds saw the big business moving to Hull and the northern ports, and Plymouth's trade slowly fell away under their competition.

SMUGGLING

Peace and the build-up of government revenue forces did not at once end smuggling. It is estimated that from 1832 to 1842 Cawsand still had fifty boats and eighty men in the French runs, and in 1839 all the houses at Laira Green were searched by the revenue men – a last echo of that Crabtree execution. By that time it was mainly a matter of meeting Frenchmen just off the coast, and by 1850 the old trade was virtually dead – though even in that year a 200-ton Plymouth vessel was being hunted. The men turned to respectable trades: after twenty years' smuggling, for instance, Dickie Kincupp from the Yealm became a Plymouth shipbroker, and his brother is said to have been an admiral in the navy. Cawsand men took to pilotage and fishing.

THE OCEAN LINERS

If Plymouth had celebrated with garlands and bands and processions when the first train arrived from London, the town celebrated even more, with better bands and bigger processions, when the first Cape mails were embarked in the steamer *Bosphorus* on 16 December 1850. The link with London and the rest of the country had been important, but the new dock and a place on the steamship map of the world doubled that importance. The port began a new life, assumed a new importance in the world of steam. Plymouth became the Australian mail port as well in 1852 and soon all the great British companies, Union, Royal Mail, Peninsula & Orient, instituted regular Plymouth calls. But it remained a port of call; Southampton or the London river were the base ports and Liverpool the Atlantic port. As time became important and the liners grew in size so they began to anchor inside the Breakwater and tenders went out to embark or land mail and passengers. At first these steamers were hired but in 1873 the *Sir Francis Drake* was specially built for the service, and in 1876 the *Sir Walter Raleigh*. A fleet of four or five tenders, all named after Plymouth's Elizabethan sea captains, were in service from 1890.

In 1869 special travelling post office sorting vans were attached to the trains carrying ocean mail from Plymouth but passengers still had to take cabs to Millbay station. In 1882 when the important P & O liners increased their use of the port, dockside facilities were much improved and ocean mail trains were introduced which passengers joined on the dock.

The big German and French liners began scheduling Plymouth calls for their American services in the 1870s and were challenging the British and American supremacy in the Atlantic. By the 1890s the Germans were building bigger and faster ships for this service, still using Plymouth. By 1902 White Star also began calling with their New York ships, and Holland–Amerika followed suit. From 1907 onwards about 500 liners called at Plymouth every year. The majority of calls and passengers were inward bound, for with the ocean mail trains a day or more could be saved in reaching London, as against steaming up-Channel to Southampton.

In 1879 3,538 passengers passed through Millbay, by 1889 10,418, by 1907 21,181 and in 1913 30,841. Mailbags handled reached a peak of 219,691 in 1913.

A side-product of the trade was three new hotels. Railway directors built the Duke of Cornwall (1862) and the Albion (which became the Albion and Continental in 1904 when it took over the former Royal Eye Infirmary premises on the corner), both alongside Millbay station. The Grand followed on the western Hoe in 1880, and with the Royal Hotel these finally put paid to the old coaching inns, like the King's Arms in Exeter Street, opposite Hawker's Avenue, where Napoleon's brother Lucien had been a lightly guarded prisoner in 1810.

EMIGRATION DEPOT

On 12 May 1839 the founder of the New Zealand Company, Edward Gibbon Wakefield, sailed from Sutton Harbour in the *Tory* with the first settlers for that colony. The following January the Plymouth Company of New Zealand was formed, with Thomas Gill and Thomas Woollcombe as the leading spirits, and they sent out six ships with 897 settlers from Devon and Cornwall, founding New Plymouth in North Island. The failure of their London bankers in 1841 led to a merger with the main company, but a new trade had been established.

The great emigration was to the United States because the passage was the cheapest and opportunities apparently greater. To siphon some of this flow into the more distant colonies the government created the Colonial Land and Emigration Commissioners in 1840, acting as agents for the colonial governments who sold land and used the proceeds to assist passages to the Cape, Australia and New Zealand. Depots were set up by private contractors at Deptford and Plymouth, in the vacated Victualling Yard premises at Baltic Wharf, close to Fisher's Nose, where emigrants waited for the chartered ships. In 1851 when the contracts were renewed the

LSW tried to steal even this trade for Southampton but Sir Frederic Rogers, the eighth baronet of the Plymouth family, had been made a commissioner in 1845 (he was eventually Permanent Under-Secretary for the Colonies and the first Lord Blachford) and no doubt supported the Plymouth depot. At first it had 500 berths; by 1883 it was 1,118, and by the time assisted passages ended around the turn of the century between 300,000 and 400,000 emigrants had sailed from Plymouth. In government eyes it was the right site because it was convenient for the Irish, and more emigrants came from Devon and Cornwall than any other English counties – a comment on the rural economy of the West Country.

SHIPBUILDING

From 1836 until the turn of the century there were more vessels registered at Plymouth than at any other port between Milford and Bridport. Shipbuilding and repairing, ropemaking and sailmaking, were inevitably important trades. The boom began in the late eighteenth century and faded in the 1870s as steam and iron ships took over the world's trade routes. The Plymouth yards built basically wooden sailing craft, with fishing boats and Tamar barges as important as the topsail schooners of the fruit trade and the 1,000-ton vessels being built by the 1850s.

Many of the shipyards were replaced by wharves and have disappeared, but Mashford's are still busy in Frank's Quarry at Cremyll. John Parkin was building there in the eighteenth century and Joseph Banks moved there from Mutton Cove in 1830. In Stonehouse Pool Hocking's were at Whitehall from 1823 until 1877; like many builders they owned vessels as well and their clippers did well in the China tea trade. A dry dock designed for paddle steamers was included in the building of Millbay's inner basin in 1857; Watson & Fox were building there until 1891 and the engineering firm of Willoughby's continued until 1969. The dock has now been filled to make a car park!

In Sutton Harbour, Moore's continued in the north-east corner until 1876, the family home at the head of their dock.

136

Then, with slums closing in and new wharves being built, William Foster Moore declared that he would never build iron ships and closed down. Shilston's were at China House from 1823 until 1905, Kerswell at Coxside from 1823 to 1850 and Gent at Teat's Hill from 1830 until 1885. Just outside the Pool, Banks moved from Cremyll in 1852 to Queen Anne's Battery and more ambitious slips; then his family were in Millbay from 1890 until 1910. Eldred Marshall was breaking up ships in Deadman's Bay until 1877 when he sold to E. Duke, who began to build Victoria Wharves there. Richard Hill & Sons were at Cattedown from 1823 until 1887 when the yard was replaced by Cattedown Wharf. At Turnchapel the Pope family took over Blackburn's yard in 1826. Members of the family were established in Prince Edward Island, Canada, building ships, as early as 1817, and they were also building at Teat's Hill from 1844 to 1857, giving up Turnchapel in 1859. Routliffe was at Mount Batten from 1849 until 1882, when W. S. Kelly took over. These were the major yards, turning out between ten and fifteen ships a year for most of the century. The biggest commercial vessel built in the port was the 1,127-ton *Nimrod* in 1870 from Banks, a speculative last fling. There were many smaller short-lived yards turning out good craft, and boatbuilders too.

All this was small beer compared with the Royal Dockyard. From 1815 until 1914 it launched 170 ships of all sizes. At first they were of wood, and in the 1820s the South Yard building slips were roofed over to protect ships while in construction. One still survives. (Its modern counterpart is the frigate complex in Keyham Yard; modern ships need the same protection.) In the transition from wooden walls to big-gun ironclads the son of a Devonport currier played a great part. William White, born in 1845 and educated at St James-the-Less national school, went into the dockyard as an apprentice, rose rapidly to national importance and was Director of Naval Construction from 1885 to 1902. Knighted in 1895, he 'saw larger additions to the Royal Navy than in any preceding period of the same length'. In 1902 he watched Queen Alexandra launch his *Queen* from one Devonport slip while His Majesty simultaneously laid the keel of the *King Edward VII* in another. White opposed the Dreadnoughts of the Fisher revolution but battleships grew to culminate in the biggest vessel ever constructed at Devonport, the 30,600-ton *Warspite* launched in 1913. Between 1898 and 1914 Devonport built fifteen battleships totalling over 300,000 tons.

EMPLOYMENT

Through the second half of the nineteenth century there were between eleven and twelve thousand officers and men of the armed services in the Three Towns. The dockyard was the biggest employer of civilian labour: 2,200 in 1830, 3,000 by 1848, 4,000 by 1879, 7,381 by 1906 and 12,075 by 1912. But with the building boom of the century – not just the government work but the explosion in houses, churches, schools and municipal works, and the dock and railway development – the building trades remained a major employer. Census returns do not distinguish places of employment and there may be some duplication with the dockyard figures, but there was a building force of 2,142 in 1831, 3,112 in 1861 and 3,937 in 1891. Hundreds of navvies, many Irish, came in for the building of the forts and railways. The Breakwater alone employed 765 men at the peak. Two thousand navvies worked on the LSW line along Tamarside in 1887–90, the last large contingent in the west. One of the two contractors for that job was 'Honest' John Pethick of Norley House, a self-made man who emerged as the biggest Plymouth builder. He built the Duke of Cornwall and the Grand Hotel, Plymouth Guildhall, Elliot Terrace on the Hoe (named after the Elliots of Barley House), and many streets of smaller houses, and was a notable contractor nationwide, building docks, bridges and railways. A Conservative alderman, mayor 1898–1900, and a pillar of the Plymouth Club, he was killed in a carriage accident at the bottom of Lockyer Street at the age of seventy-nine. But even he was overshadowed by John Jackson who came in to build the Keyham Extension and the Naval Barracks. Born in York in 1851 and trained as a civil engineer, he was knighted in 1895 after building the last eight miles of the Manchester Ship Canal. He constructed harbours all over Britain and the world, a railway across the Andes in South America, and when called to Paris for talks about a bridge over the Channel, offered to build the British half himself. In Plymouth he lived at Pounds House, Peverell, was commodore of the Royal South-Western Yacht Club and a member of the Royal Western Yacht Club, and was Unionist MP for Devonport from 1810 to 1918. By contrast there were many small firms like that of Isaac Foot, the Methodist local preacher and village carpenter who came in from Horrabridge and set up in Notte Street, with the former Scott's Hoegate Brewery as his building yard.

Occupations concerned with the sea were naturally high on the list, but again private and government employment cannot be sorted out. By 1831 some 2,000 people had employment linked with the sea, growing to nearly 6,000 (including 2,101 merchant seamen and 765 fishermen) in 1861 and falling to just under 5,000 (1,639 merchant seamen, 802 fishermen) in 1891. The other major employer, growing as the population grew, was retail trade and services: 1,409 in 1831, nearly 10,000 by 1891. After the opening of the railway Plymouth became the wholesale depot for a great range of goods for Devon and Cornwall west of a line from Kingsbridge to Hartland, and an increasingly important shopping centre.

The fourth major employer to add to sea, building and retail trades was manufacturing. Again very tentative totals culled from census returns suggest 1,477 in 1831, 3,370 in 1861 and 3,891 in 1891. No one occupation offers large figures apart from those for tailors and bootmakers, which probably indicates large contracts for fitting out the service population.

COMMUNICATION

The first railway line from London brought not only steam trains but the electric telegraph and a time problem. Mount Wise was connected to Whitehall in 1852 and the semaphore system abandoned. The Three Towns were using true local time, which was 17 minutes behind London, and not till the first Sunday in 1860 was the switch made to Greenwich Mean Time. Graham Bell, in Plymouth for a meeting of the British Association in 1877, rigged his newly invented telephone at the

Bayly home at Torr where he was staying, and in 1881 Cox & Williamson opened a telephone exchange in Plymouth. No 1 was Fox Roy of Old Town Street; the first ten numbers all went to shipping agents, merchants or manufacturers. Even the post office was Plymouth 21 and the *Western Morning News* Plymouth 31. It shows how Plymouth was still orientated to the sea and to trade.

An official Air Ministry photograph, issued in January 1946, looking down on bombed Plymouth. North Quay in Sutton Harbour can be seen bottom right, roofless Charles Church central in its churchyard and the Central Library top left. The tight street pattern of pre-war Plymouth is clearly evident.

Reconstruction: *above*, Royal Parade had been laid out but no rebuilding started in November 1949 when the crew of HMS *Amethyst* marched through the city after their escape from the Yangtse River. Note the Nissen hut shops. *Below*, New George Street carriageway reaches to the bottom of Cambridge Street; on the right the Odeon cinema has been demolished to make way for Littlewood's store. The Barley Sheaf public house was on the corner of the old Barley House estate.

CHAPTER NINE

THE YEARS OF EXPANSION: 1815–1914

IN the century from Waterloo to the outbreak of the Great War the population of the Three Towns grew from 56,000 to 209,000, at about the same rate as the national growth. In spite of one of the highest mortality rates in the country, part of the growth was by natural increase, but in the main it was from immigration. In 1841–51 Plymouth showed an increase of 2,900 by a higher number of births than deaths, but an increase of 10,000 by immigration. With agricultural wages lower than wages in the Three Towns, so people were drawn in from west Devon and Cornwall, a process speeded up as the century went on, the Cornish mines closed, and the post-1870 farming depression began to bite. In 1861 13,652 inhabitants of the Three Towns had been born in Cornwall, 4,068 in Ireland and 3,079 in London. A quarter of these Irish people may have been servicemen, and many of the Londoners too, but there was a strong civilian Irish influx, able to reach Plymouth cheaply with deck passages on the coasting steamers. A random check of the 1861 census shows that only Liverpool among the ports had a bigger Irish population than the Three Towns.

THE SPREAD OF DEVONPORT

When Devonport Guildhall was built it filled the last space left within the walls. A new working-class suburb was already growing at Morice Town, at the foot of Navy Row (now Albert Road) to serve the commercial area there. New villages were also developing at Lower Stoke, between the open 'killing area' in front of the walls (now Devonport Park and the Brickfields) and Stoke Damerel Church, and at Higher Stoke, where the turnpike to Tavistock crossed the ridge under the Blockhouse. Foulston had many commissions here, like Belmont House built in 1820 for John Norman, the Devonport banker, imposing terraces like Nelson Gardens and elegant villas as in

St Michael's Terrace. Terraces of lesser houses, many slate-hung, grew up close by, dated by their names: Trafalgar Row, Wellington Street, Waterloo Street. Slowly over the years these villages spread until they joined up, and as the dockyard spread north so did the terraces creep along outside the dockyard wall, from Morice Town to Keyham and on to Weston Mill Lake, and up the old Keyham Creek as it was filled in to become St Levan's Road.

The development of Devonport was plagued from the start not just by the St Aubyns sticking to the leasehold system, but by their working it on a 'three-lives' system with no right of renewal. People were reluctant to buy houses under such conditions and this, together with the rundown of the dockyard and the military forces after 1815, meant a static population until the beginning of the Steam Yard. The town did then increase between 1841 and 1861 from 35,820 to 50,440, and when one of the few pieces of freehold land in the borough came on the market in 1855, at Ford, the Devon & Cornwall Freehold Land Society bought it for working-class development. From 1861 to 1891 there was little change in the Devonport population, but then came a new spurt with the Keyham Extension Yard. From the 54,848 of 1891, Devonport grew to 83,678 in 1911. A Plymouth syndicate of builders bought the Keyham Barton site, north of St Levan Road, from the St Aubyn estate and covered the hillside with rows of small houses. They sold for £200 apiece; the area was nicknamed 'Klondike' as people rushed to buy, and Barton Avenue, in the heart of the area, commemorates the site of the old manor house ('barton') of Stoke which was occupied almost up to that time. On the northern side of the hill Sir John Jackson was also building houses for his workmen, as well as two mission halls with two chaplains whose stipends he paid. So the reach northwards of Devonport was completed.

Eastwards the Higher Stoke tradition of villa development spread out across Molesworth Road, while the smaller houses between the dignified parts of Lower Stoke and the church began to grow on the northern side of Millbridge, and then spread steadily eastwards along Wilton Street towards Pennycomequick.

DEVONPORT IN THE 1850s. *Part of a map showing how old Devonport was a walled town with a clear 'killing area' all round, and the new suburbs of Morice Town and Stoke developing beyond the open ground. The railway branch to the Torpoint Ferry was never constructed.*

STONEHOUSE FILLS UP

Stonehouse was also all leasehold, but the Mount Edgcumbes gave their tenants the perpetual right of renewal. It was a small area, hemmed in by Millbay, Stonehouse Creek and Plymouth. The Durnford Street elegance soon had working-class houses on either side, filling the peninsula, and from the ancient village on the east side of Stonehouse Bridge working-class streets spread eastwards so that the town was filled with houses by

1840. The population at the 1841 census was 9,712, and though it grew to a peak of 15,398 in 1891 there was little more room for houses, and the increase meant overcrowding.

The Sourpool marshes bisected by Union Street, from the town boundary where the Palace Theatre now is to Derry's Cross, were drying out enough for the Stonehouse building to cross the boundary and reach out to meet the Plymouth houses spreading westward. As early railway plans suggested that Eldad might become the heart of the Three Towns, so Wyndham Square was built, to Foulston designs, and North Road began to grow eastwards from the Naval Hospital wall. Again this was properly in Plymouth but, as lower down in Union Street, the development began at the Stonehouse end.

THE GROWTH OF PLYMOUTH

The eighteenth-century spread northwards of old Plymouth into Charlestown, up to Regent Street, and Newtown, along Cobourg Street, was continued after 1815 with good-class houses and villas. They took the healthiest sites on the south-facing slopes on either side of Tavistock Road, and good houses spread westwards from Lockyer Street towards Millbay, Foulston's new town. The better-off moved out from the old town, leaving that to be packed with the poorer new people. The Bayly family presents a case history. From the Elizabethan Island House on the Barbican, still owned by them, they had moved to the Queen Anne red brick house further along the Barbican, and then to the new (1811) Brunswick Terrace east of Exeter Street (only destroyed in 1978). As that became hemmed in by small houses various members of the family moved northwards to Seven Trees, north of Beaumont Park, and Bedford Park, off Tavistock Road. By 1882 Robert Bayly had rebuilt Torr House, right out of the town, and bought Elfordtown, Yelverton, where descendants live today.

Seven Trees still stands in its own grounds. South of it is Beaumont Park, the demesne of the Bewes at Beaumont House until 1890. Continuous with Beaumont Park on the eastern side was the 87-acre estate of the Culme-Seymour family, which did not fall to development until nearly the end of the century. On

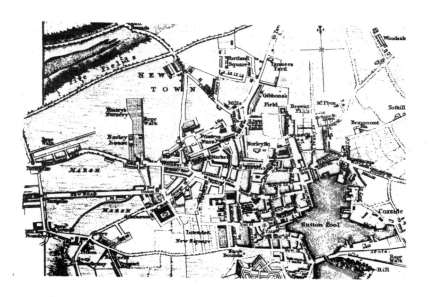

PLYMOUTH IN 1820. *Part of a map engraved by John Cooke and published in 1820.*

the other side of the town, reaching from King Street (the renamed Stonehouse Lane) up to North Road, was the Barley House estate, home of the Elliot family until the 1860s and not developed until after then. So working-class housing development was confined by these estates. It spread west along King Street and north from King Street to North Road and Cobourg Street, up either side of the Barley estate. Fingers of speculative housing also began reaching up from Regent Street between the villas – Nelson, Wellington and Waterloo, again the street names date them – until they swamped the whole hill, incorporating the better-quality houses and terraces one by one. One can still distinguish the villas among the lesser houses; the whole area makes a fascinating study.

By 1881 the streets of Plymouth packed the whole area from the Hoe to what is now Victoria Park, and east of that to the main railway line. The only break was the western end of the Houndiscombe estate, where the Derry family lived, but that soon fell and Derry Avenue cuts through the centre. Tothill and Beaumont estates still held, but the first terraces of Mount Gould, the Seymour Terrace block and the Roseberrys, were built. North Hill was housed up to the crest and down the other side, to halfway down Alexandra Road (cut in 1863, the year of the royal wedding). There were houses along both sides of Mutley Plain, and Lisson Grove was the first street running eastwards.

But the railway line west of the Plain, the western pavement of the Plain itself, and the lane just north of Connaught Avenue were all on the town boundary, and houses had been growing fast enough outside that boundary, in Compton Gifford, where the rates were lower. The Culme-Seymours had sold the Mannamead fields in 1851 and the architect Damant, who with Wightwick was carrying on the Foulston practice, designed fine villas there. These spread down Townsend Hill to College Avenue and Hyde Park Road, all built up by 1880, and between Ford Park and the railway John Pethick had built five terraces of smaller houses. Compton, with less than a hundred people in 1801, now had a population of over 6,000. There was a similar number of people living at St Budeaux, outside the Devonport boundary, and a smaller group of working-class houses just outside the Plymouth boundary at Laira.

By 1900 the Tothill estate had vanished under the massed terraces which ran to the end of Mount Gould Road, where a wall cut off Hockin's Farm – now the hospital – and right down across Beaumont Road and Prince Rock to join Cattedown. Close terraces ran from Mutley Plain to Lipson Farm. Peverell Park and its side avenues were built, and by 1914 the houses were reaching up to Beacon Park. Milehouse was still in the country but Devonport was reaching towards it slowly on the other side. The Three Towns were nearly solid, and overflowing their boundaries.

OVERCROWDING

There were in fact never enough houses. In the first half of the century Plymouth's population increased by 33,633 people, but the number of houses by only 1,396. In 1850 the Plymouth average was ten people to a house, when the national average was only five, and even in London and Liverpool it was only seven. Castle Dyke Lane, at the top of New Street, averaged 24 people to a house, and the worst house in the town had 90 inhabitants. Nor were the early speculative buildings of the King Street area any better; at the western end 825 people lived in 67 houses, and 57 had no water laid on; there were earth closets at best and drinking water fetched from a stream near No Place Inn. The 1902 Plymouth Medical Officer of Health's report said the town had 'practically a tenement population', by which he meant that most families shared a house. Six hundred and four in every thousand lived that way, and 86 people per thousand were living in one-room tenements. Even that was an improvement; in 1891 there had been 134 per thousand in single-room tenements, and forty years before that a third of the population were in one-room tenements.

The towns were insanitary as well as overcrowded. In 1847 there were no drains in 27 Plymouth streets with a total of 3,300 inhabitants. In Nichols Court on Lambhay Hill there were 13 houses, 100 people and 3 privies. In the old town, houses built for the nobility now gave partial shelter to 'the improvident, the vagrant, the vicious and the unfortunate'. The new streets were little better. Claremont Street, off King Street, averaged one privy to 66 people. The Irish were in the worst houses; they flocked over because they were destitute, escaping the famines, and took houses that landlords would not repair. They were mainly in Stonehouse, not mixing with the English and living in ghettoes.

No one had any power to make landlords improve old houses, and there was little control over new building. In some streets and courts all the household refuse and nightsoil was collected in heaps until there were two or three cartloads to be removed. Two contractors were paid £500 a year to sweep the streets and collect refuse; they removed and sold 7,000 tons a year which incidentally went to manure the fields which fed the town. The worst slums of Plymouth in mid-century were around New Street and Breton Side, and in the new housing of King Street and Stonehouse. This area was still called 'the Marsh', and parts are still below sea level. In Devonport there were appalling hovels just behind Fore Street.

Smallpox, diphtheria, measles and scarlet fever were all regular killers. Epidemics of one or the other were common. In 1832 an outbreak of cholera killed 1,031 people in the Three

Towns, 211 in one August week alone. In the 1849 outbreak the death-roll was 1,894. These were the big outbreaks; Plymouth had 702 cholera deaths in 1839 and another 900 in 1850. There was a smallpox outbreak in 1872 with 448 fatalities out of 4,500 cases. The Three Towns were not alone, of course. The villages around suffered – 52 cholera deaths in Plympton St Maurice and Underwood in 1849, for instance – and all big towns were hit. But in 1832 Plymouth's mortality rate was the seventh highest in the kingdom. A government inquiry was ordered in 1850 because the annual mortality in Plymouth for the past seven years had been over 23 in every thousand. Yet in Stonehouse it was 27, in Devonport 29. Plymouth's average for 1869–72 was only down to 21 per thousand. By 1902 the Plymouth death rate of 16.52 per thousand was just below the national average, and in 1912 the Devonport figure of 11.9 per thousand was better than the national average of 13.3 per thousand. (The fairly constant death rate of the present day is 12 per thousand.)

LOCAL GOVERNMENT AND VOLUNTARY EFFORT

It would be wrong to judge any other age, even the last century, by our own standards. The doctor's knowledge of sanitation and disease was limited, and only slowly did the idea die that poverty was a family's own fault, distress a natural punishment, and self-help the only redemption. The doctors and clergy worked themselves nearly to death in the epidemics, and indeed the vicar of Charles, Dr Carne, and his wife, did die within four days of each other in the 1832 epidemic. It was a time of voluntary organisations or private enterprise doing the welfare work, with public money minimally employed. The doctors through their Plymouth Medical Society followed their dispensaries with an eye hospital at Millbay in 1821 – it became 'Royal' in 1828 under the Duke of Clarence's patronage – and the South Devon & East Cornwall Hospital in Notte Street in 1840, originally with twelve beds.

The Poor Law was reformed with the creation of elected guardians in 1835. Each of the Three Towns had its own board, while all the parishes from Tamarside to the Yealm were formed into the Plympton Union. Their major contribution to the needs of the age was to build new workhouses – Plymouth's on old charity Trust land at Greenbank in 1849, Devonport's at Ford in 1852–4, and Plympton's at Underwood. It could be cynically added that the town councils' contribution was new prisons, Plymouth's again at Greenbank in 1849 and Devonport's at Pennycomequick the same year. The Devonport prison officers' quarters still survive as private houses opposite the central sorting office. Private enterprise helped relieve the congested old churchyards when the Plymouth, Stonehouse & Devonport Cemetery Company opened its 37-acre cemetery outside the town boundaries, between Pennycomequick and Ford Park, in 1849. In no time it was being called the best investment in the neighbourhood!

There was local concern about the state of things. The Liberal leader George Soltau had led the formation of a Plymouth branch of the Health of Towns Association in 1846, two years after its national inception. From this stemmed the notorious report by the Unitarian minister, the Rev W. J. Odgers, in 1847 which revealed the state of affairs in the slums. Odgers did manage to get bath-houses opened in Hoegate Street in 1850, with half-hearted corporation support spurred on by the 1849 epidemic. This also led to the formal government inquiry into the health of Plymouth in 1851 and three years later the corporation adopted the Public Health Act of 1848, under which it took over the work of the old Improvement Commissioners. A start was made on better drainage. The commissioners had widened a few streets during the century to let more light and air into the town, and more main streets were widened now. It did let in more air and light to congested areas, but it also removed a number of houses and so increased the overcrowding. Local authorities still had little power over new houses, and none to interfere with old houses; private property was still sacred. Devonport thought about the Health Act but did not adopt it until 1866.

Voluntary effort did open the South Devon & East Cornwall Blind Institution in Cobourg Street in 1860 (a blind man, James Gale, was the founder), and the Royal Albert Hospital at Devonport in 1862. Epidemics were still demanding temporary hutted hospitals from time to time, and from 1866 until 1929 there were one or two old naval hulks anchored in Jennycliffe Bay as isolation hospitals. There was an upsurge of interest in natural cures, and in 1870 a homoeopathic hospital started over a chemist's shop near Derry's Clock. It moved to Princess Square (so named in honour of Princess Victoria's visit in 1833, and now the site of the council chamber), where queues of patients caused obstructions, and then to Flora Place.

Public demand for better working-class housing had been growing since the mid-century, and though some Shaftesbury cottages had been built on North Hill in the 1850s there was no real activity until the 1880s. Then private enterprise took over, and people like Bulteel and Harris the bankers, Pethick the builder and Edward Bates the Plymouth MP began a number of blocks. Some survived until after 1945, looking a cross between a barracks and a prison, but they were a real contribution, and if this '5 per cent philanthropy' seems offensive to modern minds, it should be remembered that these men were taking a smaller return than they need on their money – though one can have reservations about the motives of 'Bully' Bates.

In 1884 the SD & EC Hospital was moved to its present site at Greenbank, a large healthy building but making a trinity with the neighbouring prison and workhouse, known collectively to the poor as 'the Mutley Mansions'. An ear, nose and throat hospital was opened nearby. The Blind Institution had been moved to North Hill in 1876, the Homoeopathic Hospital was purpose-built in Lockyer Street in 1893, and the Royal Eye Infirmary moved to its present building in 1900.

Now local government proper began to be involved, and the old councils were given new powers. Plymouth and Devonport became county boroughs in 1888, and six years later Stonehouse and Compton were given urban district councils, and the Plympton Union area became Plympton Rural District Council. (At Plympton the Edgcumbes had withdrawn their financial support when the borough lost its MPs in 1832, and when the ratepayers were faced with a precept for the new county police force in 1859 the town had renounced its charter.) The Local Government Act of 1888 was supplemented by the Housing of the Working Class Act of 1890 which for the first time compelled local authorities to act, whereas before they could assume some powers if they wanted. So both Plymouth and Devonport now had their first Medical Officers of Health. In Plymouth the Liberal mayor, J. T. Bond, led a slumming tour and in 1893 the council set up a Housing of the Working Class Committee. By 1896 it had built the first Council houses in Laira Bridge Road – the streets named after the committee members – and the next year, with the people rehoused, tore down the slums of How Street and rebuilt both sides with more council houses. In Devonport the editor of the *Independent*, Henry Whitfeld, launched a series of attacks on conditions there. A private Dockyard Dwelling Company was formed, and Whitfeld was elected chairman of the council's new Housing Committee. It too began slum clearing. A number of streets, notably Fore Street, were also widened.

Nor were the two new county boroughs content to see large numbers of people enjoying the benefits of their towns while living outside their boundaries. The rates in Compton Urban District were only half those of Plymouth and the inhabitants fought bitterly at being brought into the town. But in 1896 Plymouth's extension Bill was successfully through Parliament and the old medieval boundaries changed for the first time, bringing in Laira, Compton and Peverell. Devonport followed suit in 1898, taking in St Budeaux. By 1901 the total population of the Three Towns was 192,755. Other conurbations had grown more rapidly, however, and this was now the eleventh largest in England and Wales, exceeded by Liverpool, Manchester, Birmingham, Leeds, Sheffield, Bristol, Hull, Nottingham, Newcastle and Leicester, in that order.

WATER SUPPLY

The growth of population had forced attention to be paid to water supplies. Iron distribution pipes had been laid in both Devonport (1816) and Plymouth (1826) and the old conduits removed, but there were still open leats blamed for much of the ill-health. The supply was still open along the west side of Mutley Plain in the 1890s. Plymouth steadily built storage reservoirs, first at Sherwell in Tavistock road and in North Road (behind the high wall below Endsleigh Place) for the new Victualling Yard in the 1820s. Then came Crownhill reservoir (1851), Hartley (1859–62) and Roborough (1885); when the latter was constructed, 24in iron pipes were laid from there to Crownhill. But the blizzards of 1881 and 1891 froze the leats across the moor from Weir Head and troops had to be sent to clear them while Plymothians queued for water at long-forgotten wells. A great reservoir controversy developed – nothing new – and eventually the Burrator site was agreed. By 1898 it was operating with a cross-country pipe carrying water to Roborough reservoir. Stonehouse since 1593 had lived on a leat from a stream at Torr. Storage reservoirs at Peverell – their skeletons can still be seen west of Peverell Park Road – helped the nineteenth-century town growth but Stonehouse was glad to take Plymouth water from 1893 and its old system was abandoned. Devonport was not fed from Burrator until the Three Towns amalgamated in 1914. Its private water company watered the town from the leat which takes West Dart water through a tunnel under Nun's Cross Farm and so down the Meavy valley, following the old Plymouth leat. It was inadequate for most of the last century, and dangerous after the prison at Princetown became a convict establishment because its sewage was flowing into the leat. Not until the late 1870s, ten years after the first alarms, were filter works built. Various storage reservoirs were built on the leat, at Stoke and Crownhill, and Devonport Corporation bought out the water company in 1902.

PARKS

For centuries the Hoe has been the great lung of Plymouth, but even that was in danger of being lost early in the nineteenth century. The military claimed ownership of the eastern end and it took ten years of fighting before in 1818 the rights of the townsmen were established. Soon after that Gill's quarries were removing the Hoe at the western end. For most of the century the Hoe stayed a rough clifftop playground. In 1887 the military surrendered the earthworks which surrounded the Citadel. The area was laid out as formal gardens, paths were made up and down the slopes, the Promenade was constructed, and everything was neat and municipalised by 1888, the year of the Armada tercentenary celebrations, when the foundation stone of the Armada memorial was laid.

Plymouth had long paid no attention to its great Elizabethan seamen but the immense national popularity in the last decade of the history of the sixteenth century written by the Devonshire-born J. A. Froude had revived this interest. Froude made the Armada the climax of his work and applied the hero-worship of his master Carlyle; Plymouth loved it all and named Drake Circus to honour the hero, and new buildings in Tavistock Road imitated Elizabethan styles. On the Hoe the Boehm statue of Drake, a replica of that at Tavistock, had already been set up in 1884.

That year the Promenade Pier had also been completed. Its landward end rested on the Bullring, where so many political celebrations had taken place, but these were now banned. The Bullring too was formalised with a belvedere in 1891. The tower of the lighthouse which Smeaton had built on the Eddystone in 1756, and which was replaced by Douglas's Tower in 1890, was also rebuilt on the Hoe. Since then Plymouth Hoe has collected a plethora of war memorials, but it was established at that time much as we know it today.

It was a time for parks. Freedom Park, where the greatest battle of the Civil War had been fought and Plymothians had long been accustomed to celebrate, became a formal enclosure, and the mounds of soil excavated from Hartley reservoir made another park. A little pleasure ground was made with the pillars from the Shambles, the old market, just below the Drake's Place reservoir at Sherwell. Beaumont House was bought in 1890 on the death of the Rev T. A. Bewes, and its demesne was made into another park. Plymouth joined with Stonehouse and Devonport in laying out Victoria Park (opened in 1891) in the old Mill Creek above Millbridge, at last filled in. Stonehouse's only open space was Devil's Point. Devonport as early as 1858 had obtained from the military the northern part of the glacis round the town and turned it into Devonport Park. So the Three Towns did have some open spaces, though they were well away from the areas that needed them most.

LOCAL TRANSPORT

As the Three Towns expanded so local transport was necessary to get men to their work and women to the shops. There were steamers on the Tamar from 1839 onwards, and John Gilbert of Saltash dominated the traffic by the end of the century with his Saltash & Three Towns Steamboat Company's mixed fleet of eight or nine paddlers and screw vessels. There were steamers supplementing the Torpoint Ferry from 1895 to 1932, a Millbrook–Mutton Cove–North Corner steamer, and steamers on the Cremyll Ferry probably by 1858. On the Cattewater Henry Elford of Oreston started the Oreston & Turnchapel service to the Barbican in 1871, moving to Phoenix Wharf when it was built in 1895.

There were ten horse bus services surviving from coaching days, like Baskerville's bus from Roborough, but the great revolution came with tramways. The Plymouth Stonehouse & Devonport Tramways Company Ltd was the first established under the 1870 Act and laid lines from Derry's Clock along Union Street to Cumberland Road by 1872, extending to Fore Street two years later. By 1881 it was carrying over a million passengers a year. These trams were horse-drawn but in 1884 Plymouth Tramways Company (local directors, John Pethick and William Derry) ran steam trams for a couple of years on a route from which some of the very streets have now vanished, from Millbay through lower George Street, Lockyer Street, Princess Square, Westwell Street, Bedford Street, Russell Street, Richmond Street, James Street and Houndiscombe Road to Hyde Park Corner. This route avoided the climb of North Hill but the steam engines – very noisy and smelly – were replaced by horses in 1889. The town bought this company out in 1892 and by the following year Plymouth Corporation Tramways had extended the line at each end to the Promenade Pier and Hender's Corner. By 1895 they had re-aligned the middle part of the route to climb North Hill, using a third horse for the climb from Sherwell, as was done by the Devonport trams climbing from Stonehouse Bridge. PCT opened their second route, to Prince Rock, in 1896. The corporation was building a power station there primarily to electrify the tramway system, but it also gave Plymouth its first electric street lights and eventually its whole power system. Devonport was building an electricity station at Newport Street, Stonehouse.

PCT first ran electric trams in 1899 and the PS&D electrified in 1901, replacing 250 horses. In 1901 the private Devonport & District Tramway Company launched five routes reaching out from the town centre to the new suburbs. Plymouth too was opening new routes. Thus one urban area had three tramway systems. PCT in red and yellow livery, D&D in brown and the PS&D in green. Only the latter crossed borough boundaries; where Plymouth and Devonport met, as at Pennycomequick or Peverell Corner, people had to change trams. There was another hiatus; D&D built a line from Morice Square to Saltash Passage in 1901 but the old wooden bridge at Camel's Head could not carry trams, and so until the new embankment was finished in 1903 passengers had to walk from one tram to the next over the bridge.

Motor buses first appeared in 1900 with the short-lived Plymouth Motor Company's service from Derry's Clock to Salisbury Road, and in 1904 the GW began bus services from Millbay station to Modbury and Yelverton. This killed off the Baskerville horse buses, just as in 1908 the first taxis began killing the horse cabs. There was another motor bus, from Fore Street Devonport to Tor Lane, run by the Peverell Road Car Company from 1909 to 1911, but the vehicles were still not reliable enough for these companies to survive.

The LSW had started a local train service from St Budeaux to the dockyard as soon as the railway opened in 1890, and to the east the Turnchapel and Yealmpton lines started local services in 1897–8. One unusual link on the Yealmpton line was the steamer *Kitley Belle* which from 1900 to 1929 took people from the Steer Point halt down the river to Newton and Noss. Then in 1904 the GW began running steam rail coaches on its main lines between Saltash and Plympton, opening a series of halts. The LSW followed suit and by 1914 the Three Towns had a tight and cheap local transport service, by train, tram and steamer, and all three served great recreational needs as well on summer evenings and at weekends. But it is noticeable that the transport services followed the spread of houses, rather than the other way round. The one exception is Yelverton, which was only a few scattered houses before the station opened in 1885.

THE NEW PARISHES

Spiritual health was not forgotten in the nineteenth-century expansion. St Andrew's built a chapel of ease, designed by Foulston and just across Lockyer Street from the Royal Hotel, in 1823. It later became St Catherine's though never a parish church, and no controversy touched it until its demolition in 1957 to make way for the Civic Centre car park. The next two Anglican chapels were built by disgruntled parishioners, St Luke's behind the Central Library in 1827 as a church for the curate of Charles, who was not elected vicar there, and Eldad because the curate of Stoke Damerel was similarly passed over in 1828.

But the new Bishop of Exeter, Henry Phillpotts, the Tory high churchman already unpopular in the Three Towns because of his opposition to the Reform Bill, would not consecrate Eldad and John Hawker, the former Stoke curate, a son of Hawker of Charles and a true son of that Protestant church, continued to minister at Eldad as a nonconformist. The battles in Plymouth Town Council over the appointments of two vicars of Charles (the ousted curate Courtney of 1827 was elected vicar when Dr Carne died in 1832) so upset the reformed corporation that in 1842 it sold the advowsons of both St Andrew's and Charles to pay off the debts on the Royal Hotel and Theatre. After various people had made money on the transactions, both advowsons eventually ended in the hands of the evangelical Church Patronal Society.

The vicar of St Andrew's since 1824, John Hatchard, son of the Piccadilly bookseller and a strong low churchman, had long been at loggerheads with his bishop. Hatchard built Holy Trinity Church in Southside Street and when Bishop Phillpotts came to consecrate it in 1842 the bitterness between the men flared into public battle. It was not eased in 1845 when Phillpotts ordered his clergy to wear the surplice, and Three Towns protests forced him to climb down. Equally at Stoke the

Above, the end of an era: Britain's last aircraft carrier, *Ark Royal*, enters port for the last time in December 1978, steaming between Cremyll and the Royal William Victualling Yard (left) to pay off her crew and be laid up. *Below*, the new navy: David Owen, MP for Devonport and Foreign Secretary at the time, watches the frigate *Galatea*, the first vessel to be taken into the giant frigate complex, in September 1977.

Modern Plymouth: an aerial view of the new city centre looking towards the Hoe. Those who remember the maps and models of the 1943 *Plan for Plymouth* are fascinated to find them so faithfully reproduced in the reality of air photographs.

vicar, the Rev William St Aubyn, was fighting his parishioners over the graveyard and everything else.

Then Hawker of Eldad died, the Church of England bought the chapel and dedicated it to St Peter, and Phillpotts appointed a thirty-year-old Looe man, the Rev George Prynne, to the new living. He was the first Puseyite – the forerunners of modern Anglo-Catholicism – in the diocese, and there was uproar, with Hatchard of St Andrew's and Isaac Latimer, the radical new editor of the *Plymouth and Devonport Weekly Journal*, leading the opposition. There were near-riots when Prynne donned the surplice for his 1848 induction, and this state of affairs lasted for years. Nor was it eased when in the same year the bishop invited Priscilla Seddon, a naval officer's daughter, to start work among the poor of Devonport. She did wonderful work there, but she too was a Puseyite. In the cholera outbreak of 1849 she and her Sisters of Mercy ran a temporary hospital on the site of the present St Dunstan's School and there, for the first time in post-Reformation England, Prynne celebrated Holy Communion daily. In 1850 Miss Seddon started building St Dunstan's Abbey on the site and in 1856 became abbess of the first Anglican religious house since the Reformation. Since 1906 only the girl's school has survived at St Dunstan's. The disgraceful opposition of the evangelicals faded away slowly; Hatchard died in 1870 and when St Peter's was rebuilt in 1882 there were no disturbances. Prynne, who had married the admiral's daughter who paid for the 1848 conversion of the church, lived until 1903. The green-capped 1898 tower of the church is his memorial, and he saw other high church strongholds established in Plymouth, notably St James-the-Less in Citadel Road and St John Sutton-on-Plym. Not that the evangelicals weakened: in Calvinistic Charles right up into this century there was no turning to the altar for the Creed and the priest would always doff his surplice – they did come to that – before preaching.

Oddly enough the establishment of the Roman Catholic Church created no such furore. Plymouth with its Irish population became in 1850 the centre of a diocese embracing Cornwall, Devon and Dorset. The first bishop, Dr George Errington, took the little chapel of St Mary in Stonehouse as his pro-cathedral and his successor, Dr William Vaughan, built the cathedral in Cecil Street in 1856–8. Hansom, who designed the cab named after him, was the architect; when half built the whole structure fell down. It was completed with schools nearby from which grew Notre Dame High School for Girls and St Boniface's College for Boys. The Stonehouse church was taken over by the Sisters of the Poor who built St Joseph's Home in Torr Lane in 1883. By 1914 there were four Roman Catholic parish churches in the Three Towns.

Right through the century the Anglicans were also creating new parishes. When the Victualling Yard was built over the site of the ancient chapel of St Lawrence a new church, St Paul's, was built to Foulston's design in 1830 at the south end of Durnford Street. St George's at the other end continued to serve the Royal Marines and civilians, and St Peter's also took part of Stonehouse into its parish. With Robert Peel's New Parishes Act of 1843, which gave government grants to new churches and simplified the creation of parishes, there was a spate of building. In 1846 four new parishes were made in the cramped area of Devonport within the walls. Apart from Holy Trinity (from which a second parish of St Saviour, with a church on Lambhay Hill, was carved in 1870) the new Plymouth parishes were Christ Church, Eton Place, and St James-the-Less (both 1847) and St John Sutton-on-Plym (1855). Then there was a lull until Frederick Temple, later Archbishop of Canterbury, arrived as Bishop of Exeter in 1869, on Phillpott's death. He founded the Three Towns Church Extension Society and before his translation to London in 1885 (he became Archbishop of Canterbury in 1899) another eight parishes had been created. There was a further spurt under the leadership of Bishop Robertson early in this century; the location of the new churches (see Appendix A) shows the pattern of urban growth. There was even the dream that Plymouth would become a separate diocese and the Rev Gordon Ponsonby, vicar of Stoke, began a building in Collingwood Villas that was to be Devonport Cathedral. Crypt and Lady Chapel were built but war came, Bishop Robertson retired in 1916, and the project languished.

THE NONCONFORMISTS

Dissent, which had reached a low ebb in the eighteenth century, came alive in the nineteenth in a revival led by the Methodists. Old habits die hard and the earliest new buildings were tucked away. The Wesleyans' 1817 Ebenezer Chapel in Saltash Street (rebuilt in 1939 as Plymouth Central Hall) sheltered behind high railings and a heavily-treed forecourt. The new Baptist Chapel of 1847 was buried behind George Street, approached by a narrow lane. For too many years they had had to hide from the mobs. Not until the Congregationalists moved out of the old town to build Sherwell Church in 1864 did they come boldly out on a main street, and then they shocked the old people with a gothic building and a tall spire; it even looked Anglican. When Mutley Plain became the heart of the expansion northwards the Baptists (1869) and the Wesleyans (1881) dominated the new thoroughfare with their churches.

There were many denominations; even the Methodists were split into Wesleyans, Primitive Methodists, Bible Christians and later United Methodists. The town gave its name to the Plymouth Brethren, though the movement was brought to the town by its founder, an Anglican curate from Co Wicklow, in 1830. They had various meeting-places, and a number of schisms, but at first there was a strong following. Among them was George Soltau, twice mayor, whose wife cut up her drawing-room carpet to make rugs for the poor, and Samuel Tregelles who became a famous Bible scholar.

But by 1851 there were more Free Church worshippers in Plymouth and Devonport than Anglicans; on Sunday 30 March there were 23,761 at all the Anglican services and 30,900 in the Free Churches. It is interesting to see that as the old dissenters in both towns found their chapels getting cramped they moved out into the new areas. The one exception is King Street Chapel, which the Wesleyans planted in the heart of Plymouth's worst slum, just as St Andrew's established Holy Trinity and St Saviour's in the Barbican area. Parson Barnes, first vicar of Holy Trinity and creator of St Saviour's, was a hero of the battle against dirt, dissipation and ignorance.

EDUCATION

Apart from private schools for the children of the well-to-do, the Three Towns offered few facilities for education at the start of the nineteenth century. The headmaster of Plymouth's Elizabethan grammar school received just £20 to take a handful of sons of resident burgesses, and after that could take as many fee-paying pupils as he wished. Plymouth also had three charity schools, the Red and Blue (1658) founded out of the Hele and Lanyon charities, Greencoat (1714) and Lady Rogers (1764) founded under the will of the third baronet's wife, and two church schools, Batter Street (1785) and the Household of Faith, opened by Charles in 1787.

Then came the great dispute between the Lancasterians, who wanted undenominational teaching, and the National Society, which wanted Anglican principles taught. The Lancasterians took the lead locally with the Public Free Schools in Plymouth and Dock Public School, both in 1809, followed by Stoke Public School in 1819. Plymouth Public School moved to Cobourg Street in 1812 and its great years there began with the arrival of George Jago in 1842. He was headmaster for forty-three years, making it the third biggest school in the country with over 2,000 children. Stoke Public School's greatest days came later, under Alonzo Rider, who was there from 1863 until 1896, when he left to found Devonport High School for Boys.

Devonport, which had forty private schools by 1830, had three national schools and one founded by dockyard artisans by that time. Then in 1832 the national schools won government grants and the churches, old and new, in all Three Towns, began to found their schools. Charles in Tavistock Place was the first in Plymouth, in 1838. Ragged schools started too in 1849, but the census required by the Education Act of 1870 showed that in Plymouth alone there were still 2,000 children receiving no education at all.

The Act required local authorities to establish elected, rate-levying school boards and provide schools for everyone, although attendance did not become compulsory until 1876 and education was not free until 1891. After fiercely fought elections, in which Plymouth voted against spending money on denominational education, the boards began to build. By 1903, Plymouth had built eighteen schools and Devonport nine, in limestone and with a flamboyance of style which still excites in those which survive. When Bishop Temple arrived at Exeter he set out to encourage higher education and found a strong supporter in Professor the Rev F. E. Anthony of Western College, the Liberal chairman of Plymouth School Board for twenty-three years. A high school for girls was started in 1874 and one for boys in 1878. The boys' high school amalgamated with the 1854 Mannamead School in 1896 to become Plymouth College and remained independent. Plymouth High School for Girls was absorbed into the local education authority's plan for secondary education. Both towns too celebrated the Queen's Jubilee by incorporating existing art and science schools into technical colleges, with new buildings completed by Plymouth in 1892 and Devonport in 1899.

School boards disappeared in 1903 and the respective corporations became the local education authorities. In both county boroughs primary and secondary education were carved out of the old school system. Plymouth Corporation Grammar School, which had become almost completely a private school, was revived in this way in 1908 with C. W. Bracken, the local historian, as its first headmaster. At Plympton the grammar school was similarly revived as a county mixed grammar school.

SOCIAL AND INTELLECTUAL LIFE

The free intellectual and social life of the eighteenth century formalised in the nineteenth, with the well-to-do enjoying the magnificence of the Plymouth Proprietory Library in Cornwall Street and the classical solemnity of the Athenaeum for meetings of the Plymouth Institution. This body fathered the Devonshire Association in 1862 and its scholarly ranks were swelled by scientists of the Marine Biological Association after their laboratory and aquarium were opened under the Citadel walls in 1885. For the hoi polloi there were the Mechanics'

Institutes started in 1825. The Plymouth institute had its own building in Princess Square in 1827 and the Devonport institute one in Duke Street in 1844. YMCAs opened in both towns in 1848, to become strong social and educational centres. Plymouth built a new guildhall in 1870–3. It incorporated the Western Law Courts, a central police and fire station, and with the municipal buildings across a square, flanked by St Andrew's Tower to the east and eventually a new post office to the west, made a new focal point for the town. In the same way its great hall became the major centre for social events and meetings of every kind. The old guildhall in Whimple Street became a free library in 1876, and in 1882 Devonport bought out the Mechanics' Institute to make its Duke Street premises their free library and museum. (The Plymouth Mechanics' Institute merged with the Athenaeum in 1899.) Plymouth started its museum in Beaumont House in 1897 but by 1910, with Carnegie aid, had built the present library and museum in Tavistock Road.

Of the philanthropic work in the century the great innovation was that of Agnes Weston, whose mother was one of the Plymouth Baylys. She came to Devonport in 1873 working for the temperance movement among sailors and three years later opened the first Sailors' Rest; Queen Victoria later gave it the 'Royal' prefix and made Miss Weston a Dame, but to the navy it was always 'Aggie Weston's'. She set out to create 'a public house without the drink' and gave the men comfort, bright colours, mirrors and gilding. It was right outside the dockyard gates, in Fore Street, and its cabins could house 900 men.

For the gentlemen there was the Plymouth Club at the top of Lockyer Street, and the yacht clubs, led by the Royal Western, which was formed in 1827 and grew out of the first Plymouth regatta. Its earliest club house overlooked Millbay but since 1866 it has been on Plymouth Hoe. From 1880 it had a splendid block alongside the Grand Hotel, a social establishment of the first order with the finest yachts in the world racing under its burgee.

This was all gentlemanly yachting. At the other end of the scale were the regattas which every waterside community, from

Saltash Passage and Morice Town round to Sutton Harbour and the Cattewater villages, held each summer. Then there were Plymouth Races, held every August on Chelson Meadow from 1828, which matched with their showmen and sideshows the great Plymouth November Fair held in and round the market. The sport was provided at the races by the hunting fraternity, and chief among them for years was Charles Trelawny, who lived in Bedford Street. He was master and owner of the Dartmoor Foxhounds from 1843 until 1873, when at the age of seventy-four he gave up, but for all those years was a familiar sight in his pink coat, mounting his horse outside his house – where the Dingle's Royal Parade entrance is now – to ride to the kennels at Ivybridge. Very often J. R. Newcombe, the famous lessee of the Theatre Royal from 1845 to 1887, would hack off with him. With the growing naval and military establishments in the Three Towns there was strong service support for hunting and the associated point-to-point meetings.

Though there were undoubtedly social meetings between the business men, the county families and the service officers, there was a greater division than in the previous century. The Earls of Morley continued to be presidents of Plymouth Chamber of Commerce, and the Earl of Mount Edgcumbe built Winter Villa at Stonehouse in 1856 because his countess could not stand the winters at Mount Edgcumbe. The Duke of Edinburgh, Queen Victoria's second son, when Commander-in-Chief Plymouth from 1890 to 1893, played his violin in the concerts of Plymouth Orchestral Society. The Queen's son at Mount Wise, with his wife a daughter of the Tsar of Russia, brought a glitter to high life not known since the Lennox days, and before they left their eldest daughter, Princess Marie, had married the Crown Prince of Romania. But social life polarised, with county and services standing apart from the tradesmen of the town.

POLITICS

Devonport remained a staunchly Liberal constituency for most of the century. 'Bully' Ferrand with prodigious work broke through in 1863 for the Conservatives, boasting that Devonport was no longer a government pocket borough, and in 1865 he hauled his gentle partner Fleming in as well. Both were unseated on petition for bribery – they gave half a day's wages to each dockyardee who voted for them. There was such argument about the dockyard officers controlling voting in the government interest that Disraeli moved in the House that dockyardsmen should be disfranchised. That was enough to get both seats back for the Liberals, until economies in the dockyard put the Tories in from 1874 until 1892. Then, after Gladstone's great 1891 tour of the west, the Liberals were back. H. E. Kearley, founder of International Stores, was one member from 1892 until 1910, when he became Lord Devonport. In that year Sir John Jackson and Sir Clement Kinloch-Cooke won the seats for the Conservatives.

Plymouth had a similarly stormy period. Robert Collier, son of Plymouth's first Reform MP and a distinguished lawyer, was the most important of the two Liberal members until 1871, when he became a judge. There was some acrimony over Collier's judgeship; the Liberal candidate was Alderman Rooker who was held to have split the Liberal vote on a previous occasion, and Edward Bates from Liverpool took the seat for the Conservatives. Bates, one of the richest, biggest, hardest and most hated shipping owners in the world, was never known to give to any philanthropic cause in Liverpool, but in Plymouth was lavish in his presents. Just before the 1880 general election he put enough capital into the ailing sugar refinery in Mill Lane to keep it in business. That everlasting firebrand Isaac Latimer petitioned; Bates was unseated for bribery to much local indignation, and the lawyer brought down to defend him, Edward Clarke, took the seat again for the Tories. Bates was back as MP in 1885, was made a baronet in 1886 and retired in 1892. Apart from the Liberal landslide election of 1906 the Conservatives held Plymouth from 1874 onwards. H. E. Duke from Merrivale, another distinguished lawyer, was one of the members from 1900 until 1906. The members who put out the Liberals at the second general election of 1910 bore names familiar to modern Plymothians: Sir Arthur Shirley-Benn and Waldorf Astor.

LOCAL POLITICS

In the political philosophy of the times, too much government was regarded as a bad thing. The Conservatives were the arch-apostles of this doctrine of *laissez-faire* and the Liberals the more inclined to want to do things. Whatever happened, the great thing for both parties was to keep the rates as low as possible. When the guardians built the new workhouse in 1849 the corporation bought the old site and adjacent property to build a guildhall. The Liberal Alfred Rooker (he was also a deacon of Sherwell Church) was the great advocate of the scheme but not until 1873 did he see the Prince of Wales open it. A statue was put up to Rooker's honour – Drake is the only other mayor so honoured – but not all the Liberals loved him by that time, and the Tories certainly did not. So the statue finished up at the side of the municipal buildings overlooking the public lavatories, even though public subscription paid for it. The German bombs which destroyed the municipal buildings in 1941 blew the statue off its plinth and the sledge-hammer of an American demolition worker finally destroyed it. The only other piece of pure ornament in the Plymouth of those days was Derry's Clock, and though the corporation built it in 1863, most of the money was given by the mayor, William Derry, another Liberal and the son of a Sherwell deacon. (He held the contract for all local horse transport for the GW.)

For most of the century the mayors were leading members of the strongest party on the council. Generally the Liberals seem predominant, though the Conservatives had their spells. But the mayors were also men of substance, industrialists, bankers, professional men, merchants. They were the leaders of the town in the fullest sense, and very different from some of the odd choices of the previous century. The Liberals were dominant when the 1888 reforms gave the council more powers, and they set about using them. In J. H. Ellis the corporation had its first professional town clerk, and he provided the driving force. The market was rebuilt, Old Town and Ebrington Streets widened, the Hoe laid out, parks opened, a tram company bought, new sewage works and the workmen's dwellings at Prince Rock built. Burrator reservoir was in use. Compton had been dragged expensively into the town. The Plymouth rates went up to 7s in the pound. The Liberals lost their majority, the Conservatives demanded control of the main spending committees, the retiring mayor, J. T. Bond, could not find a successor and the Conservatives refused to try. After some horse-trading over committee chairmanships the Tory Alderman Pethick – 'Honest John', the major building contractor – became mayor. Is it significant that the following year saw the house-building boom in Plymouth back in full swing? From this time emerged the pattern of electing mayors from each party on the council in annual turn.

The Labour Party was not yet in existence. There had been Chartists in Plymouth in the 1840s and George Odger, the shoemaker born at Roborough, had worked in Plymouth before he moved to London and became from 1860 one of the first trade union leaders. In the 1880s unions and the associated political parties began to develop in the Three Towns. A Trades Council was formed in 1892, broke up over the idea of running candidates in local elections, reformed in 1897 and in 1899 entertained the Trades Union Congress. The Plymouth Congress passed the resolution to seek political representation – the birth of the modern Labour Party. The Plymouth Social Democratic Federation in 1900 formed the Three Towns Housing Association, pressing the local authorities for more council houses. By 1913 they were petitioning for amalgamation of the Three Towns.

The galaxy of local governments in an area where different sides of a street were under different control – Mutley Plain was so split, for instance – produced many anomalies. The Plymouth borough police of a Saturday night would push a drunk over into Stonehouse for the county police to cope with, and the county police would push him back. When Stonehouse was only a sanitary district certain contagious disease laws did not apply there as in the towns proper. So all the prostitutes flocked to Stonehouse.

With such close neighbours there were of course petty jealousies and rivalries between the three neighbouring authorities, particularly between Plymouth and Devonport. They came to a head when Admiral Sir Lewis Beaumont arrived as commander-in-chief and steadily snubbed the Mayor of Devonport, W. J. Moon, a naval outfitter. When the King and Queen visited the town in 1907 the Mayor of Plymouth was invited to lunch in the Admiralty yacht, but not Mr Moon. The Mayor of Plymouth, Sir Charles Radford, was only a draper too, but he was head of Popham's, which catered for the best people, and he had a big house at Yelverton. So Mr and Mrs Moon boycotted the royal visit, and his townsmen pointedly kept off the streets for the royal processions.

The idea of amalgamation had been mooted in 1835 and 1888 (when Plymouth also asked to become the capital of a South Devon county), and Sir Joseph Bellamy had promoted a conference on the subject in 1902 in Stonehouse Town Hall. But the 1913 ballots in Plymouth and Devonport which came from this new pressure encouraged Plymouth to make a formal representation to the Local Government Board for the amalgamation of the Three Towns.

The inquiry opened in Plymouth Guildhall on Wednesday 28 January 1914. Plymouth put up as first witness its town clerk, J. H. Ellis. Then an impressive figure appeared in the hall, Major-General A. P. Penton, CVO, CB, Officer in Command South West Coast Defences. He was in residence at Government House, Mount Wise, in effect the successor to centuries of Governors of Plymouth. Ellis stood down and General Penton took the stand as Plymouth's witness. His vital testimony was:

> In peacetime the organisation of the Three Towns into three distinct bodies does not affect us much . . . In wartime it is an entirely different question. You would have the fortress commander having to go to three different bodies . . . In fact if I was fortress commander here in wartime I should have to go to the three chief civil magistrates and say 'One of you must represent the civil community . . .'

Counsel for Devonport, the chief opponent, made heavy weather of a short cross-questioning. Ellis went back in the box, and the inquiry lasted another four days. But it was 1914. The German threat had been clear for years. War did break out six months after the inquiry ended, and from October 1914 General Penton had only one authority to deal with.

CHAPTER TEN

WAR AND PEACE: 1914–39

A UGUST 1914 came to Plymouth as so many wars before had done. The fleet was already at battle stations and the reserves mobilised. The battalions of the 8th Infantry Brigade at Crownhill and Raglan marched to the railway stations with their commanders riding at their head, to be caught almost at once in the retreat from Mons. The Territorials mobilised. Millbay Drill Hall was full, schools like Prince Rock became temporary barracks as later on other schools, like Salisbury Road and Hyde Park Road, became hospitals. The dockyard built up its labour force. As the war in France settled down to its man-eating trench warfare, so the civilians volunteered for the army, or were called to the colours, if they had not found work in the yard.

The dockyard employed just over 10,000 men at the outbreak of war; before the end it had nearly 19,000. There were war bonuses which doubled the men's wages, and much overtime: no danger and no departure from home comforts. For the men who went into the services there was poor pay, huge casualty lists, discomfort and little home leave. It was to leave a bitter taste in many mouths long after the end of the war.

The Fleet Reservists who had been the first called up were men who had done their full service and retired to live with wives and families in the ports on whose strength they had been borne. Many of these men went into the older ships also called out of reserve – the most vulnerable – and every one lost produced a large Plymouth casualty list. The Battle of Jutland at the end of May 1916, in which the Royal Navy lost fourteen ships and 6,274 men, hit the port desperately, for five of the lost ships, and at least four of those badly damaged, were Devonport-manned. There were crowds outside the newspaper offices for hours awaiting casualty lists, and for weeks after the streets seemed full of black widows' weeds. Every battle in France too, with its infinitely larger casualty lists, hit the town, but none like the Battle of the Bois de Buttes in May 1918. The 2nd Devons, long since robbed by the long war of their regular soldiers and largely made up of wartime soldiers, went down to hopeless odds with Colonel Anderson-Morshead of the old Plymouth merchant family dying with them, revolver in one hand and hunting crop in the other.

For Plymouth itself, far from the battle and out of air range, with only the sea-facing lights kept dim, there was little but the numbing wait for casualty lists. The Canadian Expeditionary Force, diverted unexpectedly into the port in October 1914 to avoid U-boats in the Channel, provided the spectacle of thirty-three liners steaming through the Sound into the dockyard to disembark 25,000 men. After the Battle of Coronel, when hundreds of reservists went down with the Devonport-manned *Monmouth* and the *Cape of Good Hope*, the dockyard had secret orders to prepare the squadron which was to avenge them at the Battle of the Falkland Islands. If the yardees had not finished the work in time, ordered Churchill, they were to sail with the ships, but as with so many Churchill orders there is a veil over the outcome.

Apart from repair and maintenance work, and fitting out the Q-ships in the latter campaign against the U-boats, the dockyard built the battleship *Royal Oak*, the cruiser *Cleopatra* and two of the weird and ill-fated K-class submarines. They were designed to steam at the same speed as the battle fleet and actually had two funnels. They were always in trouble. K-6, on trials in the basin at Keyham, submerged and sat on the bottom for two hours, refusing to come up. The defect was repaired by an inspector of engine fitters aboard, but yard men refused to dive in her again. Perhaps the major dockyard excitement of the whole war was generated by the large numbers of women employed to make up the manpower shortages. Even outside the yard there were women tram conductors.

The war penetrated the Cattewater. Submarines sailed up to Turnchapel Wharves, which the Admiralty had bought in 1905 together with the quarries behind for oil storage, to refuel. When the Americans came into the war they took over Victoria Wharves as a naval base in June 1917. Within weeks two destroyers and over sixty submarine chasers were based there, with over 3,000 men working from the port and headquarters in Elliot Terrace.

The biggest new development was at Mount Batten. The peninsula was closed to the public in 1916 and the Royal Naval Air Service set up a base. At first the little Castle Inn was the officers' mess, the petty officers were in the coastguard cottages facing the Sound, men were ferried across each day in the Oreston & Turnchapel Company's *Rapid* and a hangar housed the first Short seaplanes. A rail track was laid along Batten Breakwater to enable a crane to hoist the planes in and out of the water. Hangars and living quarters were built, with slipways for the planes and motor launches attached. When on 1 April 1918 the RNAS and the Royal Flying Corps were merged, Mount Batten became an RAF station. With the end of the war and the anti-U-boat patrols, Mount Batten went into 'care and maintenance'.

GREATER PLYMOUTH

Under the stress of war the Three Towns had merged themselves into one Corporation of Plymouth without much public concern. The mass referendum in 1914 had shown the people of all Three Towns in favour of amalgamation. Devonport Corporation had spent thousands of pounds in fighting the proposal in spite of that, and with its members the old rancour died hard. They found themselves as they feared in a minority on the new council; of the aldermen Plymouth had 11 seats, Devonport 7 and Stonehouse 2; of the councillors Plymouth had 33, Devonport 21 and Stonehouse 6. The 1913 Mayor of Plymouth, Thomas Baker, became the first mayor of the new borough and continued under the pressure of war for two years; he was a Liberal who was to be knighted in 1920. Baker's successor as mayor was Colonel J. P. Goldsmith of Devonport, to keep the balance. The first town clerk was J. H. Ellis of Plymouth. R. J. Fittall of Devonport was his deputy and took over in 1917, a robust extrovert quite capable of digging committee chairmen in the ribs and demanding: 'How can you be so stupid?'

The war, and the problems of amalgamating three councils and all their undertakings, occupied their energies. With the end of the war a burst of energy was released, an outward-looking period under Conservative control which matched the Liberal developments of the 1890s. J. Y. Woollcombe, descendant of that Reform leader of a century earlier, had been the Tory leader since 1913, exercising what the *Western Morning News* called 'a benevolent dictatorship'.

The first need was housing, for the soldiers coming home looking for 'houses fit for heroes' found a greater shortage of accommodation than even before the war. Under the 1919 Addison Housing Act Plymouth was recommended to clear nineteen insanitary areas covering 1,017 houses and 9,685 people. Houses had to be built for them first. When the Prince of Wales came to Plymouth that year to accept office as Lord High Steward, he cut the first turf at North Prospect for a new council housing estate. The Swilly estate had also been bought. The first two houses were occupied by the end of 1920, 264 more by the end of 1921 and 402 in 1922. By the end of 1924 802 houses had been built by the corporation, compared with 215 by private enterprise in the same period. The new council houses were used partly to accommodate ex-servicemen with families and unsatisfactory housing, but above all to clear the worst slum areas of the Three Towns. The housing programme went on steadily through the 1920s and 1930s – Swilly houses in 1929 were being built for £400. By 1939 Plymouth had 5,000 council houses and flats. There were patches of private house-building – a 1930s house in Stangray Avenue sold new for £850. The Great Western Railway also built an estate for its workmen at Peverell, and the Astors another estate, complete with an Institute, at the end of Mount Gould. The Admiralty built 174 houses in 1927 at Pemros Street, St Budeaux, to house men displaced by the closure of Pembroke and Rosyth Yards – hence the ugly street name.

The tramway system had been linked up in 1915 when Plymouth bought out the Devonport company (though the PS&D went on until 1922). In that year, when the Bath and West Agricultural Show was held in what is now Central Park (the idea of buying this large open space which was becoming locked in by houses generated from the show), Alma Road was widened and tramlines were laid from Pennycomequick to Milehouse. But the corporation was still paying an annual sum for its trams to cross Stonehouse Bridge, and the ha'penny gate was a nuisance to every other user.

The tolls had survived from turnpike days. Some fell into disuse when the cost of collecting became greater than the amount yielded, but not until the end of the 1850s did the gates go from Milehouse, Cattedown Corner, and the Plymouth end of Mutley Plain ('Lewis Jones's gate'). Plymouth bought the Iron Bridge and the Embankment in 1897 but kept the tolls on to recoup the cost. The tolls at Millbridge (which had caused an uproar when they were imposed in 1807) and Stonehouse Bridge had been sold by the Edgcumbes to a private company but now they too were bought out and on 1 April 1924 the mayor, Solomon Stephens, toured all four toll points and declared them free.

THE RISE OF THE LABOUR PARTY

All this had been done in typical post-war depression years. Once again men were flocking out of the forces, and the dockyard was cutting back. From the wartime peak of nearly 19,000 the labour force was back to 15,837 and still falling: 1925, 11,436; 1927, 10,854, and then 800 sacked in a few weeks. In the early post-war years it had been the wartime temporaries going out, but by 1924 men who had regarded the dockyard as their career were being discharged. There were strikes in civilian industry: a dockers' strike in 1919 which halted coal supplies and nearly left the town without gas; a builders' strike which lasted six weeks – the men wanted an extra halfpenny an hour. In 1926 came the General Strike which hit Plymouth as hard as the rest of the country. Though the strikers played a football match against the police the trams were rumbling through the streets shrouded in wire netting to stop the stones being thrown at them.

Against this background the Labour Party grew to strength in local affairs. The pioneer was J. J. H. Moses, born in

Dartmouth, leader of the Shipwrights' Union in the dockyard, a Methodist local preacher, large, shambling, sanctimonious, able to use tears to win an argument. He was a member of Devonport Town Council by 1914 and came over to Plymouth with the amalgamation. He was a guardian too – the separate Plymouth and Devonport boards remained until 1926 when their work was taken over by local authority Public Health Committees. The guardians were Labour's first target and six were elected to the Devonport board in 1919, led by H. M. Medland. He was an Okehampton boy, the leader of the Engineers' Union in the dockyard and their full-time secretary by 1921. Bert Medland fought Jimmy Moses over work allocations in the yard, refused to 'humbly petition' the Lords Commissioners when he was fighting for wage increases, and walked into the Admiral Superintendent's office smoking a cigarette. From guardians the attack moved to the town council; by the end of 1923 Jimmy Moses was an alderman and had been joined by Medland, R. R. Oke, a railwayman, J. Churchward, chairman of Plymouth Trades Council, and H. G. Mason, another dockyardee. Two years later another half-dozen socialists were elected, and they became a real force. In 1926 Jimmy Moses became Plymouth's first Labour mayor and Medland leader of the party, living up to his 'Stormy' nickname. They demanded their share of committee chairmanships, and got them, four to the twenty-two. Medland had Public Health. He had declared war on the Poor Law when he became a guardian; now he could act. His great achievement was to convert Plymouth Workhouse into the City Hospital. From now on the mayoralty went in turn around the three parties.

The council was changing in many ways. The Liberal leader, Sir Thomas Baker, who died in 1926, did much to teach and encourage the new Labour members. But the Liberals were a dwindling force, the radical torch had passed to the new men, and the Conservatives were firmly in power. In face of the Labour challenge the Tories and Liberals agreed not to oppose each other in ward elections. The Liberals suffered the fate of all minor parties in coalition.

The Tory leader Woollcombe had died in 1923. Very soon

Lovell Dunstan took over. He was a ship chandler and from the little room behind the shop in Southside Street he ran Plymouth. Callers would find him there with one or more of his cabal, all businessmen – G. P. Holmes, W. J. W. Modley, F. D. Baxter, W. H. J. Priest – all chairmen of the major committees. In the expansive years after the war rates had soared (each of the Three Towns had a separate rate until 1930, while the liabilities were ironed out) from about 8s to 14s. Now the aim was to bring them down; by 1930 a 10s rate had been achieved, and holding it at that level was to be Lovell·Dunstan's policy, watchword, guiding principle. It was good for businessmen but it was not good for Plymouth. Much that should have been done was left on one side. When in 1924 the Housing Committee approached those 1919 slum clearance areas they cut the cost to a quarter by reconditioning instead of rebuilding, and only put blocks of flats in where areas had to be cleared. It was to preserve the historic features, they said, but they still destroyed many old buildings, and even the Elizabethan House, 32 New Street, was only saved by A. S. Parker, the architect and founder of the Old Plymouth Society, after the roof had gone.

TOWN DEVELOPMENTS

Not everything stood still, of course. The capacity of Burrator was increased 50 per cent in 1928 after the dam had been heightened by 10ft (the road was carried by a suspension bridge for two years). The polo field at Roborough – the George Hotel was the club headquarters and Lord Louis Mountbatten one of the naval members – was bought as a municipal aerodrome. As early as 1923 the *Western Independent* and the *Western Morning News* were pushing the idea of an air mail service to pick up the incoming ocean mail at Plymouth. They promoted trial flights, and the Air Ministry tried running an experimental service with Alan Cobham piloting the first flight in 1923. There were rival sites at Chelston Meadow and Staddon Heights but Roborough won; the town council took an option on the ground in 1924 but the Chamber of Commerce hung back, there was no government aid, and it was seven years before Plymouth's aerodrome finally came into being.

In 1931 Central Park was opened; it was aimed to keep it as a piece of countryside with green fields and lanes between hedges but the idea has been largely forgotten over the years. Stanley Leatherby, a Conservative councillor out to make his name, began promoting Plymouth as a holiday resort. Bathing houses had been built at Tinside in 1913 and there were small bathing pools for men, women and children. In 1928–33 the large circular pool was built there with new changing rooms, sun terraces and other facilities, and various advertising schemes were launched. Madeira Road until 1933 ended at Fisher's Nose: pedestrians could only reach the Barbican by going up steps and along a passage enclosed by corrugated iron. Now the road was driven through to join Commercial Road and the last warehouses of the old Victualling Yard were destroyed to open the view. This was no loss, but the removal of the eighteenth-century pillared watch house, opposite the Admiral MacBride, was strongly but unsuccessfully opposed. The old Greenbank Prison, which had long been the responsibility of the Prison Commissioners, was demolished in 1935 and the council converted it into magistrates' courts, a central police station and a fire station, to replace the now inadequate arrangements behind the Guildhall.

PLYMPTON AND PLYMSTOCK

On the eastern and northern side the town had now grown to its boundaries. With the advent of the motor car and buses it became easier to live further afield. Plymouth was encircled by Plympton Rural District Council land; their rates were lower than those of Plymouth, and their powerful clerk, Percy Loosemore, supported every possible development in his area that would encourage housing and so push up the rateable value of the district. The RDC began providing electricity in 1926, and improved its water supply in 1928. Not only were areas like the Torr estate – old Bayly land and contiguous with the Plymouth boundary on the north – being built up, but Plympton and above all Plymstock were growing fast. The population of Greater Plymouth, static from 1911 to 1921, had fallen by 1931 from 209,857 to 208,166. The central areas of the old Three Towns showed a decrease in density of population, and the nineteenth-century suburbs were static. The city population owed its decrease to migration, while Plympton RDC showed an increase of 19.3 per cent by migration alone. Plymstock grew from 7,032 in 1901 to 12,134 in 1931 and 17,840 in 1949. The whole dormitory area was growing from Wembury to Dousland.

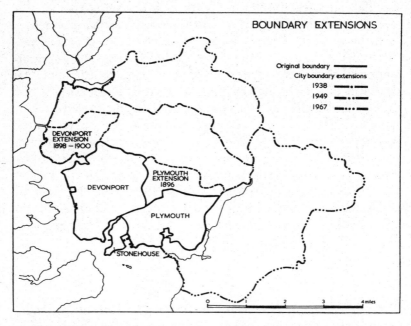

BOUNDARY EXTENSIONS. *Note how the original boundaries of Plymouth and Devonport for centuries exceeded the built-up areas, and how hemmed-in is Stonehouse. The River Plym was Plymouth's eastern boundary until 1967.*

So when Fittall retired as town clerk in 1935, Colin Campbell was appointed from Burnley, partly because he had experience of boundary extensions. He was set to work on this at once, but life was difficult. Percy Loosemore played bridge every Friday night at the Plympton home of the father of the two Leatherbys on Plymouth Council; Lovell Dunstan was another player. The editor of the *Western Evening Herald*, W. O. Mills, was in the magic circle and his Saturday 'Citizen's Diary', which could flow to eight or ten columns, was the most influential local journalism of the day. Loosemore thus had his allies in the Plymouth camp but Dunstan, against extension, was overruled (and sometimes purposely kept in ignorance). Plymouth won its boundary application in 1938, growing from 5,711 acres to 9,595. It was still hemmed in by the rivers, and the Plymstock–Plympton suburbs, as they had really become, were still outside. However, Plymouth had become a city in 1928 and its chief citizen lord mayor in 1935.

MEMBERS OF PARLIAMENT

Under the parliamentary reorganisation of 1918 Plymouth was reduced to three Members of Parliament, cut into the constituencies of Devonport, Drake and Sutton. Waldorf Astor, son of the naturalised American millionaire, had been a Plymouth MP since 1910. He succeeded to his father's title in 1919 and his wife Nancy fought and won the Sutton Division. She was the first woman to take her seat in Parliament and held Sutton for twenty-five years, longer than any other Plymouth member. In 1923 Leslie Hore-Belisha won Devonport for the Liberals. He too sat until 1945, surviving the landslides of 1919 and 1931, becoming chairman of the National Liberal Party and a minister in each successive 1930s government. As Minister of Transport he made many reforms and Belisha beacons are a memorial; then he went to the War Ministry and did more to reform the army than any man since Haldane. But his impatience, his showmanship and the necessary speed of his changes upset the generals, and they forced his resignation in January 1940. Jimmy Moses won Drake for Labour in 1929, Plymouth's first Labour MP, and survived a petition to unseat him. The allegation was that A. C. Ballard, a rich eccentric who gave weekly pocket money to every member of his vast boys' club at Millbay, had spent unexplained monies on Jimmy Moses's behalf. But he was swept out of the House in the 1931 National Government landslide.

HARBOUR WORK

After the war the work of the port went on much the same: wheat, fertiliser, timber, coal and sugar came in; china clay went out. In the 1920s the port handled between £2½ and £3 million worth of goods each year, falling away in the Depression to a low in 1932 both in imports and exports, and then climbing again, although by 1938 it was still not back to the 1920 figure. The one major increase was in petroleum imports, the 10 million gallons of 1920 climbing to 55 million gallons in 1939. New ships based on the port were the cable-layers of Cable & Wireless, which took over Turnchapel Wharf in 1922.

Fish stocks had grown in the under-fishing of the war years and the market was busy for the next ten years. There was also a winter glut of herrings that brought the Cornish boats and the east coast drifters in; from 1926 to 1936 there were up to a hundred east coast drifters and even more Cornish boats working out of Sutton Harbour. The peak year was 1930 but yields fell away after that. There were only three east coast drifters in 1938, and then they were seen no more. But in those boom years Plymouth became again the major West Country fish port, taking the title which Newlyn had regained at the turn of the century. By 1938 there were thirteen steam trawlers in the port but only one sailing trawler left.

The inter-war years were the zenith of the liner trade. Though the United States Navy's flying boat NC4 reached Plymouth in 1919 after the first-ever Atlantic flight, there were to be no trans-Atlantic passenger flights until 1939. The ocean liner was still the last word in luxurious, prestigious travel. The New York–Europe route was the most glamorous of all, with the biggest ships in the world racing to establish the fastest times. Plymouth was the nearest European liner port to New York; Cunard moved into the Channel in 1919 and all their ships, from the old *Aquitania* and *Mauritania* to the first *Queen Mary*, were anchoring in Cawsand Bay, as were the famous French, German and American ships. So too were the less renowned liners, from every corner of the globe, and there could be times with five liners having to be handled at once. Plymouth had four tenders capable of carrying 2,460 passengers, and often all had to be in service. The peak year was 1930: 788 liners called, 41,130 passengers and 307,000 bags of mail passed through the port. After 1926 it was only the two depression years of 1932 and 1933 that saw less than 30,000 passengers. Among them were the most famous people in the world: politicians, film stars, writers, sportsmen. It was the fast, smart, elegant way to cross the Atlantic.

THE SERVICES

Plymouth was still very much a service town: four battalions of infantry with brigaded corps troops, the Artillery in the Citadel, the Royal Marines at Stonehouse, the shore-based sailors at Keyham, and all still in uniform when out of barracks. In 1934 the naval supremacy was marked by the commander-in-chief moving into Government House and renaming it Admiralty House, and the senior soldier moving back to the smaller house at Mount Wise. There were still enough ships for whole fleets to be anchored in the Sound, to entertain with searchlight displays. Between 1921 and 1930 the yard converted Fisher's three giant 'light cruisers', *Furious*, *Courageous* and *Glorious*, into aircraft carriers and achieved the expertise that has made Devonport pre-eminent in such work since. In 1927 there was an echo of the K6 story, but without a happy ending, when the submarine H29 sank in dock at Devonport and seven men died. There had been two disasters before the war, A8 sinking just outside the Breakwater in 1905 with the loss of fifteen men and A7 lost in Whitsand Bay in 1914 with eleven dead. In 1927 the first Washington Treaty cruiser *Cornwall* was laid down, followed by *Devonshire* and *Exeter* among others. With the accelerated naval programme after 1937 the old battleship *Valiant* was modernised.

But the major change was at Mount Batten, which came out of 'care and maintenance' in 1928 to become the home of two flying boat squadrons of the RAF and, during 1935-7, two flights of the Fleet Air Arm. In addition to liners, cargo ships, fishing boats and warships, the Sound was enlivened by these flying boats taking off and landing. The most renowned airman ever to serve there was Aircraftman Shaw, hiding the identity of Lawrence of Arabia in his job as the station commander's runner. His experience in three fatal plane crashes in the Sound, and his experiments with his own high-speed launch, led him to bully the RAF into developing the rescue launch service which was to be so important when war came.

EMPLOYMENT

Census tabulations do not make much sense in a city like Plymouth where some 25 per cent of the working population were in the dockyard in the inter-war years, and 14 per cent in the armed forces. The 1931 returns, for instance, show a high figure in industry but much of that was in the yard, or in industries serving local needs. Biscuit manufacture had ceased, but a baker in Exeter Street, E. E. Farley, had been making rusks for babies from the recipe of a local doctor. In 1921 Farley's Infant Food Ltd was formed by the Trahair family who had bought the recipe; in 1931 they built a modern factory at Torr Lane, and in 1938 they doubled it; Farley's rusks were becoming nationally known. The soap works had closed, but the American scientist Acheson had chosen Prince Rock in 1911 as the site of his only British factory making industrial colloids – the first American factory in Plymouth. Of the pre-1914 factories serving national needs there really only remained the fertilisers and the Reckitt starch works. Their factory also did all the printing for the group, and Plymouth still had its book printing firms of national repute.

In 1931 building occupied 4,700 people but there was little major work being done. After the first council house building in the early 1920s slum clearance became a patchy affair. The oldest streets in Devonport (Cornwall Street) and Stonehouse (High Street) were cleared and flats built, and Plymouth's ancient High Street (now foolishly called Buckwell Street) was partially treated so. A new bank, several motor showrooms, three super-cinemas and a newspaper office represented the only 1930s developments in Plymouth, and these point to the city's second strength. The second largest employer was the distributive trade, employing 21 per cent of the work force compared with the dockyard's 25 per cent. But it was not a wealthy city by any means. The average percentage of unemployment in Plymouth for the years 1929–38 was 16.3, 1.5 per cent higher than the national figure.

SHOPPING AND ENTERTAINMENT

The city of a quarter of a million people was the shopping and entertainment centre for three-quarters of a million. Many people living within twenty miles came in for weekly shopping. Others would come fifty to sixty miles for special shopping – a dress 'bought in Plymouth' had a cachet none of the country towns could give. Day-out shopping, taking in a meal and a show as well, had a hinterland west of the line from Bude to Kingsbridge. A fortnightly 5*s* return excursion train from Penzance, run to coincide with Plymouth Argyle's home games, would on average bring 2,500 to 3,000 people to Plymouth. On those days the Fifty Shilling Tailors in Union Street sold an extra 200 suits.

The heart of the shopping area stretched from Drake Circus to Derry's Clock. George Street had the expensive shops and was the fashionable place; Genoni's Swiss Restaurant had world-famous customers and Nicholson's Long Bar (no women allowed on its sawdust floor) was a legend among naval officers. The smell of Goodboy's coffee (they were Southern Irish Quaker immigrants of the mid-nineteenth century) still haunts old Plymothians. Bedford Street had the four great department stores. Joseph Spooner in 1858 opened a draper's shop in Bedford Street which grew to dominate half Old Town Street as well. It was an ebullient family, with Mr Spooner's Harriers and Kenneth Spooner's amateur dramatic society, but the business was taken over by Clarence Hatry's Drapery Trust in 1927. The trust merged with Debenham's later that year, and after Hatry's crash in 1929 Debenham's took full control, although keeping the Spooner name. Next down Bedford Street was Popham's with brass plates on the front so polished over the years that 'Popham Radford' could hardly be read. The business had been founded in the 1820s by Elizabeth Radford of Plympton; Alderman Sir Charles Radford who died in 1916 was the most distinguished member of the family. Popham's was expensive, for the best people: it did not open on Saturday afternoons. John Yeo's, next door, was very different. The original John Yeo came from north Devon, learnt his trade in London and Paris, and as a good Methodist and Liberal ran the business he began in 1871 on 'cash only' lines, attracting considerably country trade. His nephew John Beckley joined him in 1893; he and his heirs maintained the family style. For the smart and fashionable there was Dingle's, run by Jack Baker and Frank Dingle whose fathers had founded the firm in the 1880s, already expanding by taking in first Underwood's the grocers and then Vickery's the outfitters. Across Russell Street in Frankfort Street was Coster's, run by the Leatherby family and very much down the price scale. At the bottom of Frankfort Street was the vast Plymouth Co-operative Society's 1894 headquarters with its clock tower, assembly hall and eductional operations over the shop. Founded in 1859 by nine working men, the Co-op had another large building at Drake Circus and by 1936 it had 140 branches, 8 farms, 78,000 members and 2,300 workers. At Devonport there were the shops of Tozer's, Boold's and Love – later Garratt's – but none had the gloss of the Plymouth stores. The eclipse was showing even in the 1920s.

While the women shopped on Saturdays, the men watched Plymouth Argyle, the city's one professional association football club. It had been started by old boys of Launceston College and their first match was against the school in 1885 (Argyle lost 2–0). Their treasurer lived in Argyle Terrace and green and black, still club colours, were thought to be the Scottish Argyle clan's colours. The club entered the Southern League in 1903; their first professional was Bob Jack who became their first manager and built up the famous 1920s team which was for six years runner-up in the Third Division, and reached the Second Division in 1930. A crowd of 20,000 at Home Park was normal, and big fixtures would attract 40,000. Argyle had taken over Home Park in 1901 from Devonport Albion, a rugby football club which had grown out of the Dockyard Technical College, started in the South Yard in 1846 to train marine engineers. In time the club became Plymouth Albion; Devonport Services drew on all service establishments and the RNEC produced a third first-class side. But rugby never drew crowds like Argyle.

THEATRES AND CINEMAS

After Argyle and shopping, there was the Palace Theatre of Varieties on Saturday night to make it a real day out. Opened in 1898, it mixed crimson plush and gilt with art nouveau, and after 1911 had the flamboyant Tommy Hoyle as owner. His widow kept this music hall going right into World War II with Jack Fitchett as manager for many years, and every major variety act played there season after season. For straight theatre there were the imposing Royal and the 1889 Grand Theatre, built by Henry Reed when he failed to get the lease of the Royal on the death of J. R. Newcombe, his father-in-law. By the 1920s, however, they were losing out to the cinemas. The Grand was converted in 1930 and the Royal finally succumbed a few years later, playing its last pantomime in 1936. The repertory company in the old Mechanics' Institute, launched by George S. King in 1914, bravely kept going until 1934, but by then the organiser of its supporters' club had started the Tamaritans, the amateur theatre group, and the 'Rep' died with its last prop removed. The story was the same in Devonport; the Hippodrome at the top of Fore Street switched to moving pictures, and the down-at-heel Alhambra around the corner collapsed in the late 1930s after a run of very fourth-rate touring companies.

The cinemas swamped the theatre; in the 1930s there were 250,000 picture-house seats a week and the *Western Evening Herald* was reviewing sixteen houses every Tuesday. They began to swarm from 1906-7 but by 1910 these penny gaffs were eclipsed by the picture house built in Union Street by Horace Andrews, the last manager of the great Victorian centre of entertainment, St James's Hall, which had been bought out and shut when the Palace opened. Billy Lindsell, Andrews's assistant, then established the Cinedrome in Ebrington Street and cinemas were opening further afield, the Ford Palladium before 1917 and the Belgrave (on the site of the mews which hired out tram horses) soon after. In 1918 Reuben Eady turned a skating rink in Ebrington Street into the New Palladium, a monster seating 3,500 under a corrugated iron roof which resounded like thunder in heavy rain. Various public halls were rebuilt as cinemas in 1921, like the Electric at Devonport and the Savoy in Union Street on the site of the St James's Hall. The Savoy was the elegant place in the 1920s, and the first converted for talking pictures in 1928. The other houses rapidly followed, and the wave of excitement brought new mammoth houses. In 1931 two local men, Guy Prance and William Mumford, head of the major motor firm in the town, built the 3,254-seater Regent in Frankfort Street and Gaumont-British built its 2,232-seater Gaumont Palace on the site of Andrews's picture house. The Royal Theatre was replaced by a 2,400-seater cinema in 1938 by the ABC Company who put Tom Purdie in as the first manager; he was to stay for thirty years. There was much wheeling and dealing by the big companies: the Odeon was negotiating for a Union Street site for another super-cinema but bought the Regent instead and changed its name; since 1945 that has been pulled down, the old Gaumont has become the Odeon and the Royal the ABC.

COUNTRY BUSES

The public for Argyle and the shops, the Palace, the pictures and the pubs now had a new form of transport. Plymouth Corporation bought its first twenty buses through Mumford's in 1920 to serve places like Laira and Mount Gould not reached by trams; between 1930 and 1939 it replaced all trams with buses except on the Peverell route, which survived until 1945. But in the post-1918 era there were army lorries for cheap sale and ex-army drivers needing work. The garage firms of A. C. Turner and Mumford's began building charabancs on the lorry chassis; one-man outfits began operating excursions with Princess Square as the base, and the Co-operative Society and Mumford's Purple Tours established touring fleets. Local services began as well, though the one-man outfits were gradually absorbed by the Embankment Motor Company.

Then in 1923 Commander E. T. Hare and his ex-service drivers moved into Plymouth with their Devon Motor

Transport Company and for nearly ten years they battled to win the country bus routes. There was fare cutting – 'Plympton 4d' – racing, timetable juggling and complete anarchy, with DMT from St Andrew's Cross winning the ascendancy. In 1927 it was bought out by the National Bus Company, which brought in the first covered double-deck buses, and in 1929 it amalgamated with the GW, which had bus interests in other parts of Devon and Cornwall, to form the Western National. A number of the smaller companies joined Hopper & Berryman, a Mumford concern; the 1930 Road Traffic Act brought rationalisation to the services, and within three years Western National had absorbed all its local rivals. Embankment reverted to tours only.

Apart from the local service battles, there had been much in-fighting for the new long-distance road transport, with fourteen companies running into the south-west by 1930. Fare-cutting reduced the London–Plymouth return fare at one point to 12s 6d (62½p). Plymouth was mainly served by the Royal Blue coaches from Bournemouth, which in 1934 joined a pool called Associated Motorways, so that co-ordination replaced competition. It made no difference when the Western National became owners with Southern National of the Royal Blue fleet.

NEWSPAPERS AND RADIO

Plymouth also saw newspaper competition removed in these years. There had been any number of short-lived weekly papers since the early eighteenth century, but the *Plymouth and Devonport Weekly Journal* eventually became pre-eminent, particularly after the arrival of Isaac Latimer in 1844, first as editor and eventually as proprietor. A Cornishman with national experience and a friend of Charles Dickens, he had established himself as a power in Plymouth and a leader of Liberal thought when in 1860 two Bath businessmen, William Saunders and Edmund Spender, in Plymouth considering another enterprise, decided to launch a daily paper. The establishment of the railway and the telegraph, and the imminent repeal of the tax on newspapers, all made the timing right. The *Western Morning News* appeared from a George Street office, opposite the

Theatre Royal, in January 1860. Within six months Latimer launched the rival *Western Daily Mercury* from Frankfort Street, and the weekly *Journal* soon disappeared. The *Mercury* was a Liberal paper as against the politically independent *Morning News*. Both fought for local causes and were served by distinguished journalists; if the *Morning News* could claim the first 'London Letter' and the first weather forecast in journalism, and a major part in the founding of the Press Association news agency, the *Mercury*, under Latimer's direction for thirty years, showed more dynamism. Albert Groser, editor of the *Morning News* from 1878 until his death in 1895, was a master of timetables and organisation and carried his newspaper into every corner of Devon and Cornwall.

In 1895 the young R. A. J. Walling, son of the *Mercury* editor, was invited by the new owner of that paper, Thomas Owen, to start an evening paper. It was done in great secrecy and the *Western Evening Herald* took Plymouth by surprise when it first appeared in April 1895. R. A. J. Walling was the first editor; when he moved into the *Mercury* chair his friend and colleague J. J. Judge took his place. The *Morning News* launched its own *Western Evening News* in reply but this lasted only a few months, and a revival in the Boer War lasted just a year. If there was no room in the Three Towns for two evening papers, equally the West Country could not support two morning papers. In 1921 Sir Leicester Harmsworth, brother of the press lords Northcliffe and Rothermere, bought the *Morning News* and a few months later the *Mercury*, which was running at a heavy loss, and the *Evening Herald*. The two mornings were amalgamated and published with the evening paper from the old *Mercury* office; the present *Morning News* premises are a 1936 rebuilding on the same site. Walling refused the editorship of the new *Morning News*, which James L. Palmer, the first news editor of the combined papers, rapidly assumed, and when a year later Lord Astor bought the *Western Independent*, the last surviving weekly (and still one of the only two provincial Sunday papers in England), Walling became its editor. Judge quickly left the *Herald* to join him in a partnership that lasted until 1949. During 1920, when Harmsworth was negotiating for the *Morning News*, Lord Astor considered buying the *Mercury* as he thought a Harmsworth *Morning News* would be 'politically very undependable'. After all, Leicester Harmsworth had been a Liberal MP for many years. However, his papers, though still in theory independent, became strongly Conservative and the Liberals never got over the loss of the *Mercury*. As late as 1936 Isaac Foot, doyen of West Country Liberals, thundered against 'the Harmsworth press' in Plymouth Guildhall; 'Devon is my washpot, and over Cornwall have I cast my shoe,' he accused them of thinking, in his parody of Psalm 60. But in their news columns these papers accepted their monopoly position in the region, and gave all sides a fair share of space.

Within three years of the amalgamation Plymouth had a new channel of communication with the opening of the BBC's radio station, 5PY. Its first broadcast was a concert given in Plymouth Guildhall by the Royal Marines Band on 28 March 1924. The studio proper was an upstairs room in Athenaeum Lane, a pedestrians-only link between George Street and Union Street, and the transmitting aerial was stretched between the two chimney stacks of the old sugar refinery in Mill Lane. Its children's hour made the greatest local impact, with amateur actors performing as uncles and aunts. Several of the men were in the dockyard and a taxi waited each day at 5 pm to rush them from the Fore Street gates.

CHURCH AND EDUCATION

The dream of Plymouth as the centre of a new diocese was revived in 1922 and a popular lecturer and writer, Dr J. H. B. Masterman, was actually offered the new bishopric and exchanged livings with Mr Ponsonby at Stoke. But Lord William Cecil, Bishop of Exeter since 1916, either changed his mind or forgot (his bad memory was a by-word), and Dr Masterman had to be content with becoming the first suffragan Bishop of Plymouth in 1923. On his death in 1933 he was succeeded as bishop by the Rev F. Whitfield Daukes, vicar of St Andrew's since 1924. The Rev T. Wilkinson Riddle was not far away at George Street Baptist Church; both were big, stately men and celebrated preachers who could fill their churches; their Sunday evening sermons were almost rival attractions.

Dr Masterman was also chairman of the Plymouth Committee of the University College of the South West. The aim was to create a full regional university with colleges at Exeter, Plymouth and Redruth. Lord and Lady Astor tried to force the pace by creating a hall of residence at Devonport and brought Bernard Shaw down to open it in 1929. But it was to be over twenty years before UCSW became a full university, and then it was concentrated at Exeter.

Under the impetus of Chandler Cook, the Secretary for Education, Plymouth made radical changes in its schools in the 1920s, creating junior and senior elementary schools, raising the school-leaving age to fifteen ahead of the nation, and ending secondary school fees. Much of this was negated by the 1931 depression and subsequent economies, and in 1937 the Education Committee marred its record by closing the Corporation Grammar School, the city's only co-educational establishment and descendant of the Elizabethan foundation of 1561. The last headmaster of the school, Frank Sandon, so badgered the committee about the inadequate premises that they accepted his view and closed the school.

THE APPROACH OF WAR

But sterner issues were at hand. Under the threat of Nazi Germany the dockyard was building up again with the re-armament programme. That, and falling world prices, brought a renewal of prosperity. The city had its taste of fascism with the creation in Plymouth of a strong branch of Oswald Mosley's Fascist Party. Their demonstrations brought the Plymouth Communists on the streets too; meetings broke up in brawls, and there were police baton charges outside Fascist headquarters in Lockyer Street. Thugs imported to beat up opponents finally disgraced the Fascists in local eyes and the organisation disappeared. The Munich crisis brought a scurry of activity with the mobilisation of the naval reservists. Within a few minutes of Chamberlain's broadcast on the morning of Sunday 3 September 1939 air raid sirens wailed over the city. The all-clear soon followed, but those sirens had signalled the death knell of the old city.

CHAPTER ELEVEN

DESTRUCTION AND RECONSTRUCTION: 1939–79

BLACKOUT, gas masks on shoulders, rumours, the City Museum a services recruiting centre: the war had an eerie start. Within two weeks rumour became reality. The aircraft carrier *Courageous*, Devonport-manned and with many reservists in her crew, was torpedoed at the mouth of the Channel. It made hundreds of widows in Plymouth.

The council set up a War Emergency Committee of the three party leaders, Dunstan, Churchward and Solomon Stephens. The town clerk, Colin Campbell, took over as Air Raid Precautions Officer and found little prepared, shortages all round and little money: the danger areas were supposed to be in the south-east. It was agreed that the next lord mayor should serve for the duration of the war and Lord Astor was persuaded to accept office. Alderman Modley became his deputy, and was to hold the fort loyally and modestly in Astor's absences.

Early in 1940 first *Ajax* and then *Exeter*, victors in the *Graf Spee* battle, limped into port to heroes' welcomes, with the First Lord of the Admiralty, Winston Churchill himself, down to greet *Exeter*, Devonport-built and manned. 'A flash of colour,' Winston said, but there were desperate days to come. Germany overran western Europe and Churchill became Prime Minister. As the shattered armies came out of Dunkirk nearly 80,000 French troops were brought to Plymouth and shipped back to western France to continue the struggle. Before the last had gone the civilian refugees from western France were crowding into the Sound in all shapes and sizes of craft. The 1st Division of the Canadian Army was embarked at Millbay for France, and disembarked, and a fresh wave of refugees poured in from St Nazaire and the Biscay ports – French and British civilians and units of the British Expeditionary Force. The greatest test for the Plymouth emergency services were the thousands of survivors of the liner *Lancastria*, sunk from the air off St Nazaire with an estimated 3,000 killed – nearly the worst marine disaster of all time.

France surrendered on 25 June, and the German Air Force was now just across the Channel. Within a fortnight the first bombs fell on Plymouth, killing three people at Swilly. The raids went on all that summer, while the Battle of Britain raged to the east. Mount Batten, which had been taken over by No 10 Squadron of the Royal Australian Air Force on 1 April, was among the targets. Men flocked to join the new Home Guard and an Invasion Committee began planning resistance.

Plymouth had twenty-one raids by the end of October and then the Luftwaffe switched its main offensive from London to the munition towns and ports. The pattern was set at Coventry; the raids on Plymouth grew heavier and at the end of the month the oil tanks at Turnchapel were hit and burned for days, marking the city by day with a vast pillar of smoke and floodlighting it with flames at night. Hospitals were hit, gas supplies cut, electricity intermittent; hardly an area was free from damage. The death-roll was mounting. The city was already so stricken that the King and Queen came down on 20 March, and there was an alert before they had left.

That night, and the next night, the heart of Plymouth was wiped out. Three hundred and thirty-six civilians were killed. High explosives cut the water mains and incendiaries completed the damage. The ARP control had to abandon their headquarters in the cells under the Guildhall when the building above them was burnt out. From Drake Circus to the Octagon just a few modern buildings were left in the devastation. Twenty thousand properties were destroyed or damaged.

For a month Plymouth struggled to recover. Only the shopping centres of Devonport and Mutley Plain survived, and every kind of administration had to find a new home. There were a few raids to keep nerves on edge, and every night people who had no duty in the city made their way out into the countryside around. Then for five nights out of nine at the end of April the bombers were back in force, completing the destruction of central Plymouth, flattening the heart of Devonport, severely damaging the South Yard of the dockyard and the Naval Barracks, wrecking whole blocks in every residential suburb. Five hundred and ninety civilians were killed, even more injured, and an unknown number lost without trace. One thousand five hundred dwellings were destroyed or damaged beyond repair, and another 15,000 damaged.

How much death and damage the services suffered has remained hidden. In his war history Churchill said that the dockyard was saved by false fires, at the expense of the city. Mass Observation, a survey group working for the government, upset the Cabinet by reporting that at Plymouth, where the civil and domestic devastation and the dislocation of everyday life exceeded anything they had seen elsewhere, panic lay close behind the surface of local confidence. It was the chaotic and primitive flight of evacuees (to use their words) that most upset these observers. Yet in these raids there was a warden service alone of 2,500, nearly all part-time, and a normal 90 per cent turn-out in raids. The untrained were better out of the city; for those who stayed it was a time of terror, and much heroism.

The French writer André Savignon, winner of the *Prix Goncourt*, went through the Plymouth Blitz. Even before the March raids he wrote of 'the almost physical impression that a city is slipping away from under one's very feet'. Of dawn on 21 March he wrote, 'in this town that was wasting away in reddish trails of smoke, only a few citizens wandered: the others were still in hiding; or lay, all distress ended, under the ruins'. That evening: 'The silence returned, but not to last. A great breath of fear soughed through the town: "they" were coming.' Later: 'Ashes, mud, dust . . . this poignant acrid smell . . . this effluvia of death.' As night fell in Plymouth in those Blitz days it was unnerving to walk the narrow path between the shattered buildings of once fine streets, frightening in their emptiness. Those who were staying were snatching sleep before the bombers came; those who could were walking, or waiting silently for lorries, on the main roads out of town. Stanley Goodman has written of leaving the burning YMCA on the night of 20 March:

Nobody wanted to move much because the noise outside was hellish, but we did file out through the broken front . . . to find that the whole of Spooners on the opposite side of the road was alight. It was burning steadily and evenly like the wide wick of an oil lamp with a great crackle and roar, and the heat was so great that we could not look at it . . . it was lighter than day and great bombs were falling every few seconds.'

He then went off to look for his bicycle!

On 1 May it was decided to evacuate the children: whole schools were moved. On 2 May Winston Churchill came down to cheer the people. Air-raid victims were buried at Efford cemetery in a common grave. Dancing was started every evening on the Hoe. A fighter airfield was constructed at Yelverton, the rubble of destroyed Plymouth the foundation for its runways, and opened by 15 August. As a direct result of the Plymouth experience, where fire brigades from other towns stood by helpless because their equipment would not fit that of Plymouth, or anywhere else, the National Fire Service was set up. Plymouth's balloon barrage and the gun defences were strengthened, the ARP strength built up to 3,500. ARP control, burnt out again, found a third base at Pounds House, as did the town clerk's office. The administration found homes in many queer places, and the big shops were spread from Drake Circus to Hyde Park Corner. Raids continued for the rest of the year, on a lesser scale, and then for 1942 the city was left in comparative peace. It was needed.

Not until February 1943 did Germany change its tactics again and resume night bombing, but now defences were stronger, and a number of times the citizens saw enemy planes shot down. That spring 29 Division of the United States Army was garrisoned in Plymouth and the American Navy established a Cattewater base from Sutton Pool to Laira Bridge. They increased the polyglot population of wartime Plymouth, which already had Free French, Dutch, Norwegian and Polish servicemen – even Spanish refugees from the Civil War. The Americans set up their own anti-aircraft guns around the city and on city bomb sites and constructed camps and embarkation hards on every waterfront. The Second Front, the way back, was imminent.

With the new confidence the children were coming back, to the embarrassment of the education authority. By midsummer 8,000 of the evacuated 12,000 were home again. There were still air raids, some of them sharp, but the last – though Plymouth could not know it then – came on 30 April 1944. The waterfront and railway lines were the main targets. Nine people were killed in Plymouth, eighteen at Oreston.

The fleet for the invasion of Europe was already building up, and V and VII Corps of General Omar Bradley's 1st US Army embarked at Plymouth for the bloody landings on Tuesday 6 June at Omaha and Utah beaches. After the initial bombardments some of the American battleships came into the dockyard for repair, including the *Arkansas* which had been in the Sound only a few years earlier on a courtesy visit. By the beginning of August the armies were breaking out of Normandy, by the end they were over the Seine and the war was moving eastwards. In September Plymouth relaxed the blackout, in November the Home Guard stood down, and on 8 May 1945 Plymouth joined in the celebrations of Victory in Europe. It was time to count the cost.

There had been 602 air raid alerts, 59 actual bombing attacks, 1,172 civilians killed and altogether 4,448 civilian casualties. Apart from the two main shopping centres, two guildhalls, a theatre, 6 hotels, 8 cinemas, 26 schools, 41 churches and 100 public houses, 3,754 houses had gone and another 18,389 were in need of major repair. All told the houses damaged – not counting just broken windows – were 72,102, more than the number of houses in the city because many had been damaged more than once. So many people had been forced to find homes out of the city that the population was down from 208,000 to 127,000.

THE PLAN FOR PLYMOUTH

The planning for the future had already been done. Lord Astor and Colin Campbell had begun talking of the need for it within days of the end of the Blitz, but who was to do it? The officers were fully stretched with a myriad new problems, and exhausted. Jamie Paton Watson, city engineer since 1938, was the obvious man but Lord Astor wanted the most eminent authority possible and called in as consultant Professor Patrick Abercrombie, who was already working on a plan for Greater London. Lord Astor's value to Plymouth throughout his long association was his intellect and his knowledge of people and developments in high places. The limelight always was Lady Astor's, who could inspire but also infuriate. The strength was in her husband.

Paton Watson produced a mass of plans. Abercrombie came down, walked the city alone and studied the schemes, and the result was an amalgam of several Watson plans. Paton Watson later said there were thirty-seven drafts, and that his job in all the talking was to keep his poet–architect partner's feet on the ground. *The Plan for Plymouth* was published in 1943, and approved by the council in principle in August 1944. It had to deal not just with war damage but with all the pre-war defects of the city. A quarter of the working-class population had still been overcrowded before the war, twice as many as in Liverpool. The horse-age streets were already saturated with motor traffic; St Andrew's Cross had the highest traffic density in southern England outside London.

Abercrombie was not just the doyen of town planners but the virtual father of the Council for the Preservation of Rural England and his plan was for a region, with a central city and satellite towns, each a self-contained residential district with all social facilities and industries, a minor version of his Greater London Plan from which emerged the New Towns of post-war England. His area stretched from Portwrinkle on the west through Pillaton, Plaster Down, Burrator, Cadover and Hemerdon to the mouth of the Yealm. The towns were to be separated by green belts and Dudley Stamp the great geographer did the land utilisation study for the agricultural areas. They were not planning for any population increase but to give the people proper amenities. It was not as big an area as that which the present-day Department of Employment calls the 'Plymouth-Travel-to-Work-Area'.

The city put this up to the Boundary Commission, who turned it down. Had it been accepted it would have obviated all the turmoil which preceded the 1951 boundary extension which moved Plymouth's boundary north to the Tamerton–Roborough–Plym Bridge line, and the 1967 extension which brought in Plympton and Plymstock: it would also have obviated the black comedy of all those people west of the Tamar who live off Plymouth and shout like Cornish nationalists. But by 1967 Plymouth had incorporated all its new suburbs save Saltash and Torpoint, and covered 19,936 acres.

BUILDING THE HOUSES

Before anything else Plymouth wanted homes. The ultimate target to replace the war-destroyed and the pre-war substandards was put at 20,000; the immediate need was as many roofs as soon as possible. Prefabricated buildings served the stopgap purpose, and the thousandth 'prefab' was occupied by November 1946. It was a crash programme and the driving force was W. A. Miller, a Labour veteran first elected to the council in 1925. Grandson of a freed slave, this dockyard electrician had himself been bombed out of East Street, Stonehouse, where he was born. When the Labour Party won its first-ever majority on the city council in November 1945, 'Darkie' Miller became chairman of housing, and it became his life's work: he even refused the lord mayoralty in 1947 so that he could stay at the job. Harold Pattinson, who took the housing chair when the Conservatives were in power, had also been born in a poor home, in the north of England, but he came to Plymouth in 1940 as an insurance company branch manager with a house in Mannamead. Fire guard organiser during the war, his ambition when in office was to build more houses than Miller. From 1951 to 1957 over a thousand permanent council houses were built each year.

The first estate started was Efford, in December 1945, closely followed by Ham, Honicknowle, King's Tamerton, Pennycross, Ernesettle and Whitleigh. In the 1950s smaller developments were started at Manadon Vale and the Barbican, with Southway and Egg Buckland started in the early 1960s.

The major estates were laid out on the lines of the Plan, acquiring in time their own schools, shopping centres, churches, and public houses. Ham, in the parkland around the old home of the Trelawny family, became a showpiece and the only blot was the seventeenth-century mansion at its heart, still decaying and neglected. By 1964 Plymouth had passed its housing target with 2,250 prefabs, which the corporation was beginning to replace, 13,542 permanent council houses, 853 permanent houses built by the Admiralty and 3,586 built by private enterprise: a total of 20,231. Apart from the estates there were medium-rise blocks of flats in central areas and three tower blocks at Devonport. Since then housing has been developing at Chaddlewood, Leigham, Estover, Mainstone and Bellever, and a start has been made on modernising the older, structurally sound houses in central areas. By 1978 the corporation stock of houses of all kinds totalled 23,881. Some of these had been built by Plympton RDC and taken over.

In the early 1960s too the Ministry of Defence found a great need for service quarters as overseas bases began to close down. By 1978 the ministry had 4,489 married quarters in the Plymouth area, of which nearly 4,000 were for naval families. Over 1,500 houses were bought from private developers so that service families should be mixed into the civilian population.

Since the war about 19,500 houses have been built in the present city area by private developers, but twice as many have gone up in the Plympton–Plymstock area as in the pre-1967 city. In 1951–64 alone 4,652 private houses were built in that area. The estates, council and private, are still spreading but there is still much sharing of houses. In 1971 10.5 per cent of the houses in Plymouth were occupied by more than one family.

THE DOCKYARD AND THE SERVICES

The replanning of Plymouth was bedevilled for years by the indecision of the Admiralty. In 1939 it had been finding the dockyard cramped and had acquired Keyham Quarry for new building, and taken over the Gun Wharf from the War Office and rechristened it Morice Yard. War damage sent various departments to odd corners of Plymouth and the neighbouring countryside; even Buckland Abbey became a stores depot. The Americans had set up a hutted camp in the ruins of Fore Street.

In 1945 the Admiralty wanted an extra 220 acres, with an irregular perimeter that had Paton Watson tearing his hair. The new party leaders on the council were Harry Mason, a dockyardee, and Clifford Tozer, a Devonport shopkeeper and last survivor of Devonport Town Council, neither conditioned by his background to fighting the Admiralty. The extension area kept changing but by 1950 the final decision was reached, just 50 acres. Mainly it was the Fore Street area and another outside the old Keyham gates, the eventual destruction of which was possibly the biggest loss. But in spite of all fears the yard kept busy. For many years there were major refits to the big aircraft carriers and by the time they were being phased out Devonport had been established as the biggest of all naval dockyards. When the last carrier, HMS *Ark Royal*, was paid off in the Hamoaze in December 1978 there was a nuclear submarine base in the Keyham Extension and a massive frigate refit complex just north of the Torpoint Ferry which could take three Advanced Leander class frigates into dry dock, all standing, under cover. The two developments had cost £83 million, and the annual yard wage bill was over £50 million. Apart from these major developments in 1975-7 there has been an extensive new building programme over the years of offices, engineering shops and warehouses. In 1963-4 flyover bridges linked all three yards by road.

The navy was also spreading its wings. In the 1950s a new Royal Naval Engineering College was built at Manadon, with the old mansion turned into the captain's house. In 1959 the Royal Dockyard College moved into the vacated Keyham college. The hutted camps built west of Torpoint during the war became HMS *Raleigh*, training all new entrants to the navy, and HMS *Fisgard*, training the artificers. A gunnery range set up at Wembury in 1940 was built up to become HMS *Cambridge* in 1956, the Naval Gunnery School. In 1970 the Royal Naval Barracks were extensively modernised with new blocks.

In 1971 the last infantry battalion marched out of Plymouth and the army had virtually departed. Raglan Barracks had been demolished in 1969 and in the next few years service married quarters were built there, with only the imposing gateway left as a monument. Crownhill (Plumer) Barracks had already been torn down to make way for a dual carriageway out of Plymouth. But in 1973 the city became the Royal Marine commando base, with headquarters at Mount Wise and commandos at Stonehouse, Seaton Barracks (the 1914 hutted camp at Crownhill, rebuilt between the wars), and Bickleigh (a World War II hutted camp, rebuilt since). A commando regiment of the Royal Artillery normally occupies the Citadel. Even before the soldiers, most of the airmen had left. Flying boats died with the end of the war, and though Mount Batten remained the headquarters of No 19 Group RAF Coastal Command, that too went in 1968 leaving only marine craft and some small units. The service element has changed all round, but by no means disappeared. The biggest change to the appearance of the city is the absence of uniforms from the streets; for apart from the new entrants of the Torpoint establishments all servicemen wear civilian clothes when out of barracks.

THE CITY CENTRE

From the start Paton Watson expected the dockyard to swallow up the old Devonport shopping area and planned the new city with one centre, having room for all the shops, administrative and business premises. Only a handful of buildings survived in working order in the area and so he swept away the old outgrown street plan and designed a new city heart. The grid pattern he based on two main axes, a north–south line (Armada Way) from Cobourg Street to the Hoe, and an east–west line (Royal Parade) from St Andrew's Cross to the eastern end of Union Street. Municipal offices, banks and the like were to be south of Royal Parade, and the shopping area to the north. An inner ring road was to enclose the whole, leaving just local traffic in the streets. Armada Way brought the green slopes of the Hoe down into the centre after it had been lost behind houses for a century or so, and the Royal Naval War Memorial on the Hoe made a focal point. Paton Watson even persuaded the Imperial War Graves Commission to pattern their additions to the memorial to complement his plan, and the now nationalised railways to build a tower block at the station to set off the other end.

The 1944 Planning Act was specifically designed to enable bombed towns to control redevelopment, and Plymouth was the first to take advantage of it. Preliminary notice was given for

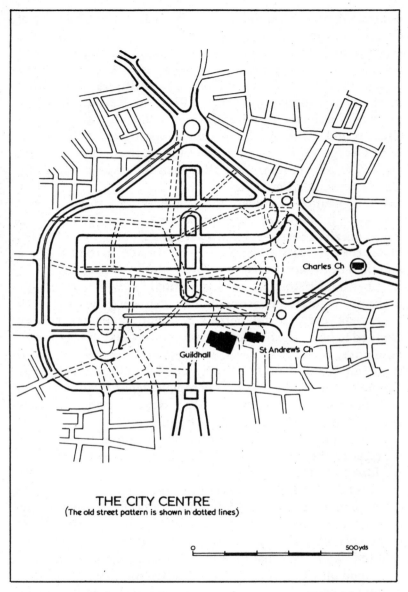

THE CITY CENTRE
(The old street pattern is shown in dotted lines)

0   500 yds

THE CITY CENTRE. *The layout of the city centre, superimposed on the old street plan.*

Declaratory Area No 1 in February 1946, which sought the compulsory purchase of 178 acres in the city centre at 1939 values. (A similar procedure was used to obtain the housing estates.) A public inquiry was held at which the Chamber of Commerce was the main opponent; when the order was granted the chamber appealed to the High Court and not until that appeal was withdrawn on 10 February 1947 could the city go ahead. The first kerbstone of the new city was laid on the morning of Monday 17 March 1947, in Raleigh Lane. It survives – wrongly dated 21.3.47 – in the edging of Derry's Cross roundabout. Work went on so fast that on 29 October King George VI dedicated the flagstaff set in a reproduction of Drake's Drum at the Armada Way–Royal Parade crossing, the formal ceremonial opening.

Colin Campbell's was the legal brain which guided Plymouth through the maze of new legislation. A new chief officer post had been created, Estates and Development Valuer, to buy the mass of bits and pieces which made up the 178 acres, and then negotiate the leasing of new sites to developers. W. K. Shepherd, a Bristol man, was appointed in 1946, borrowing a desk and creating a department as he went along: he was to stay twenty-six years. He did more for Plymouth than has ever been credited to him. The first major decision was that the big stores, Popham's, Spooner's, Yeo's, Dingle's and the Co-op, should stand on Royal Parade roughly on their old sites. In 1951 Dingle's opened, the first new complete departmental store to be rebuilt in the country. By 1955 Royal Parade and New George Street were 80 per cent completed.

It was time to be rehousing the city's administration. For years after the war argument raged as to whether the 1870 Guildhall should be rebuilt or completely replaced. A new city architect, H. J. W. Stirling, arrived in 1950 and won acceptance for a plan that kept the Guildhall exterior to comfort the sentimentalists and gave a modern interior without the defects of the old hall. He was a sensitive artist whose work was always civilised and well-mannered. A co-ordinating committee examined all city centre plans submitted and tried to balance one building with another; it was vital but was producing monotonous results. Portland stone was being insisted upon; there was for instance a great battle with Montague Burton, who wanted their standard black exterior, and Burton's had to give way. Stirling managed to some extent to liberate the architects, though he was never strong enough to manage committees well. His greatest achievement was to break away from the blocks-round-a-courtyard concept which Paton Watson had sketched in for the municipal buildings, and persuade the council to adopt the city's first high-rise building, of fourteen storeys. Its height and whole approach dramatised the civil engineer's stolid masses of even roof levels. In the end, because Stirling's department was so loaded with work, the design was completed by Alan Ballantyne of Messrs Jellicoe Ballantyne and Coleridge.

In 1959 the rebuilt Guildhall was opened by Field-Marshal Lord Montgomery and that year the new Pannier Market, designed by Walls & Pearn with an exciting roof, was also in business. The Queen opened the new Civic Centre in 1962 and the following year Lord Denning, Master of the Rolls, opened the new Law Courts which, with the Guildhall and Civic Centre, completed the administrative precinct. Since 1972 the Law Courts have been the home of the newly-created Plymouth Crown Court and 3 Elliot Terrace, the Astor home which they left to the city, has been the Judges' Lodgings. New magistrates' courts in St Andrew's Street were opened in 1979.

The shopping area gradually spread northwards up the hill. There was a long delay before the pedestrian-only shopping complex was completed at Drake Circus in 1971, but with this the new city centre was virtually complete. No one really thought when the Plan was produced that twenty-five years would see this done, or with so few departures from the original concept. There have been modifications and new thinking. The new city can be exposed to wind and rain as the old streets never were, but it is efficient and is growing its own personality. What is more, it is all on land owned by the city.

Of the big stores Popham's alone failed, though Dingle's took it over and tried for some years to keep it alive. When Edwin Beckley retired in 1964 he sold John Yeo's to Debenham's whose then chairman, John Bedford, had been a next-door neighbour for years when he was managing Spooner's. In 1977 both stores were renamed Debenham's. Dingle's had grown and built up an empire of stores through the west of England, mainly under the leadership of Wesley Brimacombe, who had first left his Cornish village to be a draper's apprentice in Plymouth. When in 1971 Dingle's was taken over by the House of Fraser, Brimacombe joined the central board, and of the great stores only the Co-op remained in local hands. Coster's closed down in 1978 when Geoffrey Leatherby retired. Of the major Devonport shops, only Tozer's made the move to the new city centre, but it closed down in 1971.

With the increased mobility of the motor car Plymouth built up its strength as a regional shopping centre, and as new shopping centres developed at Plymstock Broadway, Plympton Ridgeway and Estover, and the older centres of Mutley Plain and St Budeaux maintained their strength, so more and more food shops in the city centre gave way to what the planners called 'sophisticated durable goods'. But what shops remained at Devonport became just neighbourhood shops: Stonehouse had never had anything more.

THE NEW FACTORIES

As early as 1942 the Chamber of Commerce was saying that more industry would be wanted in Plymouth after the war, and was bewailing the departure of so many firms. Reckitt's, for instance, lost its factory in 1941 and resolved to concentrate on Hull. By 1943 the city labour force had been reduced by 10,000 as a direct result of the bombing. At the end of the war the dockyard was employing 17,793 people but this figure was bound to fall – in fact it was down to 15,338 by 1950.

In 1946 the Board of Trade sent three firms looking for new factories to Plymouth. They were found sites – Tecalemit, lubrication engineers, at Marsh Mills; Rank, makers of television sets, at Ernesettle; and Berketex, dressmakers, at Honicknowle. They were all in business by 1948 and grew rapidly: by 1978 they were employing 5,000 people between them.

In 1953 Sir Colin Campbell (he had been knighted the previous year) retired and his successor, Stuart Lloyd Jones, arrived from prosperous and booming Nottingham. In spite of the massive building programme in the city centre and in housing he found unemployment twice that of the national figure. The city was still heavily dependent on the dockyard. He made the economy his major concern and found an ally in Dick Shepherd, who had broken the back of the city centre sites. They began an advertising campaign, earmarked more land for industry at Burrington, Southway and Estover, and in 1957 three more new arrivals, C. & J. Clark, shoemakers, Slumberland mattresses and Browne & Sharpe machine tools were settled at Crownhill and Ernesettle. This group was to produce eventually 1,400 jobs.

Then, because of the high unemployment, in 1958 Plymouth was given Development Area status, which meant government aid to firms moving in. This, on top of the local initiative, brought seventeen more factories and when they were all in production over 10,000 new jobs had been created. Over half were for women, but there had been little local tradition for women to work, and this did bring the number of women in work up to the national norm. The number of jobs estimated by the incoming firms was always optimistic and because of these inflated figures Plymouth ceased to be a Development Area in October 1960. In fact the unemployment figure never fell as had been forecast. The need for work remained.

In spite of strenuous efforts in the next four years only one new factory was won (Jaeger's clothing in Union Street), although a number were extended. The takeover of Plympton brought the Newnham industrial estate into the city, but Fine Tubes stood in solitary state at Estover. Constant pressure eventually wheedled Intermediate Development Area status out of Whitehall in 1969, which meant grants on a lesser scale than before, but still grants. In 1970 Wrigley's chewing gum factory was in operation at Estover and by 1972 another eight were coming, mainly for Estover. Nearly 3,000 people were working there, in sixteen factories, by 1978. In contrast Newnham had as many establishments but smaller, employing just under 700. All told Plymouth had 65 new factories, 14 American-controlled and one, Rank, in part-Japanese ownership.

The post-1974 recession saw many of the new plants cutting back, and from a peak of about 15,000 the numbers employed there were down to just over 12,000 by 1978. The total unemployed, nearly 10,000, was 9 per cent of the labour force. But the eggs were no longer in one basket. In ministry classifications shipbuilding now employs 13 per cent, the shops 13 per cent, manufacturing 12 per cent and building 8 per cent. Inevitably the construction industry has been a major employer and some Plymouth firms, like Dudley Coles, builders, and Blight & White, steel construction engineers, have had contracts right across the south of England.

Apart from attracting factories as sources of employment, Plymouth also tried very hard to get one of the new universities but had to settle for a polytechnic. It has had more success in bringing office work to the city but the towering city centre office blocks have not pleased everyone. Equally a great many people echo the sentiments of the Plan, that growth is not for the city's good, but this concept is ruthlessly pushed in all future planning.

THE PORT

With the end of the war the ocean liners were moving back into Plymouth Sound as if the world was unchanged. But mail contracts were already going to the new air routes and though the Plymouth total built up to 437,000 bags in 1949 there were no more contracts going to shipping companies. Mail figures began falling but passenger numbers still climbed, to a peak in 1955 of 187 ships calling and 29,000 passengers through the port. Then jet aircraft began to make trans-Atlantic air traffic reasonable, the liner trade fell off, and one by one the tenders went out of service. All the big ships had come again, and gone, and last-ditch efforts to make cruising liners take their place came to naught. The last tender was laid up in 1963, and an epoch had ended.

Yet ten years later, with Britain's entry into the Common Market, a French company from Roscoff began a cross-Channel service. A million-pound roll-on-roll-off jetty was built in Millbay Docks and what had been intended primarily as a freight service became so popular that by 1977 there were three ships, serving St Malo as well and carrying 200,000 passengers in the year, about five times as many as in the palmiest days of liner traffic. But in 1976 the Frenchmen also opened a Portsmouth–St Malo service which they envisage as becoming more important than Plymouth–Roscoff. In 1978 an additional service was added from Plymouth to northern Spain. In 1977 Millbay Docks handled 309,000 tonnes of cargo, 109,000 more than in the last pre-ferry year, but it was all lorry-borne, going straight through the city.

In fact the total tonnage through the port that year was 79,000 tonnes down on 1972, and basically it consisted of grain for the silo built beside West Wharf, Millbay, during the war, house coal into Sutton Harbour, petrol to Cattedown Wharves and china clay out from Victoria Wharves. The last Coast Lines vessel used Victoria Wharves in 1967. A second Plymouth power station had been built at Prince Rock in 1945–51 but by 1967 its coal was coming in by rail and now it is virtually in reserve. Another power station planned near Millbrook was first going to be nuclear-powered, then oil-fired, and by 1978 the plan was abandoned. The old-style gasworks using coal at Coxside was closed in 1969, two years after a new gas plant using oil distillate opened in the old Breakwater Quarry at Pomphlett. After a few years that was stopped with the piping in of North Sea gas, but is is kept on standby in case oil is found in the south-west approaches. Such a find might revitalise the port, just as the new road planned to link all the Cattewater wharves will make them more efficient.

Fishing had a quick revival after the war, with the 1947 landings up to the 1927 figures. By 1963 however the fleet was down to half a dozen trawlers. The 1967 extension of territorial waters to twelve miles brought a revival and the Sutton Harbour company modernised the fish quay that year. New fishing methods brought increasingly larger landings, the entry into the Common Market opened European markets, and by 1977 the fleet was up to 150 vessels with such congestion that Coxside Creek, Millbay and Cattedown were being used to land catches. Ocean-going craft from the north which had been driven from Icelandic waters were joining in a mackerel boom and 1978 landings were 46,000 tonnes, valued at £4.6 million. How long stocks would stand up to this kind of depredation was another matter.

Yatching too boomed. In addition to the bi-annual Fastnet Race the Royal Western, which had absorbed the breakaway Royal South-Western Yacht Club, launched the Single-handed Transatlantic Race and a Round Britain Race, and welcomed Francis Chichester back from his epic single-handed voyage round the world. Each race crowds Millbay inner basin with a world fleet of yachts. Sutton Harbour established a marina in 1972 which by 1974 had pontoon berths for 200 yachts, and at Ocean Quay another marina was opened in 1973 with over 200 berths, all filled, backed by a block of eighty-two luxury flats. So the port has a vitality which brings employment and considerable cash, even if the pattern has radically changed.

COMMUNICATIONS

The railway network, unnecessarily complicated by the railway rivalries, had been shrinking since 1930 when the suburban services began to wither and the halts closed down. The war saw the veteran Mutley station close in 1939 and Millbay in 1941; post-war years saw the branch lines going down to the competition of first buses and then private cars. The Yealmpton line went in 1947, Turnchapel in 1951 and Tavistock in 1963. That year saw the Beeching Report urging concentration on main-line traffic.

The old LSW lines had become part of the Southern Railway in 1922 and Southern Region under nationalisation; in 1963 all their West Country lines passed to Western Region. The last passenger train to Exeter on the LSW route was in 1968, though the line to Bere Alston and the branch to Calstock remained open. North Road station's temporary wooden buildings of the 1877 rush were finally rebuilt in 1956–61 and renamed 'Plymouth' in 1958, when Friary became a goods depot. By 1971 all the quayside railways to Stonehouse, Sutton Harbour and Millbay, which had caused so much strife, were closed, and in 1975 the railway embankment from North Road to Millbay was removed, opening a vista lost for over a century. Plymouth is now only a major station on the main Penzance–Paddington line, but the best trains reach London in

$3\frac{1}{2}$ hours and a faster service still is promised.

For twenty-five years after the war Plymouth dreamed of a better airport than the grass field at Roborough. A Bill was promoted in Parliament to acquire the wartime aerodrome at Harrowbeer but the Lords rejected that in 1961. The target then became the wartime barrage balloon headquarters at Collaton Cross, but that was killed because it would interfere with the naval gunnery school at Wembury. A third plan for Winston Beacon, west of Saltash, roused Cornish tempers and finally in 1974 it was agreed that Roborough could be improved after all. Plym Bridge Lane was closed to lengthen the runway, but modernisation was minimal. Various small companies had worked airlines since the war of which Brymon, which began operations in 1972, is still in being and expanding. In 1978 Brymon carried over 60,000 passengers.

The road traffic problem was obvious to Paton Watson when he came to Plymouth in 1936 and by the following year he had plotted and preserved from development a route from Marsh Mills to Saltash Passage. This was shown in the 1943 Plan as the northern ring road, and the basis of the city centre plan was an inner ring road which would keep through traffic out of the shopping and administrative areas. The Ministry of Transport cut Paton Watson's main artery, Royal Parade, down to half the width he planned but otherwise he drove ahead, bullying Whitehall and the council where necessary, starting roads before obtaining ministry permission in some cases, bulldozing his way on.

The first move for a Tamar road bridge came from Cornwall County Council and together that council and Plymouth finally built it in 1959–61 as a toll bridge in the absence of government money. Two months after the Queen Mother opened the Tamar Bridge a new Laira Bridge was opened, replacing Rendel's Iron Bridge. The third and greatest road achievement was getting the M5 motorway extended from Bristol to Exeter, and the A38 on to Plymouth made a dual carriageway of near-motorway standard. By May 1977 Plymouth was finally linked to the national motorway system: the city was no longer at the end of 'the longest country lane in England'. The Roscoff ferry and local industry gain, and there is one more inducement to industry to move to the area. But forty years on there is still opposition to the northern ring road, though a start seems imminent. The Tamar Bridge is already taxed by its traffic load, and a better road west out of Saltash desperately overdue.

SOCIAL LIFE

Public and social life was slow to return after the war, but then most of the old centres had gone. The city council was meeting in the Art Gallery, mayor-choosing had to be in the Central Hall, and the first large-scale balls had to make the most of the Tecalemit canteen or the RNEC gymnasium at Manaton.

For years the area within the roofless walls of St Andrew's Church was laid out with lawns and flower beds; not until 1957 was rebuilding completed and the church rededicated. Charles was left in ruins, isolated at the centre of a roundabout as a memorial to the war dead. With few people left living in the city centre there was little need of downtown churches and those that were rebuilt had new sites. King Street Methodist Church is now in the Crescent, Old George Street Baptist Church in Catherine Street, and the Roman Catholics show their flag in the city centre with the Church of Christ the King on Armada Way. The new churches are properly on the new estates, though some with old names; St James-the-Less from the Hoe and Morice Baptist Church from Devonport, for example, are both at Ham. Dwindling congregations have reduced the need for the Victorian plethora of churches and the Methodists in 1975 set about cutting down to new conditions. Mutley, Greenbank and Embankment Road are among the best-known churches now closed.

Again in education the new need was on the estates and there in the main have gone the rebuilt primary schools. With the new ideas in education the old elementary schools became 'secondary moderns', but the long resistance of the local Tories to the comprehensive idea makes Plymouth one of the last strongholds of grammar schools in England. Because of the uncertainty most of them still struggle on in antiquated buildings, though Plympton and Plymstock had 'gone comprehensive' before being taken into the city.

The new Polytechnic, which also embraced the fast-growing School of Navigation and stretches from the old 'Tec' site right across Portland Square, was started in 1965. Its School of Art moved into a new building below the Central Library in 1978 and the former Technical College, now a College of Further Education and incorporating the Dockyard Technical College, moved to a new building on the old Devonport Southern station, opposite Devonport Technical College, in 1974–5. The Derriford site earmarked for the university that never came was taken over by the teacher's training college of St Mark and St John, which arrived from Chelsea in 1971, soon to be crippled by government cuts in the numbers of teachers wanted. A multi-million-pound complex was also opened in 1977 at West Hoe for the Government-funded Institute for Marine Environmental Research, whose oceanologists complement the work of the Marine Biological Association.

On another Derriford site the new Plymouth General Hospital is going up, reduced to 890 beds from the 1,750 planned back in 1971. Freedom Fields, Greenbank and Mount Gould will serve as branches of the new scheme but Devonport is scheduled to close and the Lockyer Street hospital is already closed.

A powerful force in the post-war city has been the Guild of Social Service, which grew out of the Civic Guild of Help founded in 1907 to co-ordinate the work of the various Plymouth charities. J. P. Brown and his son C. P. Brown, between them, were the chairmen for forty years; the guild's work expanded vastly in World War II with the drive of Ernest English as secretary, and since the war it has helped in almost every facet of welfare and communal life.

The theatres and cinemas that survived the war have since suffered the onslaughts of television and bingo. The BBC's Broadcasting House is a Victorian villa in Seymour Road and commercial television comes from Westward's 1961 building at Derry's Cross, shaping as the entertainment centre of the city. The Athenaeum, rebuilt at the same time on its old site and next door to Westward, gave most of its interior to a modern theatre which it was hoped that Westward TV would use for its productions. It was a false hope but has given the city a decent small theatre. The corporation provided first a tent theatre on the Hoe, replaced by a 'temporary' building which has steadily become more permanent, doing more damage to its surroundings than good to the community. A real theatre has long been the city's aim but demands from the amateur operatic companies for a 1,500-seater, against all modern provincial experience, so confused the issue that only after ten years was the Derry's Cross site fenced off. In 1972 the corporation set up, on a shoestring budget, a Plymouth Theatre Company which has come through with improving productions and audiences. The argument did, however, revive the Palace Theatre with live theatre in 1979: it had closed in 1959 to become a bingo hall and nightclub. Plymouth also acquired two or three other nightclubs, mainly run by Greek Cypriots, after gambling was legalised. Against this the Arts Centre in Looe Street which grew out of a wartime cultural centre set up by the Astors has been a boon to the young, and the amatuer theatre companies still flourish.

Three big cinemas survived the bombing and the Drake at Derry's Cross was built in 1958 to cater for the then novel wide screen. Of the survivors the Odeon/Regent was pulled down in 1963 and Littlewood's store in New George Street was built on the site. In 1975–6 the ABC/Royal, the Odeon/Gaumont and the Drake were all carved into two- or three-screen cinemas, and of the outer houses only the Plaza and Belgrave keep going. The regular queues of the 1930s are rare now, even as the huge crowds at Argyle have fallen to the thousands rather than the tens of thousands. The club in 1962–3 was still in Division Two and talking about the First Division but has been back in Division Three for most of the time since. Boardroom battles and sackings of managers have all added to the excitement.

Plymouth gained its first indoor swimming bath with the building of the Ballard Youth Centre near Derry's Cross, and a second larger indoor pool in Central Park. Close by a covered sports centre grew out of the 1970 Mayflower celebrations, but it has not all been gain. Of Central Park's original 234 acres, only half remain as open space. Perhaps Plymouth's lung is now Dartmoor, designated a National Park in 1951, and with Buckland Abbey, Saltram and Antony all now in National

Trust hands (as is Drake's Island) those parks and gardens provide outdoor recreation. Mount Edgcumbe Park became a Country Park in 1975, administered jointly by Plymouth and Cornwall County Council. The earl retains Mount Edgcumbe House and the Carew-Poles still live at Antony, but the Morleys have moved from Saltram to Pounds House, Yelverton. Both Lord Mount Edgcumbe and Lord Morley continue the active role of their predecessors in Plymouth life.

Plymouth also administers Buckland Abbey as a Drake Museum and Drake's Island as an adventure training centre, and all these facilities swell the city's growing share in the tourist industry of Devon and Cornwall, the most popular British holiday area. The pre-war hotels flourish, with the Grand on the Hoe owned by the millionaire Berni brothers who in the mid-1930s started with a little all-night coffee shop in Courtenay Street and another in Exeter. The number of small hotels and boarding houses has multiplied, and on the Hoe the Holiday Inn and Trust House–Forte's Mayflower Post Hotel, both opened in 1970, have set new standards in comfort and size.

POLITICS AND LOCAL GOVERNMENT

By mid-1944 the end of the war was in sight. Politicians began flexing their muscles again. Lord Astor was glad enough to leave the mayoral chair but would have accepted an alderman's seat without party attachment. The Conservatives would have none of this; they wanted every vote, and so Lord Astor went. Harry Mason was the Labour lord mayor 1944–5 and Isaac Foot followed him. Fourth son of the Notte Street builder, he had earlier spent twenty years on the council and eight in Parliament, making a remarkable national reputation for so short a career in the House. The Liberals had to bring him in from outside the council, and there has not been a Liberal lord mayor since, and scarcely a Liberal councillor.

The general election of 1945 with its Socialist landslide saw Labour men returned for all three Plymouth seats. At Devonport Michael Foot, Isaac's fourth son, defeated the formidable Hore-Belisha. Ten years later Michael in turn was

215

put out by Joan Vickers, who was to sit for nearly twenty years. Michael took the Ebbw Vale seat after Aneurin Bevan's death and the leadership of the Labour Left in the House until 1974 when he joined the government and in 1976 became vice-premier and Leader of the House. It was a remarkable time for the Foots. Sir Dingle, Isaac's eldest son, was in the House for twenty-seven years, a wartime minister and Solicitor-General 1964–7. Lord Caradon, the second son, was the last Governor of Cyprus and Minister of State at the United Nations 1964–70. John Foot, the fourth son and only unswerving Liberal, became a life peer in 1967.

In 1945 too Bert Medland captured the Drake seat and was invaluable as Plymouth's man in Westminster, fighting the reconstruction battles and making friends with vital ministers and civil servants. In Dame Evelyn Sharpe he found an ally who was to do much for Plymouth until her retirement in 1966. It was a tragedy that the reduction of Plymouth to two seats in 1950 ended Medland's parliamentary career, but Michael Foot and J. J. Astor, Nancy's son, who sat for Sutton 1951–9, took over his role. In 1966 young David Owen, son of a Plympton doctor, was elected as Labour member for Sutton, moving to Devonport when the revision of boundaries and the restoration of the Drake seat made Sutton unsafe for him. Dr Owen had become Navy Minister by 1968 and rapidly rose to Foreign Minister in 1977. Dame Joan Vickers, the painstaking constituency member whom he unseated at Devonport, went to the House of Lords with a life peerage.

In 1945 the Labour Party had also captured the city council for the first time. Harry Mason was the leader, Harry Wright the chairman of finance and with Bert Medland in Parliament made a powerful and driving triumvirate. Clifford Tozer the Conservative leader had as good a grip on his party as Mason and their bi-partisan policy meant few divisions in the council. Mason was a modest man who would have been happier left as chairman of the Museums and Libraries Committee, and the gentlemanly Tozer was no quick thinker. Though party control of the council changed regularly over these years, there was basic harmony.

The 1950s were the great years, with the city centre and the housing estates forging ahead and by the end of the decade the Guildhall, Civic Centre, Tamar Bridge, Laira Bridge and the augmentation of the water supply by a dam at Lopwell on the Tavy were either completed or under way. In 1961 the new factories were going up and the Chamber of Commerce (which had just amalgamated with the two mercantile associations to give the business community one voice) in its annual report declared that 'Plymouth is enjoying a prosperity unknown to herself in her long history'.

It was not to last. In the 1960s it seemed as if the city had exhausted itself by its efforts. Resurgent Plymouth was no novelty in the city or the great world. The basic great concept of the Plan was complete, the details were being filled in, and there seemed no one to prepare for the future. Nor was there, for the hard-pressed chief officers were too stretched to deal with more than immediate problems. The end of Development Status in 1960 cut off the factories, and 1961 brought defeat over the first attempt at boundary extension, the rejection of the Harrowbeer Bill, and no university in the first granting of new charters. The Conservative government in Whitehall had no regional policy so local initiative was needed. Plymouth persuaded Devon to take the lead in setting up the 'Committee of Six', representing Cornwall, Devon, Somerset and Dorset county councils, and Plymouth and Exeter county boroughs, to fight for a share of the national cake. It did establish the need for a major spine road into the west, and that its route should be south of Dartmoor, through Plymouth. By the time the Conservatives established a Department for Regional Planning and Edward Heath as its Secretary of State (David Serpell of the Plymouth family was the Second Permanent Secretary) was getting things moving, the government was defeated. The new Wilson government's concern was with the socialist cities of the North. In their new Regional Economic Planning Councils the 'Six' were overshadowed by Bristol and Gloucestershire, and all that came from the South-West Council was the Tress Report (named after its chairman) which agreed that Plymouth was the natural growth centre of Devon and Cornwall.

There were internal troubles. Paton Watson who had always

been the great driving force retired in 1959. The Tories captured the council in 1963 and in spite of bi-partisan policies they had never viewed reconstruction with the same urgency as the socialists. The original leaders were getting old; Mason and Tozer both retired and their successors, Wright and Pattinson, were not only of the same generation but quarrelled fiercely. Party politics became increasingly vehement, and young Turks on the Labour side forced their elders to break the old tradition which shared committee chairs between the parties. So instead of chairmen being the best men on the council, they were henceforward the best men in the dominant party. In turn Ron King, who had been among the leading Turks and (true to tradition) was district secretary of the strongest dockyard union, took over the Labour leadership and George Creber, a prominent estate agent, the Tory leadership. These men were natural leaders in their own sphere but increasingly the political parties were taking over, and rank and office on the council went to the most assiduous party workers. Those who kept aloof from local politics, and this included many of the business, professional and intellectual leaders of the city, had no part in its government.

The pursuit of a new airport, for which the much-sought American companies in particular clamoured, the boundary extension obtained in 1967, and then the fruitless battle for a new reservoir at Swincombe on Dartmoor, meant that Plymouth had antagonised all its neighbours by the end of the 1960s. The little neighbours had all through history been jealous of the growing Plymouth, and their residents, while happy to enjoy its wealth and facilities, wanted no share of its financial responsibilities. The county councils had grown to maturity, and their leaders were no longer country landowners but vigorous professional men who had adopted the new-style country life. Both counties had bigger populations than Plymouth, bigger rateable values, and these were the things that mattered in Whitehall. When the Plymouth police force was swallowed up in the two county forces in the dictated amalgamation of 1967 the natural headquarters would have been Plymouth, in the heart, but it went to Exeter. When the South-West Water Authority was created in 1974, taking over

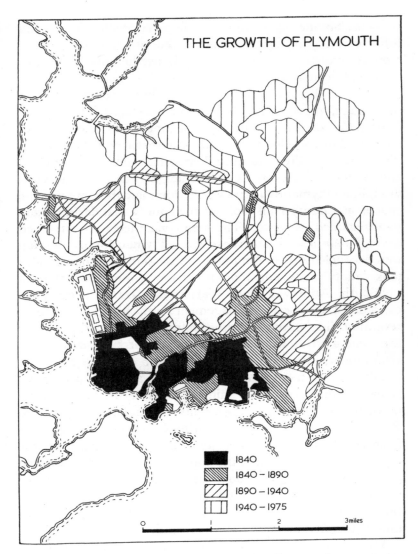

THE GROWTH OF PLYMOUTH

■	1840
▨	1840 – 1890
▧	1890 – 1940
▥	1940 – 1975

O   1   2   3miles

THE BUILT-UP AREA. *The diagram shows how the Three Towns spread to meet each other, and then expanded northwards.*

the Plymouth supplies, the headquarters again went to Exeter.

In 1974 too the Tory government reorganisation of local government tore up the Redcliffe-Maud Plan, which would have given Plymouth one-tier government over an area almost that of the 1943 Plan, and touched its hat to the county councils. Six metropolitan boroughs were created for the big conurbations and the remaining county boroughs were reduced to district councils with half their functions shifted to the county councils.

Now the best of the city councillors became county councillors, representing Plymouth, or else did both jobs. George Creber, Tory leader of the council, was also leader of Devon County Council. The Conservatives had ruled Plymouth since Plympton and Plymstock had been brought in, and dominated Devon. It looked for a time as if the well-disciplined Plymouth Tories would dominate the Conservative caucus at County Hall too, but the county mandarin system soon regained its power. The men concerned were stretched beyond their powers, and those with a Plymouth-only function were second-line men. A number of Plymouth chief officers also took county posts, and though the new young town clerk of Plymouth, Andrew Forbes Watson, has built up the fresh concept of corporate management with his chief officers, several of them have overriding county responsibilities. There are some gains, but great losses. After over 500 years of self-government, Plymouth is now ruled from outside.

Yet it is now a city of over a quarter of a million people. Its rateable value is over £26 million. Outside the metropolitan boroughs it is the fifth largest city in England. Apart from Bristol it is the largest city south of Birmingham. Its new factories provide as many jobs as the dockyard or the distributive trades. Yet, of the population of 259,000, of whom over 100,000 form the 'labour force', the Ministry of Defence believes that there are 20,000 servicemen of all ranks living in the city, and another 20,000 civilian employees in all its various establishments, including the dockyard.

Much has changed. A new city has arisen on the ashes of the old, acquiring after a quarter of a century its own personality and vitality. Housing estates run out across the once green hills. Among them the clean and elegant factories shine in park-like surroundings.

Much is still the same. Plymouth is still the distributive, shopping and entertainment centre of the West Country, its mercantile capital and, through its newspapers and television stations, the information centre. Apart from the economic value of the new factories, and to a lesser degree the port, all these operations depend in the long run on that strong naval and dockyard population. Plymouth may have grown out of all recognition, but fundamentally it is the military and naval base that it has been since the Plantagenet kings ruled England.

In spite of all its growth Plymouth is still a beautiful city, worthy of its magnificent setting.

ENVOI

The writing of history is never done. Not only does Plymouth go on, but there is so much that has gone before that is still hidden. It is twenty years since I started this work, thirteen since I published the first volume. Some choice spirits who urged me on at the start have died along the way, and I have not enough time left to research all the nooks and crannies that I should; all those nineteenth-century newspaper files, those 314 volumes of Devonport Dockyard records in the Public Record Office, for instance. 'If you wait until you know it all,' W. G. Hoskins told me years ago, 'you will never write a word.' Some things we shall never know; some records have gone for ever through fires and bombs and just plain foolishness. But perhaps I can give some pointers for future researchers who will tackle special aspects of the Plymouth story, for that is the way of the future.

Over the years many people have helped; many named in Volume One have continued their help. Some others deserve a special word. In pursuing the family histories I have had great kindness from the Earl and Countess of Mount Edgcumbe, Sir Michael Culme-Seymour, Mrs Passey of Blachford, Captain H. P. Chichester-Clark with the Ourry and Treby families, and Mr Val Insley of the St Aubyn Estate Office. In municipal affairs there have been many friends over the years among councillors and officers who have given me their confidence, and of them I am particularly grateful to three Town Clerks, Sir Colin Campbell, Stuart Lloyd Jones and Forbes Watson, for the time they have given me.

In the libraries and museums there has been much generous assistance. In Plymouth James Barber, the Director of the City Museum, and his archivist wife Jennifer, John Elliott the West Devon Area Librarian, Kenneth Burns the Local History Librarian, and a succession of archivists have helped with my problems. Living in Oxfordshire for the past nine years has had the one advantage of bringing the Bodleian Library and the great national institutions close to hand. Mr C. S. A. Dobson of the House of Lords Library, Dr Helen Wallis of the British Library Map Room, my old friend Basil Greenhill, Director of the National Maritime Museum, and his colleagues, and tolerant officers of the Public Record Office and the Census Office have all eased my path.

Major F. W. Woodward led me to valuable Citadel documents and Captain J. D. G. McCrae, RM, was a great help at Stonehouse. Over the years many officers of the armed forces and the dockyard have been kind, as have been so many people in various corporation departments, the Custom House and the Plymouth harbour authorities.

I was indeed fortunate to have a retired hydrographer, Captain C. R. K. Roe, RN, to draw specially a number of maps. Mrs Cynthia Margetts made the typescript a work of art. Finally (the *vale* of all writers, but none the less sincere) I have been sustained and encouraged by my long-suffering wife Betty. To them all, and to those unnamed, my deepest gratitude.

APPENDIX 1

THE MAIN NEW PARISHES OF THE THREE TOWNS AND NEIGHBOURHOOD, 1815–1914

Date of Parish	Church and Location	Mother Church	Notes
1846	St Paul, Morice Square	Stoke Damerel	Consecrated 1851
1846	St Mary, James Street (near Mutton Cove)	Stoke Damerel	Consecrated 1852
1846	St James-the-Great, Keyham Road	Stoke Damerel	Consecrated 1850
1846	St Stephen, George Street (Mount Wise)	Stoke Damerel	Consecrated 1858
1847	Christ Church, Eton Place (near top of Armada Way)		Consecrated 1846
1847	St James-the-Less, Citadel Road, Millbay	St Andrew	Consecrated 1861
1847	St Peter, Wyndham Square	St Andrew	Took in part of Stonehouse parish
1854	Holy Trinity, Southside Street	St Andrew	Built 1842
1855	St John Sutton-on-Plym (Exeter Street)	Charles	
1856	St John Hooe	Plymstock	Built 1855
1870	St Saviour, Lambhay Hill	St Andrew	Carved from Holy Trinity
1870	Emmanuel, Mannamead	Charles	
1873	St Michael, Stoke (Albert Road)	Stoke Damerel	Built 1845
1875	All Saints, Harwell Street	St Andrew	Carved from St Peter
1876	St Matthew, Clarence Street, Stonehouse	St George	
1876	St Jude, Beaumont Road	Charles	
1882	St Aubyn, Chapel Street (Old Devonport)	Stoke Damerel	Built 1771
1885	St Mark, Ford	Stoke Damerel	Built 1874–82
1887	St Matthias, North Hill	Charles	
1887	St John Baptist, Duke Street (Old Devonport)	Stoke Damerel	Built 1779. Chapel of ease to St James-the-Less
1891	St Michael, West Hoe	St Andrew	
1904	St Barnabas, Wilton Street	Stoke Damerel	Building started 1886
1904	St Augustine, Lipson Vale	Charles	
1907	St Simon, Mount Gould	Charles	Carved from St Jude
1910	St Gabriel, Peverell	Pennycross	
1911	St Mary, Cattedown	Charles	Formed from St John

APPENDIX 2

OTHER PRINCIPAL CHURCHES BUILT IN 1815–1914

Date of Parish	Church and Location	Denomination	Notes
1816	Mount Street, Devonport	Congregationalist	
1816	Ebenezer, Union Street, Stonehouse	Baptist	
1817	Providence, Home Park, Stoke	Baptist	
1817	Crownhill	Wesleyan	Replaced 1871
1817	Ebenezer, Saltash Street	Wesleyan	Now Plymouth Central Hall
1819	Princes Street, Devonport	Bible Christian	
1829	Stoke	Wesleyan	Replaced by Belmont 1875
1831	Raleigh Street, Plymouth	Brethren -	
1833	Bethesda, Ebrington Street	Universalist	
1834	Seamen's Bethel, Barbican		
1836	Union Street, Stonehouse	Calvinistic Independents	
1845	George Street, Plymouth	Baptist	Replaced Hows Lane
1845	Union Chapel, Courtenay Street	Congregationalist	
1845	King Street, Devonport	Bible Christian	
1848	Princess Street, Plymouth	Catholic Apostolic	Rebuilt 1867
1852	Zion Street, Plymouth	Bible Christian	
1854	Tamerton	Wesleyan	Society founded 1814
1856	Wycliffe, Albert Road	Congregationalist	Replaced Mount Street
1857	Ebrington Street	Primitive Methodist	Former Brethren chapel
1858	St Budeaux	Wesleyan	To Saltash Road 1893
1859	Herbert Street, Morice Town	Primitive Methodist	
1861	Cattedown	Wesleyan	Replaced 1897
1861	Ebenezer, Union Street, Stonehouse	Baptist	First Baptist in Stonehouse
1862	Eldad	Presbyterian	Replaced Devonport Church
1862	Mount Zion, Ker Street	Calvinists	
1864	Sherwell, Tavistock Road	Congregationalist	Replaced Norley
1866	King Street, Plymouth	Wesleyan	

1868	Ridgeway, Plympton	Wesleyan	Society founded 1814
1868	Ford	Baptist	
1868	Colebrook, Plympton	United Methodist	
1869	Mutley	Baptist	
1869	St Michael, James Street, Devonport	Roman Catholic	
1874	Ford	Wesleyan	
1876	Hooe	Baptist	
1878	Millbridge	Prim Methodist	
1879	Wesley, Ebrington Street	Wesleyan	Replaced Buckwell Lane
1881	Mutley	Wesleyan	
1882	Holy Cross, Beaumont Road	Roman Catholic	
1886	Congress Hall, Martin Street, Plymouth	Salvation Army	
1886	Estover Mission Chapel	Objectors	
1886	Greenbank	Bible Christian	
1890	Johnstone Terrace, Keyham	Wesleyan	Moved to Admiralty Street 1903
1892	Laira	Wesleyan	Replaced 1906
1896	Peverell Park Road	Wesleyan	Moved 1905
1900	Granby Street, Devonport	Salvation Army	
1900	Compton	Wesleyan	Rebuilt 1939
1902	Holy Redeemer, Keyham	Roman Catholic	
1904	Embankment Road	Bible Christian	
1904	Honicknowle	United Methodist	
1904	Mount Gould	Wesleyan	
1905	Salvation Army Hall, Exeter Street	Salvation Army	
1907	St George's Terrace, Devonport	Bible Christian	
1907	Salisbury Road, Plymouth	Baptist	
1907	Pennycross	Wesleyan	
1907	Camel's Head	Wesleyan	
1908	Cobourg Street	Prim Methodist	
1910	Barton Avenue, Keyham	Prim Methodist	
1911	St Edward the Confessor, Peverell	Roman Catholic	
1915	Laira	Congregationalist	

SOURCES AND REFERENCES

Abbreviations: *Trans DA* = *Transactions of the Devonshire Association*; *Trans PI* = *Transactions of the Plymouth Institution*; *WMN* = *Western Morning News*

1 THE PURITAN TOWN: 1603–42

Baker, J. P., *Church of Plymouth called Charles* (Plymouth, 1915)
Barber, Jennifer, 'Plymouth's Seventeenth-Century Merchant Adventurers', *WMN* (1 Sept 1970)
Beckerlegge, J. J., 'Plymouth Muniments and Newfoundland', *Trans PI* Vol 18, p 3 (1944)
Brushfield, T. N., 'Devon Briefs', *Trans DA* Vol 27 (1895)
Cornish, W. H., 'Sir John Gayer', *Trans PI* Vol 21 (1949)
Davey, F. A. and Watts, S. G., 'Devon Pioneers and Pilgrims', *WMN* (autumn 1969)
Davis, Ralph, *Rise of the English Shipping Industry* (1962)
Dictionary of National Biography
Dredge, J. I., 'A Few Sheaves of Devon Bibliography', *Trans DA* Vol 21 (1889) and Vol 24 (1892)
Duke, H. E., 'Some Metamorphoses of James Bagge', *Trans PI* Vol 13 (1903)
Elliott-Drake, Lady, *Family and Heirs of Sir Francis Drake* (1911)
Gill, Crispin, *Mayflower Remembered* (Newton Abbot, 1969); *Plymouth: a New History* Vol 1 (Newton Abbot, 1966)
Groves, Robert, *Story of Pennycross* (Plymouth, 1964)
Harris, Rev S. G., 'Samuel Heiron', *Trans DA* Vol 24 (1892)
Holt, K. D., *Sir Ferdinando Gorges* (Plymouth, 1965)
Oppenheim, M. M., *Maritime History of Devon* (ed Minchinton, Exeter, 1968)
Purchas, Samuel, *Pilgrims* (Maclehose ed, 1906, Vol 19)
Rowe, R. B., *Ecclesiastical History of Plymouth* (Plymouth, 1876)
Rowse, A. L., *England of Elizabeth* (1950)
State Papers Domestic, 1625
Stephens, W. B., 'Foreign Trade of Plymouth in the Early Seventeenth Century', *Trans DA* Vol 101 (1969); 'West Country Ports and Newfoundland Fisheries in the Seventeenth Century', *Trans DA* Vol 88 (1956); *Seventeenth-Century Exeter* (Exeter, 1958)
Stevens, John, *Plympton in the Seventeenth Century*, typescript, West Devon Area Record Office, Plymouth
Welch, Edwin, *Plymouth Building Accounts, Sixteenth and Seventeenth Centuries* (Devon and Cornwall Record Society Vol 12, 1967)
Williamson, H. A., *The English Channel* (1959)
Williamson, H. R., *Sir Walter Ralegh* (1951)
Willan, T. S., *English Coasting Trade* (Man UP, 1938)
Worth, R. N., *Calendar of the Plymouth Municipal Records* (Plymouth, 1893); *History of Plymouth* 2nd ed (Plymouth, 1890)

2 CIVIL WAR: 1642–6

Andriette, E. A., *Devon and Exeter in the Civil War* (Newton Abbot, 1971)
Coate, Mary, *Cornwall in the Great Civil War* (Oxford, 1933)
Jewitt, L., *History of Plymouth* (Plymouth, 1873; taken from 1644 pamphlet)

3 COMMONWEALTH AND RESTORATION: 1646–88

Allen, W., Diary, Plymouth Public Library
Barber, Jennifer, op cit.

Barnes, R., 'The Mutiny of the Plymouth Garrison in 1688', *Trans DA* Vol 101 (1969)
Beckerlegge, J. J., 'Charles II at Plymouth', *Trans DA* Vol 100 (1968)
Bracken, C. W., 'Huguenots in Plymouth', *Trans DA* Vol 66 (1934)
Calendars of State Papers Domestic
Calendar Treasury Papers, 1557–1696
Coate, Mary, op. cit.
Cope, R. Pearse (ed), *Early Tours in Devon and Cornwall* (1918; reprinted Newton Abbot, 1967)
Copeland, G. W., 'Charles Church', *Trans DA* Vol 81 (1949)
Davis, Ralph, op. cit., *Rise of the Atlantic Economies* (1973)
de Gomme, Sir Bernard, Plans of Royal Citadel, British Museum Add MSS 16371 (a–k)
Dictionary of National Biography
Duke, H. E., op. cit.
Elliot-Drake, Lady, op. cit.
Nicholson, H. Y., *Authentic Records relating to the Christian Church now meeting in George St and Mutley Chapels Plymouth, 1640–1870 (Baptists)*, Plymouth Local History Library
Oppenheim, M. M., op. cit.
Parish Registers, St Andrew's Church
Selleck, A. D., 'Plymouth Friends, a Quaker History', *Trans DA* Vols 98 and 99 (1966 and 1967)
Stephens, W. B., 'Foreign Trade of Plymouth'; 'West Country Ports'; *Seventeenth-Century Exeter* op. cit.
Stevens, John, *History of Plympton*, typescript, West Devon Area Record Office, Plymouth
Welch, C. E., *Edmund Pollexfen, Town Clerk of Plymouth, 1665–99* (Plymouth Corporation, 1960); *Plymouth City Charters* (Plymouth Corporation, 1962)
Worth, R. N., *History of Plymouth*, 2nd ed, op. cit.; 'Puritanism in Devon', *Trans DA* Vol 9, 1877; *Calendar of the Plymouth Municipal Records*, op. cit.
Yonge, James, *Plymouth Memoirs* (ed Beckerlegge, J. J., Plymouth Institution, 1951)

4 PLYMOUTH DOCK: 1688–1750

Blight, F. S., 'Hail and Farewell to Devonport', *Trans PI* Vol 21 (1951)
British Museum Add MSS 16370, folio 41, 1665; Lansdowne MSS 847, F.26–51; Misc docs BMM 13; MS Kings Mar 43 and 45
Bryant, Arthur, *Samuel Pepys, The Man in the Making* (1933)
Burns, K. V., *Plymouth's Ships of War*, Maritime Monographs and Prints no 4 (Greenwich, 1972)
Calendars of State Papers, Commonwealth, Charles II, James II, William
Collins, Greenvile, *Great Britain's Coasting Pilot* (Harrap's facsimile of 1753 ed)
Cope, R. Pearse (ed), op. cit.
Copeland, G. W., 'Notes on Puslinch', *Trans DA* Vol 75 (1943)
Dicker, George, *Story of Devonport Royal Dockyard* typescript (1967), Office of Secretary to the Dockyard, Devonport
Donn, Benjamin, Map of the County of Devon, 1765 (Exeter, 1965)
Gray, Patricia, *Stoke Damerel Parish Church: A History* (Plymouth, 1974)
Hooley, J. M. P., *Growth and Development of HM Dockyard, Devonport*, lecture to summer conference, Institute of Structural Engineers, Torquay, 1939
Lewis, Michael, *History of the British Navy* (1957)
Oppenheim, M. M., op. cit.
Stevens, A. E., *Plymouth Haven, Late Fourteenth Century to 1693* (University of London thesis, 1936); *Development of Dockyard in Hamoaze during Sailing Ship Days* (University of London thesis)
Treasury Papers, 1557–1696
Worth, R. N., *History of the Town and Borough of Devonport* (Plymouth, 1870)
Yonge, James, *Plymouth Memoirs*, op. cit.

5 THE ADMIRALTY TAKES OVER: 1688–1750

Carson, Edward, *The Ancient and Rightful Customs* (1972)
Chandler, George, *Liverpool Shipping* (1960)
Collins, Greenvile, op. cit.
Cope, R. Pearse (ed), op. cit.
Copeland, G. W., 'A Visist to Plympton', *Trans DA* Vol 71, p 177 (1939)
Davis, Ralph, op. cit.
Dictionary of National Biography
Elliott-Drake, Lady, op. cit.
Captain Hambly's Book, Plymouth Record Office MSS
Hoskins, W. G., *Industry, Trade and People in Exeter, 1688–1800* (Exeter, 1935)
Jasper, R. C. D., *Parliamentary Representation, Plymouth, Devonport and Stonehouse 1812–37* (Leeds University thesis, 1938; typescript, Plymouth Local History Library)
McGrath, Patrick (ed), *Bristol in the Eighteenth Century* (Newton Abbot, 1972)
MacInnes, C. M., *Bristol: a Gateway of Empire* (reprint, Newton Abbot, 1968)
Parkinson, C. Northcote, *Trade Winds* (1948)
Rogers family papers, Blachford, Cornwood, near Plymouth
Rowe, J. Brooking, *History of Plympton Erle* (Exeter, 1906)
Sedgwick, R. R., *History of Parliament: the Commons, 1715–54* (1970)
Shore, H. N., *Smuggling Days and Smuggling Ways* (1892)
Stevens, J., *Old Plympton*, typescript, Plymouth Local History Library
Welch, C. E., *Edmund Pollexfen*, op. cit.; *Plymouth City Charters*, 'Municipal Reform in Plymouth', *Trans DA* Vol 96 (1964)
Williams, Neville, *Contraband Cargoes* (1959)
Willan, T. S., op. cit.
Woollcombe, Henry, *History of Plymouth*, manuscript, Plymouth Local History Library (*c* 1835)
Worth, R. N., 'Early Commerce of Plymouth', *Trans PI* Vol 6 (1878)
Yonge, James, *Plymouth Memoirs*, op. cit.

6 THE GREAT AWAKENING: 1750–1815

Acts of Parliament: Public General Acts, House of Lords Library
Albert, William, *Turnpike Road System in England 1663–1840* (1972)
Armstrong, Col G. W., RMLI, 'Plymouth Division Royal Marines', *Globe & Laurel* (1893–4)
Beckerlegge, J. J., 'Eastern Plymouth Yesterday and Today', *Trans PI* Vol 18 (1944)
Blight, F. S., 'Stoke and Morice Town', *Trans PI* Vol 22 (1951)
Bracken, C. W., 'Plymouth Streets and Place Names', *Trans PI* Vol 71 (1937)
Burt, William, *Review of the Port of Plymouth* (Plymouth, 1816)
Charnock, John, Rogers, Sir F., Ourry, Paul, *Biographica Navalis* Vols V and VI (1797–8)
Cornelius, David B., *Devon and Cornwall, a Postal Survey* (Postal History Society, 1973)
Crimp, S. H., 'The Post in Plymouth', *Proceedings of the Plymouth Athenaeum* Vol II, p 41 (1971)
Culme-Seymour family papers, West Devon Area Record Office, Plymouth; archives of Sir Michael Culme-Seymour
Dawe, John W., 'John Foulston', *Proceedings of the Plymouth Athenaeum* Vol II (1971)
Dicker, George, *Short History of Devonport Dockyard* (Plymouth, 1969); Mr Dicker's notebooks
Everett, R. V., *History of Lodge of Sincerity, 1769–1969* (1969)
Gill, Crispin, *Sutton Harbour* (Plymouth, 1970); 'Stonehouse', *Trans PI* (1969); 'Woven into Plymouth's History: the Bayly Family', *WMN* (15 Dec 1971)
Gray, Patricia, op. cit.
Griffiths, Stanley, 'History of the Batter Street Congregational Church 1704–1921', *Trans PI* Vols 9, 10 (1944)
Guide to Antony House (1953)
Hall, P. L., 'History of the Cremyll Ferry', *Royal Cornwall Polytechnic Society Report* (1963)
Hamilton-Edwards, Gerald, *Twelve Men of Plymouth* (Plymouth, 1951)

Harris, Gladys and F. L., *Making of a Cornish Town: Torpoint* (Institute of Cornish Studies, Redruth, 1976)
Hicks, C. E., 'Banking Crisis of 1825 in SW Devon', *Trans DA* Vol 81 (1949); 'Devonshire Bank Notes', *Trans DA* Vol 80 (1948)
Hine, J., 'A Few Notes on Old Plymouth', *Trans PI* Vol 16 (1878)
Hoskins, W. G., *Industry, Trade and People in Exeter, 1688–1800*, op. cit.; 'Ranking of Provincial Towns', *Local History in England* (1959)
House of Commons Journal, June 1784 etc
Hoxland, *Guide to Dock* (1792)
Hudson, Derek, *Sir Joshua Reynolds* (1958)
James, Adml Sir William, *Old Oak: The Life of John Jervis, Earl of St Vincent* (1950)
Kingston, Jack, 'History of the Torpoint Ferry'; *Old Cornwall* Vol VII No 5 (autumn 1969)
Larks, Dr George, *The Plymouth Medical Society in the Nineteenth Century* (Plymouth, *c* 1968)
Leonard, A. G. K., 'Edward Pellew, Lord Exmouth', *WMN*
Lewis, Michael, op. cit.
Map of Plymouth–Exeter road with 1819 improvements, Devon County Record Office
Marshall, William, *Rural Economy of the West of England* (1796)
Namier and Brooks, *History of Parliament: the Commons, 1754–90* (1964)
Noall, Cyril, *Smuggling in Cornwall* (Truro, 1971)
Oppenheim, M. M., op. cit.
Ormsby, Col R. D., RM, 'Plymouth Division Royal Marines', *Globe & Laurel* (193?)
Ourry/Treby family papers, Capt H. P. Chichester-Clark, New Grenofen House, Whitchurch Road, Tavistock
Pearce, A. Preston, Presidential Address 1923, *Trans PI* Vol 17 (1937)
Pollard, Frank, 'Smuggler, Captain Harry Carter', *Journal of the Royal Institute of Cornwall*, new series, Vol 5 (1968)
Pugh, Surgeon Capt P. D. G., 'History of the Royal Naval Hospital Plymouth', *Journal RN Medical Services* Vol 58 (1972)
Rogers family papers, op. cit.
St Aubyn Estate Office papers, Devonport
Samuel, Edgar R., 'Plymouth's Bicentenary', *Jewish Chronicle* (9 June 1961)
Sedgwick, R. R., op. cit.
Selleck, A. D., op. cit.
Sherborne Mercury
Shore, H. N., op. cit.
Spinney, David, *Rodney* (1969)
Stevens, A. E., *Plymouth Haven*; op. cit. *Development of Dockyard in Hamoaze*
Stevens, J., op. cit.
Vancouver, Charles, *General View of the Agriculture of Devon* (1808)
Vosper, D. C., 'West's Postal Service', *WMN* (1 Oct 1951)
Welch, C. E., 'The Iron Bridge', *Trans DA* Vol 98 (1966); 'Andrew Kinsman and Eighteenth-Century Free Churches', *Trans DA* Vol 97 (1965); 'Early Dissenters' Meeting Houses in Plymouth', *Trans DA* Vol 94 (1962)
Williams, G. H. and Matthew, L. J. L., *History of the Lodge of Fidelity No 230* (Plymouth, 1960)
Woollcombe, Henry, op. cit.
Worth, R. N., *History of the Town and Borough of Devonport*, op. cit.; 'Notes on Early History of Stonehouse', *Trans PI* Vol 9 (1887)
Wright, W. H. K., 'Some Further Peeps at Old Plymouth', *Trans PI* Vol 14 (1911); 'Plymouth 100 Years Ago', *Trans PI* Vol 5 (1918)
Wycisk, Godfrey, 'Governors of Plymouth', *WMN* (18 March 1969)
Zeigler, Philip, *King William IV* (1971)

7 POLITICAL REFORM: 1750–1835

Dictionary of National Biography
Jasper, R. C. D., *Parliamentary Representation, Plymouth, Devonport and Stonehouse 1812–37* (Leeds University thesis, 1938; typescript, Plymouth Local History Library)
Namier and Brooks, op. cit.

Oldfield, T. H. B., *The Representative History of Great Britain and Ireland, being a History of the House of Commons* . . . (1816)
Rogers, Edmund, manuscript history of Plymouth (1864) at Blachford, Cornwood, near Plymouth
Welch, C. E., 'Municipal Reform in Plymouth', op. cit.
Whitfeld, H., *Plymouth and Devonport in Times of War and Peace* (1900)
Woollcombe, Henry, op. cit.
Worth, R. N., *History of the Town and Borough of Devonport*, op. cit.

8 THE AGE OF STEAM: 1815–1914

Allen, Douglas, 'Changes in Brewing', *WMN* (24 March 1970)
Billing's *Directory of Plymouth* (1857)
Boulton & Watt engine books, Birmingham City Library
Brindley's *Guide to Plymouth* (1830)
Brock, Rear-Adml P. W., and Greenhill, Basil, *Steam and Sail* (1973)
Burns, Lt-Com K. V., *Plymouth's Ships of War* (Greenwich, 1972)
Census Returns and Statistical Tables, 1831–1911
Cock, R. F. E., 'Millbay Docks', *WMN* (30 Jun, 1 July, 2 July 1970); 'Early Plymouth Hotels', *WMN* (26 Aug 1969)
Colonial Land and Emigration Commissioners, General Reports, 1842–71
Custom House Registers, Plymouth
Devonshire, Mate's County Series (1907)
Dicker, George, *Story of Devonport Royal Dockyard*, op. cit.
English, E. T., *The Browns of Plymouth* (Plymouth, 1971)
Farr, Grahame, 'Custom House Registers of the West Country', *South West and the Sea* (Exeter, 1968); *West Country Passenger Steamers* (Prescot, Lancs, 1956)
Flintoff's *Directory to Plymouth and Devonport* (1844)
Forbes, L. M., *Captain R. F. Scott* (Plymouth, 1965)
Gaskell Brown, C. (ed), *Industrial Archaeology of Plymouth* (Plymouth, 1973)
Gentry, P. W., *Tramways of the West of England* (1952)
Gill, Ald H. D., *Random Notes on the Tavistock Gills* (published privately, 1957)
Gill, Crispin, *Plymouth as a Liner Port*, unpublished paper (1970); 'When Napoleon's Brother stayed at a Plymouth Inn', *WMN* (20 Sep 69); 'New Plymouth Pioneers', *WMN* (7 Oct 1970)
Hicks, C. E., 'Banking Crisis of 1825 in SW Devon', op. cit.
House of Commons Accounts and Papers, Vol 38, 1849; Vol 50, 1851
Obituary, Sir John Jackson, *The Engineer* Vol 128 (1919)
Kellaway, F. W., 'The Growth of Devonport Dockyard', *Trans PI* Vol 20 (1948)
Kendall, H. G., *The Plymouth & Dartmoor Railway and its Forerunners* (Lingfield, 1968)
Kingston, Jack, op. cit.
Latimore, Dr Margaret, *Economic History of Plymouth* Vol II, typescript, Plymouth Local History Library
Laws, Peter, 'A Journey by Railway from Plymouth to Gunnislake', *Old Cornwall* Vol VIII No 10 (Spring 1978)
Leonard, A. G. K., *History of Woodland Fort* (Plymouth, 1951)
Lewis, M. J. T., *Early Wooden Railways* (1970)
Lewis, Samuel, *Topographical Dictionary of England* (1844)
MacDermot, E. T., *History of the GWR* Vol 2 (1927; revised Clinker, C. R., 1964)
Map of Plymouth–Exeter road, op. cit.
Merrett, L. H., 'The Building of Plymouth Breakwater', *Maritime History* Vol 5 No 2 (Tavistock, 1977)
Murray's *Handbook, Devon and Cornwall* (1830)
Nettleton's *Guide to Plymouth* (1836)
Noall, Cyril, op. cit.
O'Brien, Capt F. T., 'Introduction of Steam Navigation in the Solent', *Mariners' Mirror* Vol 55 No 3 (Aug 1969)
Pigot's *London and Provincial New Commercial Directory* (1823–4)
Rendell, Joan, 'Partnership that Struck it Rich' (Bryant & May), *WMN* (30 Oct 74)
RN Dockyard, Plymouth, typescript researched by Plymouth Public Library Staff (1960)

Sambourne, R. C., *Plymouth: 100 Years of Street Travel* (Falmouth, 1974)
Shore, H. N., op. cit.
Sparrow, K., 'James Peek's Prizes', *WMN* (7 May 74)
Sutton Harbour Improvement Company Minutes
Thomas, D. St J., *Regional History of the Railways of Great Britain*, Vol 1, *The West Country* (Newton Abbot, 1960)
Vosper, D. C., op. cit.
Welch, C. E., 'The Iron Bridge, op. cit.
White's *Devon Directory* (1850)
Woollcombe, Henry, Diary, Woollcombe family papers
Wycisk, Col G., 'Devon's Pioneer Volunteers', *WMN* (17 April 1973)

9 THE YEARS OF EXPANSION: 1815–1914

Atkinson, Alan, 'Water Supply of Plymouth and the Burrator Reservoir', *Trans PI* Vol 19 (1944)
Billing's *Directory of Plymouth* (1857)
Blight, F. S., 'Hail and Farewell to Devonport'; 'Stoke and Moricetown',; op. cit.
Bracken, C. W., 'Plymouth Grammar School', *Trans DA* Vol 76 (1944)
Census Returns and Statistical Abstracts
Charles Parish Magazine (Sep 1965)
Cook, E. Chandler, 'Growth of Education in Plymouth', *The Book of Plymouth* (NUT Conference, Plymouth, 1910)
Culme-Seymour family papers, op. cit.
Denbow, Fernley J., 'Puritan Charles Church', *WMN* (27 Sep 1965)
Fenton, Cecil A., 'No Cheers for Royalty', *WMN* (3 April 1968)
Festival History of Plymouth (Plymouth Communist Party, 1953)
Ford, W. J., *An Amusing History of Plymouth* (Plymouth, 1924)
Gill, Crispin, 'Woven into Plymouth's History: the Bayly Family', op. cit.; *Plymouth 1848–1958: A YMCA History* (Plymouth, 1958)
Gray, Patricia, op. cit.
Griffin, Stanley, *History of Union Congregational Church, Plymouth* (Plymouth, 1956); *The Sherwell Story* (Plymouth, 1964)
History of St Philip's Church, Weston Mill
Hoskins, W. G., *Devon* (1954)
Jennings, Valerie, 'St Dunstan's Abbey', *WMN* (3 Nov 1964)
Kelly's *Directories*
Lane, Peter, 'The Day the Railway Came to Plymouth', *Christmas Cheer* (Plymouth, 1956)
Larks, Dr George, op. cit.
Map Collection, Plymouth Local History Library
Matthews, Coryndon, *Chronicles of the Royal Western Yacht Club of England* (Plymouth, 1919)
Medical Officer of Health Report, Devonport, 1912
Medical Officer of Health Report, Plymouth, 1902
Mortimer, Bishop Robert, 'George Rundle Prynne', *Exeter Diocesan Leaflet* (June 1968)
Odgers, Rev W. J., *A Report on the Sanitary Condition of Plymouth* (Plymouth, 1847)
Orchard, B. G., 'Sir Edward Bates', *Liverpool's Legion of Honour* (Liverpool, 1893)
Rawlinson, Robert, *Report on the Health of Plymouth* (1853)
Report of the Inquiry into the Plymouth Representation for Union with Plymouth and Devonport, 1914
'The Roman Catholic Cathedral', *Plymouth Diocesan Year Book* (1958)
Rooker, Alfred, 'Sanitary Legislation', *Trans PI* Vol 4 (1873)
Rowe, J. Brooking, op. cit.
Smallcombe, H. R., *Retold Stories of Charles* (Plymouth, 1960)
Stephens, Walter, *Highways and Byways of Plymouth* (Plymouth, 1943)
'A Survey of the Plymouth Trades Council', *Souvenir of the 68th Trades Union Congress* (Plymouth, 1936)
Treby, Paul Ourry, sporting journals and private papers with Capt H. P. Chichester-Clark, New Grenofen House, Whitchurch Road, Tavistock

SOURCES AND REFERENCES

Trethewey, Clifford, *The Master Builders: A Story of St Jude's Church, Plymouth* (Plymouth, 1976)
Walling, R. V., 'Hospital Ships in the Sound', *WMN* (19 Feb 1966)
Welch, C. E., Introduction, *Guide to the Archives Department of Plymouth City Libraries* (Plymouth, 1962)
White's *Directory of Plymouth* (1850)
Winton, John, *Hurrah for the Life of a Sailor* (1977)
Worth, R. N., *History of the Town and Borough of Devonport*, op. cit.; 'The Tything of Compton Gifford', *Trans DA* Vol 28 (1896)

10 WAR AND PEACE: 1914-39

Ainsworth, Robert, 'The Showman-Engineer', *WMN* (20 Sep 65); 'Cinema Pioneer who loved the Spectacular', *WMN* (9 Dec 66); 'Showman who gave City a Cinema with 3,500 seats', *WMN* (10 Oct 68)
'Capital Region of the West – once slum-ridden Plymouth', *WMN* (5 Jan 60)
Cheeseman, A. D., 'Seaplanes in Plymouth Sound', *WMN* (date unknown)
Cock, R. F. E., 'Death Knell of Plymouth's Tolls', *WMN* (2 Apr 74); 'Pioneers of the Cinema', *WMN* (27 May 71); 'Early Days of the Silent Screen', *WMN* (20 May 75); 'Pioneer Plymouth Editors', *WMN* (3 Apr 69); 'Radio Yesterdays', *WMN* (14 Nov 1972)
Corina, Maurice, *Fine Silks and Oak Counters: Debenham's 1778-1978* (1978)
Dicker, George, *Story of Devonport Royal Dockyard*, op. cit.
Dodd, Pat, 'Cornish Growers fight the Breton Invasion' (Roscoff ferry), *Farmers' Weekly* (23 Feb 1979)
Doyle, Katie, 'Lawrence of Arabia and Mount Batten', *The Independent* (29 Jan 67)
Grills, Beatrice, 'When a Packet of Pins came in the Change', *Christmas Cheer* (Plymouth, 1961)
Hibbs, John, *History of British Bus Services* (Newton Abbot, 1968)
Hoskins, W. G., *Devon* (1954)
Hurd, Archibald S., 'The Western Morning News', *Cornish Magazine* Vol 1 No 4 (1898)
Medland, H. M., 'They called me "Stormy" ', *Christmas Cheer* (Plymouth, 1961)
'Notes on the West', *WMN* (16 Oct 76)
Palmer, J. L., 'Plymouth's Daily Newspapers and their Founders', *Trans PI* Vol 20 (1948)
'RAF Mount Batten', *WMN* (26 Aug 66)
Report of the Royal Commission on the Press, 1947-9
Sambourne, R. C., op. cit.
Smale, Rosa M., 'Plymouth and the Co-operative Movement', *Souvenir of the 68th Trades Union Congress* (Plymouth, 1936)
Toy, H. Spencer, *History of Education in Launceston* (1965)
Tozer, Sir C., 'Fifty Years in Public Life', *Christmas Cheer* (Plymouth, 1962)
Trewin, J. C., *Portrait of Plymouth* (1973)
Walling, R. A. J., *The Story of Plymouth* (1950); 'The Western Daily Mercury', *Cornish Magazine* Vol 1 No 4 (1899)
Walling, R. V., 'The Battle that put Devonport into Mourning', *WMN* (27 May 1966)
Watson, J. Paton, and Abercrombie, Patrick, *A Plan for Plymouth* (1943)
Wycisk, Col G., 'From Peace to War', *WMN* (2 Aug 1973)

11 DESTRUCTION AND RECONSTRUCTION: 1939-79

British Transport Dock Authority Annual Reports
Cattewater Commissioners' Annual Reports
Corina, Maurice, op. cit.
Davies, Eric, 'Ally of the Homeless', *WMN* (7 May 1970)
English, E. T., *Pilgrim to Plymouth* (Plymouth, 1967); *The Browns of Plymouth* (Plymouth, 1971)
Front Line 1940-41 (HMSO, 1942)

233

Goodman, Stanley, 'While It Stood, It worked', Plymouth YMCA Report (1939–46)
Harris, W. Best, 'The City of Tomorrow', additional chapter to Bracken's *History of Plymouth* (Wakefield, 1970)
Mildren, James, 'Plymouth, a Mecca for Marine Research', *WMN* (4 May 1977)
Millbay Dock Manager's Office manuscript volumes, 1879–1936
Plymouth Blitz (Plymouth, 1946)
Plymouth Chamber of Commerce Annual Reports (1947–63)
Plymouth: Housing, Planning, Reconstruction (City Planning Department, 1965)
Savignon, André, *With Plymouth Through Fire* (Hayle, 1968)
Sutton Harbour Improvement Company Annual Reports
Twyford, H. P., *It Came to Our Door* (Plymouth, 1945)
Watson, J. Paton, 'The Rebuilding of Plymouth', *Town and Country Planning* (Nov 1955)
Watson, J. Paton, and Abercrombie, Patrick, op. cit.
Winfield, D. E., *An Outline of Post-War Planning in Plymouth* (1974)

INDEX